Transatlantic Spiritualism
and Nineteenth-Century American Literature

Transatlantic Spiritualism
and Nineteenth-Century American Literature

Bridget Bennett

palgrave
macmillan

TRANSATLANTIC SPIRITUALISM AND NINETEENTH-CENTURY AMERICAN
LITERATURE
Copyright © Bridget Bennett, 2007.

First published in 2007 by
PALGRAVE MACMILLAN™
175 Fifth Avenue, New York, N.Y. 10010 and
Houndmills, Basingstoke, Hampshire, England RG21 6XS.
Companies and representatives throughout the world.

PALGRAVE MACMILLAN is the global academic imprint of the
Palgrave Macmillan division of St. Martin's Press, LLC and of Palgrave
Macmillan Ltd. Macmillan® is a registered trademark in the United
States, United Kingdom and other countries. Palgrave is a registered
trademark in the European Union and other countries.

ISBN-13: 9-781-4039-7800-4
ISBN-10: 1-4039-7800-X

Library of Congress Cataloging-in-Publication Data
Bennett, Bridget.
   Transatlantic spiritualism and nineteenth century American litera
   ture / Bridget Bennett.
         p. cm.
   Includes bibliographical references and index.
   ISBN 1-4039-7800-X (alk. paper)
   1. Spiritualism in literature. 2. American literature—19th century—
History and criticism. 3. Spiritualism—United States—History—19th
century. 4. Literature and spiritualism—United States—History—19th
century. 5. Occultism in literature. I. Title.
   PS217.S65B46 2007
   810'.9384—dc22
                                    2007060005

A catalogue record of the book is available from the British Library.

Design by Scribe, Inc.

First edition: June 2007

10 9 8 7 6 5 4 3 2 1

Printed in the United States of America.
Transferred to Digital Printing in 2008.

For Ayesha and Iona

CONTENTS

ACKNOWLEDGMENTS

I would like to thank the following presses for allowing me permission to republish early versions of this work: Cambridge University Press for "Spirited Away: The Death of Little Eva and the Farewell Performances of 'Katie King,'" Journal of American Studies 40 (Spring 2006): 1–16; MIT Press for "'Sacred Theatres': Shakers, Spiritualists and Performing the Indian in the 1830s and 1840s," TDR: The Drama Review 49, no. 3 (Fall 2005; T187): 114–34; Manchester University Press for "'Crossing Over': Spiritualism and the Atlantic Divide," in Special Relationships: Anglo-American Affinities and Antagonisms, 1854–1936, ed. Janet Beer and Bridget Bennett, 89–109 (Manchester: Manchester University Press, 2002).

I would like to offer my deep gratitude to the Leverhulme Trust for a one year Fellowship that supported the early part of my research and allowed me to visit libraries in Britain and the United States, the Arts and Humanities Research Council for awarding me a Research Leave Award, the British Academy for its generous travel award, and the School of English at the University of Leeds for granting me study leave and a period of teaching remission, which greatly assisted me at a crucial time.

Many, many, generous people have contributed toward the making of this book. They include friends, family, colleagues, students, conference and seminar organizers and attendees, librarians, and anonymous and known readers. I hope they will forgive me for not giving an exhaustive list of names, dates, and places. I have a long-standing suspicion of over-lengthy acknowledgments. I thank them all and think they know who they are. They should not doubt for a moment that I do. I would like to offer my very particular thanks to Janet Beer, Susan Castillo, Hermione Lee, and Helen Taylor for unstinting and much-appreciated support of various kinds over a long period. My immediate colleagues at Leeds—Denis Flannery, Mick Gidley, Jay Prosser, Andrew Warnes, (and more recently) Hamilton

Carroll—have shown me the many different ways it is possible to be an Americanist: for this, and for much more, I am deeply grateful. Other colleagues, past and present, have read parts of my work and helped me sharpen my arguments and think differently about what I was doing: Elleke Boehmer, Kate Dossett, Robert Jones, Ed Larrissy, Sonny Kandola, and Gail Marshall have all challenged me in various ways as they have read and responded to parts of this book. Long may it continue. Sarah Meer offered useful scholarly advice at an important time. Julia Cohen, Katie Fahey, Erin Ivy, and Farideh Koohi-Kamali at Palgrave, as well as Dale Rohrbaugh at Scribe, have been all that an author could hope for, and for this I am very thankful. Once again Martin Hargreaves has stepped in and done a great indexing job. Many thanks are due to him. The memory of Dominic Montserrat, whose enthusiasm for, and knowledge of, so many subjects, including spiritualism, has enlightened and inspired many of us, must be acknowledged too. I wish he could read this, since we talked about it so much together. Duncan and Josephine Bennett have continued, as ever, to provide loving support and encouragement, for which I profoundly thank them both. Sanju Velani has long transformed every part of my life. Ayesha and Iona Bennett have continued, and extended, that transformation. They make it all worth while. Thank you, all three of you, for everything.

Introduction

The Apparitional Past

I had a very dear friend, who, I had heard, had gone to the spirit-land, or perdition, or some of those places, and I desired to know something concerning him. There was something so awful, though, about talking with living, sinful lips to the ghostly dead, that I could hardly bring myself to rise and speak. But at last I got trem-blingly up and said in a low and trembling voice:

"Is the spirit of John Smith present?"

(You can never depend on these Smiths; you call for one, and the whole tribe will come clattering out of hell to answer you.)

"Whack! whack! whack! whack!"

Bless me! I believe all the dead and damned John Smiths between San Francisco and perdition boarded that poor little table at once! I was considerably set back—stunned, I may say. The audience urged me to go on, however, and I said:

"What did you die of?"

The Smiths answered to every disease and casualty that men can die of.

"Where did you die?"

They answered Yes to every locality I could name while my geography held out.

"Are you happy where you are?"

There was a vigorous and unanimous "No!" from the late Smiths.[1]

America was the only Great Power of the nineteenth century that produced three new religions, all of global scope, Spiritualism, Christian Science, and Mormonism, and Mormons were as *imperial in their claims on the material world as Christian Scientists and Spiritualists were in their claims on the 'Spirit Land.' The mind-over-matter philosophy was not simply an American product or tradition but the identity, the actual history of a people who patented much of modern technology and conquered a continent in a brief century or two.*[2]

[T]he American 1848, a moment that continues to haunt the present.[3]

This is a book about the ways in which, and reasons why, communicating with the dead was so popular in the nineteenth-century United States. In seeking to trace spiritualism's emergence, meaning, and spread within the United States as well as beyond its borders, this book locates it within a complex set of identities and identifications. I argue that spiritualism, as it emerged in the United States in the nineteenth century, bore the traces of its origins in the nation's circum-Atlantic past. Further, by the period this book concentrates on (roughly from the Revolution to the Civil War), spiritualism was largely a transatlantic phenomenon. While this distinction does not hold absolutely, it does allow us to understand some of the key features of the spiritualism that is at the heart of this book. By using the term "circum-Atlantic," rather than the more familiar coinage "transatlantic," to think of the prehistory of spiritualism, this book engages with recent critical work by Joseph Roach, which prioritizes a geopolitical history that acknowledges "the centrality of the diasporic and genocidal histories of Africa and the Americas, North and South, in the creation of the culture of modernity."[4] It is from the work of Joseph Roach that this book found its early impetus in his argument that "While a great deal of the unspeakable violence instrumental to this creation may have been officially forgotten, circum-Atlantic memory retains its consequences, one of which is that the unspeakable cannot be rendered forever inexpressible: the most persistent mode of forgetting is memory imperfectly deferred."[5] Such an imperfect deferral produced, among other things, the set of cultural and religious practices here described as spiritualism. The different ways in which the living and the spirit worlds communicated, the meanings ascribed to such communications, and the forms that govern and mold them are among the subjects this book considers.

Throughout the book I use the word transatlantic to describe the movement of spiritualism across the Atlantic in both directions. This is not an act of critical perversity. Using this term reflects the book's particular focus on spiritualism's relation to white subjects and subjectivities whose own trajectories were largely, though not exclusively, based around Europe and the United States. So, while I argue that spiritualism draws from a history that includes the presence of, (often violent) collisions with, and beliefs of nonwhite subjects—chiefly Africans and Indians with whites—I contend that it is not just that past but its disavowal that contributed to the formation and structures of spiritualism. While the past that it draws from is explicitly shaped by the circum-Atlantic, by slavery, and by its impact on mercantilism, economic and political structures, and imperialism, it is chiefly the transatlantic exchanges of nineteenth-century spiritualism that are investigated here. This book shows a pattern of survival through syncretism: the spiritualist practices of the nineteenth century are the result of a cultural and political commingling that resulted from the processes of colonial settlement and their continuation which included removals and slavery, and also from the territorial expansion and ambition that has marked U.S. imperialism. I use the term "American literature" in the title of this work with some self-consciousness, following and borrowing Shelley Streeby's argument about her use of the adjectival use of the word American in her recent work *American Sensations* (2002) and acknowledging Wai Chee Dimock's profound meditations on the consequences of using that adjective.[6] Dimock writes, "I have in mind a form of indebtedness: what we call 'American' literature is quite often a shorthand, a simplified name for a much more complex tangle of relations. Rather than being a discrete entity, it is better seen as a crisscrossing set of pathways, open-ended and ever multiplying, weaving in and out of other geographies, other languages and cultures. These are input channels, kinship networks, routes of transit, and forms of attachment—connective tissues binding America to the rest of the world."[7]

The very good scholarly work that has been done on spiritualism to date powerfully reveals many important details about a subject that was once regarded as both esoteric and marginal. Logie Barrow and Alex Owen have both produced seminal work on British spiritualist culture and, respectively, plebeian radicalism and women's relation to mediumship. Ruth Brandon has written a well researched popularizing book on British spiritualism and Philip Hoare's book on Victorian utopias including much entertaining material on spiritualism and related subjects. Roger Luckhurst, Janet Oppenheim, and Pamela

Thurschwell have each written on psychical research in nineteenth-century Britain. Ann Braude has shown the significant interactions between women's rights, abolition, radicalism, and spiritualism in the nineteenth-century United States. Bret Carroll has provided a comprehensive reading of the religious foundations of U.S. spiritualism as well is its core ideologies. Howard Kerr and R. Laurence Moore have both produced pioneering work on U.S. culture and spiritualism. John J. Kucich's recent book on nineteenth-century U.S. spiritualism develops this body of work still further. Work on mesmerism and its impact from the late eighteenth century onward has made connections between mesmeric trances and the cultures of mesmerism and spiritualism.[8] Though this body of research answers many key questions, other questions persist. What is the relationship between spiritualism and traditions of occult and magic, which often survived on the margins of mainstream culture, within folklore, for instance? How can spiritualism's rapid expansion beyond the United States be understood and what is its relationship to the Atlantic? How did the beliefs of many African Americans and Indians help to form and inform spiritualism?

This book addresses these and other questions through an examination of the materialist and historical underpinnings of spiritualism, particularly as they can be known through the literary culture of the period. The central focus of the book is spiritualism—the emergence of which, in the late 1840s in upstate New York, is mapped. I argue that an investigation of a transatlantic spiritualist culture as practiced in the United States demonstrates two of this book's claims. The first asserts that U.S. culture is built upon a history that includes, alongside what conventionally exists within cultural memory, the relics of what refuses to be repudiated and forgotten. Nineteenth-century U.S. culture can be read as a series of responses to the intervention of the past on the present. The past often surfaced at moments of trauma or transformation, exposing an inadequate process of mourning that Freudians theorize using the concept of the return of the repressed. Spiritualism provided an outlet in which the spirits of the dead spoke with and through the living, often exposing such relics. Through spiritualism, the past could be reconstituted and reclaimed according to the political, social, and cultural needs of the moment. An examination of the ways in which the spirits of the dead appear within the nineteenth-century United States allows for re-readings of the country's troubling colonial past and its ongoing relationship with its imperial present. The second claim is that discourses associated with spiritualism permeated nineteenth-century culture to a remarkable degree. Once this is comprehensively recognized, the past becomes more readable. One aim of the book is to register and explore that legibility, to show the ways in which the past looks different once the impact of the rhetoric, tropes, and practices of spiritualism are revealed.

First, I will review some definitions. Spiritualism is a broad term that covers a complex and sometimes heterodox system of beliefs and practices that have at their center a conviction in the proximity of a spirit world to the material world and of the possibility of communication through personal interactions between the two. This book examines a wide range of different kinds of beliefs and practices, all of which could be described as spiritualist in some way. It might be more accurate to describe beliefs in such communications in the plural as "spiritualisms," as some critics do, since practitioners could have very different ideas about the role of conventional organized religion, for example—especially Christianity—within their own spiritual worldview. They could also have conflicting notions about the best ways in which such ideas could be articulated or expressed. Mediums often had particular specialties that they cultivated.

Within the broad definition of spiritualism that is used in these pages are many differing potential definitions that are not pursued. The word spiritualism follows the usage established by a wide range of individuals who claimed it for themselves. It is taken to indicate a set of beliefs and their expression that begin with the events of 1848 known as the "Rochester rappings." These have conventionally been read as the start of a type of cultural practice that took place with increasing frequency in the decades that followed, by individuals who claimed special powers for themselves. The Fox sisters, Margaret and Kate, claimed that they were able to communicate with the spirit world through a series of sharp raps. These percussive noises—extensively investigated by doctors and others who were interested in both scientific and supernatural explanations and the conjunctions and disjunctions between the two—later turned out to be the product of cracking their toe joints against hard surfaces. But the Rochester rappings (the subject of extensive discussion both then and now) were the trigger for an explosion of interest in spirit communication, which rapidly spread throughout the nation and then across the Atlantic and beyond.[9] What started off as a local, private, experience of engaging with the dead in limited and primitive ways rapidly gained in sophistication and impact.

Early methods of communication—systems of rapping or knocking—developed slowly into sentences as spirits responded to the letters of the alphabet so that communications could be spelled out in painstaking detail, though the contents of some of their messages seemed, to some observers, not to be worth the trouble it took to record them. As will be discussed later in this book, others thought differently. Some spirits directed mediums to write their communications down. Others began to speak through mediums, literally borrowing their vocal chords and putting words into their all too willing mouths. This significant development was overtaken by an even more astonishing phenomenon as spirits began to materialize in séances and move and walk freely around the rooms in which people gathered to experience spiritualism firsthand.

Once rapping had begun to seem both dated and limited, the Fox sisters pioneered this development of communication and performance in the United States . Like other aspects of spiritualism it spread across the Atlantic. The first medium to produce so-called full body materialization in Britain was the young medium Florence Cook. This was not until 1873, some time after such materializations were established in the United States.[10] The practices of mediums repeatedly demonstrate that patterns of performance that were pioneered in the United States traveled with varying degrees of rapidity beyond its borders. Specialist spirit photographers emerged quite early in the inception of photography itself, producing images of spirits that suggested the invisible could be rendered visible through new technologies. Later still, mediums produced substances such as ectoplasm from their bodily orifices, astounding some and outraging others. This was in some ways a development from earlier séances in which flowers and a range of other gifts (often called apports) would be given by spirits to the living within séances. Yet flowers are a far cry from a semi-mysterious substance that apparently was produced from the bodies of mediums. Why did such a change happen?

The self-conscious transformation of spiritualism over a period of a few decades, and the ability to produce new and startling effect (or proofs as they were sometimes known) fascinated the public. I argue that many spiritualists had a profound understanding of the market value of the performances they put on and that developments in communication and special effects, such as previously outlined, were prompted by attempts to engage new audiences while entertaining and maintaining existing ones. This book considers several examples of the varied and often sophisticated ways in which spiritualists saw themselves as involved in a commodity culture that was undergoing considerable change in the early decades of the nineteenth century. Spiritualism was a protean phenomenon: part religion, part entertainment. To some it was an extension of their Christian beliefs. Such figures often conceived of it as demonstrating biblical truths in the contemporary era—an extension of an era of miracles into the present. To others it was a secular set of practices that could take place outside of, and separate from, any religious worldview. Some of its practitioners were fundamentally conservative; some used their interactions with the spirit world to further their already existing radical agendas.

Given spiritualists' reluctance to get involved in formal organizations it is unlikely that it will ever be possible to get an accurate figure for the numbers of people who thought of themselves as spiritualists. In 1854 the U.S. Senate received a petition with thirteen thousand signatures asking for the appointment of a scientific committee to investigate spirit communication.[11] This remarkable figure suggests the extent to which a phenomenon that emerged only a few years prior to this had taken hold of the popular imagination. Spiritualism became increasingly fashionable on both sides of the Atlantic within households where members of a family and their friends would attempt to contact the spirit world, as well as a form of popular public entertainment in which séances were staged by itinerant mediums. The losses associated with the Civil War also helped to produce an increasing interest in the attempt to bridge the gap between the living and the dead by communication with spirits, and they also produced consolatory emotional writing that aimed at suggesting ways for the grieving living to accept the deaths of healthy young men. Novels such as Elizabeth Stuart Phelps' *The Gates Ajar* (1868), whose protagonist is a young woman confronting her despair over the death of her brother in the war, aimed at an emerging market of mourners, many of whom were women.[12] The need for some way to cope with the grievous personal losses associated with the war led to a range of methods being used to communicate with the beloved dead, including séances. By the 1890 census the number of people who considered themselves spiritualists was 45,000. Figures going as high as eleven million (when the population was twenty five million) have also been claimed.[13] Why did so many Americans turn to spiritualism from the late 1840s onward, and why, eventually, did many of them move away from it? What did it provide them with and why did it stop providing it? Or did it? Where did spiritualism emerge from and how did it relate to forms of engagement with the supernatural also current in the same period? These are some of the questions that this book addresses and answers. Reading through newspaper accounts of séances, diary entries, autobiographies, biographies, poetry, and fiction as well as looking at photographs and magic lantern slides and other visual artefacts, I discovered the remarkable extent to which spiritualism permeated the culture more broadly. Spiritualism's infiltration into U.S. culture and the ways in which it was represented and debated in novels, poetry, lectures, newspapers, and visual culture is an important part of what is traced here.

Spiritualism depended on an understanding that the world of the living and that of spirits could engage with each other through individuals who were particularly sensitive in some manner. The mid-nineteenth century was a particularly fertile moment for the emergence of spiritualism due to a renewed interest in the processes and power of rhetoric, inherited from an earlier period; a focus on the individual and subjective experience and expression, which came from Romantic philosophy and thought; and a renewed emphasis on inner light and individualistic responses to a God (conceived of in a variety of different ways which came from challenges to Calvinism).[14] Finally, new modes of conceiving of death that had been taking place since the late eighteenth century but found particular expression in the culture of sentiment of the nineteenth. The emergence of a newly professionalized funerary market, among other factors, challenged existing ways of thinking about the dead and their places in the lives of the living.[15] The coalescence of these modes of thought and the discourses they produced prepared the way for the emergence of a form that frequently focused on the power of the voice and of personal inspiration from mysterious sources. They also allowed for a variety of interpretations regarding the meaning of spirit communication.

Spiritualism is, in part, an extension of a range of supernatural beliefs inherited from earlier periods. Many of the ways in which the supernatural is envisaged in the literature of the early Republic until the 1850s or so are constructed around ideas of contact, however loosely defined. The definition of the supernatural used throughout this work is that of the *Oxford English Dictionary*: "above nature; belonging to a higher realm or system than that of nature; transcending the powers or the ordinary course of nature." Such an expansive definition allows for the incorporation of a range of phenomena and ideas that contemporaries thought of as exceeding the boundaries of the natural world or in some ways defying rational explanations.

Extant accounts of spiritualist performance allows for a consideration of the séance as an arena with powerful analogies to Mary Louise Pratt's influential term a "contact zone." Pratt uses the phrase to "refer to the space of colonial encounters, the space which peoples geographically and historically separated come into contact with each other and establish ongoing relations, usually involving conditions of coercion, radical inequality, and intractable conflict."[16] This definition certainly suggests such space's affinities with some of the earliest forms of encounters the book investigates. Though these are not strictly colonial, in terms of the period in which they take place, they can be read through a consideration of a type of colonial mapping, which they implicitly gesture to by invoking figures precisely located in histories of contact in the colonial period, such as the appearance of William Penn and Pocahontas in the Shaker manifestations discussed in chapter 3. This points to a national drama conceived of in terms of negotiations between competing groups with very different and uneven access to power, as we will see.

The spectral figures of the returning dead that appeared within the cultural productions of white subjects in the nineteenth century were often used to critique, subvert, authenticate, or comment on contemporary U.S. concerns. They had a position of special privilege, that of being simultaneously inside and outside of it, literally insubstantial yet profoundly and materially substantiated by the occasions that produced them and gave them form. Their shadowy presence, unacknowledged though powerful, has always been there.[17]

Benedict Anderson has argued that many "'second-generation'" nationalists believed that it was possible to speak for, or ventriloquize, the dead "with whom it was impossible or undesirable to establish a linguistic connection."[18] He contrasts this with figures such as nineteenth-century Colombian Fermín de Vargas who "still thought cheerfully of 'extinguishing' living Indians, [while] many of his political grandchildren became obsessed with 'remembering,' indeed 'speaking for' them, perhaps precisely because they had, by then, so often been *extinguished*."[19] As we will see, many of the ways in which the dead were invoked and ventriloquized by spiritualists, particularly dead Indians, followed a very similar pattern to this. Once Indians could be regarded as being well on the way to being extinguished, speaking for them (to use de Vargas's terms) became an attractive prospect to some. While the mediums who worked in this way would not necessarily have regarded themselves as nationalists, their actions followed a pattern adopted elsewhere by individuals who were, explicitly so.

It is beyond the scope of this book to trace in detail the history of the complex circum-Atlantic legacies that produced spiritualism, though they are alluded to as appropriate. The legacies of slavery and of the treatment of indigenous peoples and others help to account for the ways that some nineteenth-century performances of spiritualism legitimate narratives of U.S. history that challenge existing hegemonies. Profound engagement with the spirits of ancestors and ideas of ghosts within African American writing has led to remarkable literary achievements in the twentieth century: Toni Morrison's *Beloved* (1987) is the most celebrated example.[20] There are very significant relationships between the spiritualist practices and expressions of the white Americans with whom the book is largely engaged and those of African Americans, including spirit possession and the role of women as mediums.[21] The appropriation and reversal of white Americans ideas about Indian spectrality that Leslie Marmon Silko subverts in *Ceremony* (1977) and *Almanac of the Dead* (1991) neatly corresponds to the opposite impulse traced here—the repeated invocation of Indian spirits and ideas of Indian spirituality by whites.[22] Indian and African American ideas about spirits permeated into the practices of white subjects who remade them by incorporating them into belief systems with which they were more familiar and comfortable: mainly emerging from a Protestant worldview. It is those practices with which the book is primarily engaged, and the issue of how cultures respond to, and shape, each other.

Indian spirits have always featured significantly within the practices of white mediums, particularly as spirit guides.[23] Their relationship to an evolving cultural tradition of representing Indians on the stage, in novels, and in poetry is close. This has continued well outside the boundaries of the United States, though undoubtedly it originated there. Indian spirit guides were frequently credited with significant power by white mediums. Their presence was an accepted and common part of spiritualist culture. They were usually believed to be highly perceptive, capable of significant insight, and possessed with powerful oratorical gifts. However some white mediums claimed to have their séances disrupted by the riotous behavior of Indian spirits whose pantomime-like performances were thought of as being both entertaining and shocking.[24] Indian spirits, within the performances of white mediums, largely conformed to one or the other of these stereotypes, which already had broader cultural valency.

Yet why does such Indian spectrality cross the Atlantic in the manner it does? In other words, how does an argument that focuses on the specific geopolitical circumstances that produce Indian spirits within the séances of white mediums in the United States explain their persistence in séances beyond its borders? And, while the appearance of Indian spirits does appear to be a kind of cultural residue of spiritualism's origins within the United States, what does it mean for Indians to be spirits at all? Recent work on the significance of the dead, or of ideas of ghostliness, in relation to nationhood has built on seminal accounts of U.S. literary culture and cultural memory to suggest the extent to which Indians have both been rendered ghostly and have themselves appropriated positioning as ghosts.

Renée Bergland argues that Indian ghosts are overwhelmingly invoked for nationalist purposes within U.S. culture, though they can also represent a resistance or counternationalism, especially when Indians themselves produced such haunted metaphors.[25] She shows, through examples drawn from a range of texts drawn largely from the late eighteenth to mid-nineteenth century, that a repeated motif for whites to represent Indians is to depict them as ghosts. Further, Indians are often represented as themselves choosing to "ghost" themselves through noble acts of disappearance, which points to a white belief that Indians were in the process of vanishing.[26] Her analysis of Indian ghosts, and ghosting within national consciousness, also acknowledges the extent to which other kinds of haunting, by slaves, women, and workers needs to be a part of the understanding of the construction of an identity in which haunting (in fact being haunted) was a defining aspect of national self-consciousness, particularly of white subjects.[27] The repeated motif within spiritualism of the Indian spirit guide appearing to a young, white, working-class woman medium, for example, suggests that for many of these mediums imagining a self that included a relationship to others who were also in danger seemed particularly appropriate.

The medium had also to engage in an act of self-abnegation in order to allow the spirit of others to speak or appear through her- or himself in a further self-conscious association with the vanishing Indian. In addition, the many surviving pieces of Indian oratory that made reference to a spiritual existence and a continued life beyond the grave seemed to demonstrate a connection between spiritualists and Indians. The ways in which Indians were imagined as already partially disembodied allowed them to be incorporated into transatlantic spiritualism with some ease. That process must be conceived of as one that has its origins in the ideological construction of the Indian during a period that saw Indians violently and forcibly moved from their homelands.

African American spirits did not play such a central part within white mediumship, though they were certainly visible. Nevertheless African American spirits also conformed to particular stereotypes. A significant degree of racial theatre was reproduced within séances. Minstrelsy and blackface performance were hugely popular on both sides of the Atlantic in the decades around spiritualism's earliest appearance and could constitute performances in themselves or be co-opted into other theatrical performances. The stereotypes produced and popularized in such shows offered mediums a kind of template from which they could work. A black spirit known as "Hambro" who repeatedly appeared in séances in Southampton Row in London, for instance, was described by the spiritualist and novelist Florence Marryat as "a very comical Negro," "humourous and full of native wit and repartee, as negroes generally are."[28]

The notion of generic characteristics, casually reproduced here as a generalization, suggests that Marryat, a professional actor at one point in her life, may well have taken her cue from stage stereotypes. It is very probable that traditions of blackface minstrelsy with their emphasis on what Eric Lott has described as "minstrel devices (ventriloquized dialect, racial burlesque)" were crucial to informing the modes of performance that took place within séances.[29] Séance goers witnessed a form of performance that was at least in part familiar to them because it corresponded to aspects of culture they had experienced or knew of. Disruptive spirits could offer light relief and important distractions within a séance but could also be blamed when messages failed to get through from the other side. Both possibilities were important for mediums, and both were repeatedly used, becoming a stock part of mediumistic technique.

Yet Indian spirits play a more central role in the culture of spiritualism than African American spirits raising questions about why white subjects found engagement with Indian spectrality easier or more efficacious than with black spectrality. Since the Atlantic is already indelibly marked by the history of slavery, black bodies are always embodied to a degree that Indian bodies are not. The process of ghosting can never be as fully successful for black subjects as it can for Indians, since they cannot be envisaged as disappearing in the same manner. At the same time, embodied black subjects are frequently constructed as being threatening, both physically and in terms of the social and political order. To some degree, the African American presence drops out of transatlantic spiritualism to a far greater extent than the Indian presence since it has its basis in a memory that can be only imperfectly and problematically invoked.

Spiritualists seemed to have engaged with an ethnic group comprised of subjects who were perceived as being already disembodied or in the process of becoming disembodied. This is not always a stable form of representation, though. By the 1840s—the period of spiritualism's emergence—theatrical representations of blacks and Indians seemed to display a binary tendency. Paul Gilmore argues that blacks and Indians "tended to be gendered as polar opposites— blacks as femininely submissive and emotional, in need of protection from (or victims of) the market, Indians as masculinely stoic and resistant to the market."[30] Yet he also notes that black and Indian representations could operate far outside this range, so while "in the sentimental realm Harriet Beecher Stowe evokes minstrel stereotypes in figuring [Uncle] Tom's inherent spirituality and goodness, in the arena of literary manhood William Wells Brown uncovers a revolutionary potential still buried within sentimental minstrelsy to figure a model of black manhood."[31]

Other critics have engaged with related arguments about the connections between U.S. citizenship and ideas of death—a number of them borrowing from Orlando Patterson's influential argument that slavery constitutes a sanctioned form of social death.[32] These kinds of preoccupations echo the interests of scholarship that considers subjectivity in relation to national and political representation and the politics of selfhood more centrally than this book does. Metaphors of the ghostly abound in such work. Sharon Holland asks,

> What if some subjects *never* achieve, in the eyes of others, the status
> of the "living"? What if these subjects merely haunt the periphery of
> the encountering person's vision, remaining, like the past and the
> ancestors who inhabit it, at one with the dead—seldom recognized
> and, because of the circum-Atlantic traffic in human cargo or because
> of removal, often unnamed?"[33]

The idea of subjects who remain as haunted beings, on the margins,
is a powerful metaphor for the kinds of social, ethical, and political
injustices that characterize and permeate U.S. history in terms of citizenship and representation. Russ Castronovo argues that the United
States likes its citizens to be maintained in a position of death-like
quiescence, but that they can be, and are, recuperated. He writes, "at
the edges of legal incorporation and political dispossession, the dead
walk, too: citizens are reanimated by republican, feminist, and
Africanist senses of subjectivity that materialize in the seams of
abstract personhood."[34] In both examples marginal figures are seen
as being in some way ghostly. Though they are dead, they have not
gone away; they remain to trouble the social and political order.

A further example of the use of a metaphor of haunting allows us
to see that such unruliness can be conceived of as structuring the
foundations of empire itself. Amy Kaplan uses the following ghostly
metaphor to consider the ways in which the imperial is constructed
through and out of the anarchic: "anarchy becomes an integral and
constitutive part of empire, central to the representation of U.S.
imperialism in dispersed locations and at different historical
moments. Anarchy is conjured by imperial culture as a haunting
specter that must be subdued and controlled, and at the same time,
it is a figure of empire's undoing."[35] In each of these examples the
ghostly or haunted is associated with disruption, suggesting that it
exists beyond the frame of more controlled and rationalist discourses
and structures of power.

PERFORMING SPIRITS

The kinds of beliefs that might be described as spiritualist were usually
articulated through some kind of performance or performances.
These might vary considerably in the form they took. They were frequently communal; at the very least (when successful), they involved

more than one person—the medium, or person in a trance, and the spirit who spoke or acted through the medium, for which he or she was a vehicle—and they always involved a belief that death was not the end of life. Clarke Garrett writes that "spirit possession is a kind of theater, communicating the experience of the sacred through culturally comprehensible words and gestures to the believing community."[36] Spiritualists learned from the technologies that produced ghosts or used the dead as their subjects. They also developed techniques from the theater, from sentimental novels and from melodrama. One crucial element of the séance was that it was highly performative: one scholar has recently called the Fox sisters "performance artists."[37] Though *Transatlantic Spiritualism* does not primarily focus on the performative aspects of spiritualism it does recognize that acknowledging its performativity is crucial.

Richard Schechner has defined performance as existing between ritual/efficacy and theatre/entertainment. He writes that

> Efficacy and entertainment are not so much opposed to each other; rather they form the poles of a continuum. . . . The basic polarity is between efficacy and entertainment, not between ritual and theater. Whether one calls a specific performance "ritual" or "theater" depends mostly on context and function. A performance is called theater or ritual because of where it is performed, by whom, and under what circumstances. If the performance's purpose is to effect transformations—to be efficacious—then the other qualities listed under the heading "efficacy" will most probably also be present, and the performance is a ritual. And vice versa regarding the qualities listed under "entertainment." No performance is pure efficacy or pure entertainment.[38]

Schechner's definitions of ritual/efficacy and theater/entertainment are instructive when thinking about the range of practices considered here. They allow us to see the extent to which they exemplify his notion of a continuum. Thinking of a performance as ritual entails recognizing certain characteristics. The performance must aim toward achieving certain results, involve audience participation and belief, represent "collective creativity," not invite criticism, take place within "symbolic time," and have a "link to an absent Other." In contrast, a performance at the other pole, that of theatre, centers on "fun" or entertainment, exists for those who witness it at that time, has an emphasis on the present, is performed by figures cognizant of what is taking place, has an audience in the position of watching and appreciating, and functions within the context of active criticism and of "individual creativity."[39]

When viewed within these parameters, the performances of spiritualism considered here begin to reveal themselves partly as efficacious rituals (the Shaker possessions of chapter 3) and partly as theatrical entertainment (séances involving Katie King in chapter 4). This movement away from "ritual" and toward the kinds of occasions best thought of as forms of "entertainment" helps to account for spiritualism's roots in the ritualistic practices of magic, the occult, and organized religion, as well as its movement as the nineteenth century progressed into an engagement with commodity culture. In that transition, which took place over several decades, the meanings of spiritualism altered in ways that this book investigates.

Yet this is only a partial account for the development of the kinds of patterns that can be traced within spiritualism. It does not fully address the relation between spiritualism and other forms of contemporary cultural practice that this book engages with and sees spiritualism as being intimately connected to. One powerful example of a process that the spiritualist performances discussed here have connections to is Joseph Roach's account of the relation between "memory, performance, and substitution" that makes up the processes of surrogation that he sees as central to performance.[40] Roach suggests that surrogation is an ongoing process within communities in which losses caused "through death or forms of departure" produce a need for a substitute. Yet the substitute can never be an exact fit for what they aim to replace, and the difficulties resulting from either the "deficit," the "surplus," or division they cause—combined with the anxiety produced from "the very uncanniness of the process of surrogation" itself—lead to a need for some mode of dealing with the crisis this causes. He writes that in this case,

> selective memory requires public enactments of forgetting, either to blur the obvious discontinuities, misalliances, and ruptures, or, more desperately, to exaggerate them in order to mystify a previous Golden Age, now lapsed. . . . [T]he process of trying out various candidates in different situations—the doomed search for originals by continuously auditioning stand-ins—is the most important of the many meanings that users intend when they say the word *performance*.[41]

Highly performative methods of communicating with the dead are part of U.S. cultural practice in ways that are not always recognized. Indeed performance was a central part of the ways in which colonizers encountered indigenous peoples in the colonial period, as new work by Susan Castillo has elegantly demonstrated. She shows, through scholarship that engages multilingual texts, the significance of performance within the early Americas. A distinction between the precontact performances of indigenous peoples and European traditions was that "they were embodied (in that they were enacted by actual human bodies) rather than scribal. European performative traditions were both: they were embodied in actual stage performance by actors, and scribal as well."[42] Spiritualist performances—by which I largely mean the activities of mediums within séances and the processes of speaking while in a trance—were also unscripted and, in Castillo's sense of the word, embodied. That aspect of spiritualism was particularly remarked upon. While what went on in such situations might be transcribed, each performance was essentially a new occasion, albeit one that took place within certain parameters. This suggests elements in common between spiritualism and earlier forms of performance that took place within preliterate societies. These included the performance of rituals such as magic and healing.

SPIRITS, GHOSTS, MAGIC, AND THE OCCULT

In *The Female Thermometer* (1995) Terry Castle argues that the eighteenth-century displacement and discrediting of supernatural and magical explanations led to an "historic Enlightenment internalization of the spectral—the gradual reinterpretation of ghosts and apparitions as *hallucinations*, or projections of the mind—[which] introduced a new uncanniness into human consciousness itself."[43] Many of the examples considered in this book show that the haunting qualities of the dead are not just invoked figuratively or metaphorically. The dead often literally or materially appear to come back and speak to the living and appear in their midst, somewhat crudely turning the uncanny consciousness back into a materialized form that seems to reanimate the popular beliefs that Enlightenment rationalism had claimed to discredit and undermine. The occult continued to shape both late eighteenth-century notions of the rational and conventional nineteenth-century religious beliefs, rendering them more complex and unstable—even baroque—than they have sometimes been taken to be.[44] As the nineteenth century continued, the occult ("that protean phenenomenon," as Susan Gillman has called it)[45] developed along new lines. She has shown how by the turn of the twentieth century the occult could be conceived of in terms of its complex racial possibilities. It could simultaneously (and paradoxically) suggest "an intensely nationalist spirit of the *Volk* or a transnational and pan-racial consciousness."[46] The popularity of spiritualist séances in the nineteenth century and their emphasis on the visibility of spirits, and access to them, makes such spirits distinct from the ghosts of the past. Scientific explanations for what went on within séances allowed for what today might seem to be distinct modes of explanation working comfortably together.

In her earlier book *The Apparitional Lesbian* (1993) Castle used the motif of "ghosting" to explain the ways in which lesbians have been made to vanish within cultural practices. This form of disappearance ("derealization") allowed for a process of exorcism that renders the lesbian powerless and hence safe.[47] Her analysis of the ways in which lesbians were made spectral within literary texts, in particular, as a way of legitimating and reinforcing the status quo might be applied to the complex ethnic impersonations of spiritualism. Non-white subjects could similarly be rendered safe through a process in which certain kinds of disruptive behavior could be legitimated and reined in.

Paradoxically, in some sense what spiritualists achieved was to make the dead less exotic. By bringing the spirits of the dead into the houses of the living and engaging them in the kinds of conversations that might have taken place if they were still alive, spiritualists could make even the dead seem quite banal. Whereas once ghosts had been awe-inspiring visitants from the afterlife, and angels moved in celestial realms far beyond that of mortals, the spirits that appeared or communicated in séances frequently lacked their grandeur, glamor, or ability to produce fear. They were frequently engaged by the material conditions of the world they had left behind to a remarkable degree, dispensing advice about the hiring and firing of servants and other matters just as if they were still alive.[48] This suggests a continuum in which spirits could remain actively interested in the living and this was profoundly comforting to many. It may be one explanation for spiritualism's rapid expansion. Another is its accessibility: anyone could, in principle, be a medium.

Underlying this book's approach and arguments are questions about why spiritualism was so popular, what motivated Americans to invoke and perform the spirits of the dead, and what molded and shaped such performances. Ideas about ghosts, the occult and magic, and the power of the supernatural that still had a currency in the 1840s also assisted its popularity. Joseph Smith, who received *The Book of Mormon* from the angel Moroni in 1827, used a magical seer, or peep stone, to translate them and was immersed within popular syncretized notions of magic.[49] The ideas of the Swedish mystic Emmanuel Swedenborg and of the Austrian pioneer of animal magnetism, Franz Anton Mesmer, still had significant relevancy in the period. Mesmerism enjoyed particular popularity in the 1830s and 1840s. The two pioneers were linked in an 1847 work by Swedenborgian professor George Bush, pithily titled *Mesmer and Swedenborg*. This work emerged from Bush's fascination for Andrew Jackson Davis ("The Poughkeepsie Seer," as he was known) who had published a collection of lectures in 1847 that supposedly came from the spirits of Swedenborg and the physician Galen, a figure of significance to some occultists.[50] Davis's autobiography, *The Magic Staff* (1857), explicitly invoked traditions of magic and the occult in its title. His work was one source for spiritualists.

TECHNOLOGIES OF THE GHOSTLY

Though spiritualism rapidly evolved into a central part of the lives of many within the United States, it was important to spiritualists to identify themselves as being on the margins. This is indicated by the spirits who largely communicated through mediums: children, Indian spirit guides, wives, sisters, brothers, and parents whose main significance to the bereaved concerned their location within the familial. Even when spiritualism became increasingly mainstream, even commonplace, it was often significant to them to use what R. Laurence Moore has called a "rhetoric of deviance."[51] It is as if the mediums themselves wanted to inhabit the shadowy realms that have been traditionally associated with spirits—though in fact many of them moved within far more conventionally material domains, such as drawing rooms, lecture halls, kitchens, and lodging houses. The origins and legacy of spiritualism are both on the margins and in the material—in a conceptually broad range of cultural forms, including séances, theatrical performances, ventriloquism, political oratory, and poetry.

In addition they could be found in technologies that aimed to produce or replicate spirits, such as magic lantern shows, phantasmagoria, and spirit photography. Magic lantern shows had long included ghostly subjects. In the hugely popular phantasmagoria shows that were popular during the early decades of the nineteenth century, ghosts were produced, through lighting and other special effects, to the delight and sometimes fear of assembled audiences. The shared subject matter of magic lantern and phantasmagoria shows and séances, of vaudeville and more voyeuristic performances in private rooms, went further than just the subject of ghosts to reveal other connections between them. The commodification of spirits—first through visual forms, such as these shows and then through séances—made them increasingly well-known to audiences. In addition, the images of far-away lands, such as the biblical Holy Land, began to make these places imaginable to audiences in new ways. Visual culture contributed to the formations of séances. For example, the combination of spirits and foreign places, which can be seen in magic lantern and phantasmagoria shows, passed into some early spirit manifestations. Spirits were sometimes asked to describe the places they now inhabited. Such exchanges between spirit and medium were analogous, on the one hand, to early American accounts of foreign travel and travels to the West, and on the other, to the representations of tourist destinations that took place within the shows. When spirits described the other worlds they encountered, they were in part helping their listeners to validate or critique the experiences they had of their own, rapidly changing world.

Some of the early séances that this book deals with, such as those attended by the abolitionists Amy and Isaac Post, included the spirits of a number of significant public celebrities. To some degree this echoes the kinds of juxtaposition of well-known individuals that magic lantern shows and other performances engaged with in which U.S. history was rendered up for commercial exploitation and consumption. But there was one crucial difference, of course: in the séances these figures appeared as spirits, not as eminent, dead figures from the past as they did in other cultural productions. As spirits they had in some way transcended death: spiritualists believed that such figures maintained, augmented, and extended the status they held in life. Skeptics often argued that they made themselves seem trivial or commonplace by the banalities they uttered and, some-times, the company they kept. The growing disillusion with the manner in which the ghosts of the past were brought into public consciousness may have paved the way for a desire to see apparitions in new ways, such as in séances. Theodore Barber has argued that by the 1830s Americans were so thoroughly familiar with magic lantern and phantasmagoria performances that they were starting to tire of them.[52] Spiritualism found a primed incipient audience amongst a public who had engaged with the phantasmal and the gothic through the new technologies and the broader culture of the late eighteenth and early nineteenth centuries.

The public appetite for such ghostly performances in the period leading up to this point helps to explain why spiritualism was both enormously popular as well as visually legible to contemporary audiences. Such technologies also carried the legacy of beliefs about the occult into the modern period, forming one of the connections between such practices and those of spiritualists. Innovative forms of entertainment were already emerging. By 1839 the first daguerreo-type was taken within the United States and within a decade, the photographic industry had emerged. These were producing significant images of the famous: By 1843 Edward Anthony photographed all the members of Congress. Matthew Brady began collecting photo-graphic images that would culminate in his *Gallery of Illustrious Americans* (1850). Spiritualism made good use of photography very early on—including the appropriation of Indians as frequent subjects—with results that are now infamous.[53]

The rhetoric of the ghostly and mesmeric was used to try to explain the mystery of the photographic process from very early in its inception.[54] Some photographers explicitly drew upon this as an important part of their aesthetic. The British photographer Julia Margaret Cameron was a significant pioneer in this regard. Writing of Cameron's relation to spirit photography, Marina Warner notes that such "photographs seem to . . . be picturing the dead, not in person as ghosts, but as prints of thought emanating from the subject in sym-biosis with the photographer."[55] Roland Barthes sees the emergence of the photograph as being associated with challenges to religion that were being experienced in the nineteenth century. He writes,

> Death must be somewhere in a society; if it is no longer (or less intensely) in religion, it must be elsewhere; perhaps in this image

which produces Death while trying to preserve life. Contemporary with the withdrawal of rites, Photography may correspond to the intrusion, in our modern society, of an asymbolic Death, outside of religion, outside of ritual, a kind of abrupt dive into literal Death."[56]

If photography emerges as a way of preserving life through the production of death, as Barthes argues,[57] then this reflects changing cultural understandings of both religion and death, and does so in a form that offers a way of reflecting and utilizing those changes (as well as contributing to them). Strikingly, though, the relationship between photography, spiritualism, and magic is repeatedly invoked throughout Barthes' text. Peggy Phelan notes that "Invoking terms such as *magic* and *alchemy* throughout his work, Barthes comes close to suggesting that photography is a medium, not only in the sense of an art form but also in the sense that it consorts with spirits."[58] The idea that technologies of the visual, such as photography, are in some way spiritist is one that has persisted since their inception. It is the relationship between the subject as both a living presence and one who is dead but will be maintained within the photographic realm exactly as they had once seemed that allows for the mediatory function of the photograph.

The reframing of the consequences of death within Christian ideology in the mid-nineteenth century allowed for a transformation in an understanding of the place and significance of the dead in the lives of the living. A more secularized understanding of death, informed by a variety of sources, was emerging by the late eighteenth century on both sides of the Atlantic.[59] Though this was challenged by the religious revivals of the Second Great Awakening, the increasing belief in the reunion of the family in the afterlife by the mid-nineteenth century was one that had a great impact on spiritualism.[60] Postmortem photography, which often placed the dead within an entirely or overwhelmingly secular realm, was both a symptom and a cause of this development. The history of postmortem photography, a widely used form of remembering the dead, is often linked to the photographs of the casualties of war, and the subsequent circulation of images of the dead into popular culture via newspapers and journals. The development of new visual technologies around the period helped augment the connection between spiritualism and photography. The deaths due to the Civil War led to a particular interest in spiritualism.

Séances, like postmortem photographs, took the dead into the homes of the bereaved.

The connections between spiritualism and photography took a number of other forms that ranged from the ways in which such images were staged and arranged to the meanings ascribed to the dead subjects or the spirits. The Civil War photographs of Alexander Gardner and Matthew Brady brought what were conceived of as the realities of the war back into the domestic lives of Americans. Though we now know that some of these photographs were carefully staged (using the same dead body more than once in different images and moving it to form a more pleasing composition), many Americans at the time saw these as highly realistic.[61] The kinds of things that went on within séances were also often appealed to as irrefutable evidence of the reality of spirits. The idea of witnessing was itself central to this.

The following *New York Times* editorial from October 20, 1862, suggests something of the experience that seeing Civil War photographs had on Americans:

> Mr. Brady has done something to bring home to us the terrible reality and earnestness of war. If he has not brought bodies and laid them in our dooryards and along the streets, he has done something very like it. At the door of his gallery hangs a little placard, "The Dead of Antietam." Crowds of people are constantly going up the stairs; follow them and you will find them bending over photographic views of that fearful battle-field, taken immediately after the action. Of all objects of horror one would think the battle-field should stand preeminent, that it should bear away the palm of repulsiveness. But on the contrary, there is a terrible fascination about it that draws one near these pictures, and makes him loathe to leave them. You will see hushed, reverent groups standing around these weird copies of carnage, bending down to look in the pale faces of the dead, chained by the strange spell that dwells in dead men's eyes.'[62]

What were these people trying to see in the eyes of the dead? What was it that they wanted from these dead men—comfort or explanation, reassurance perhaps? Surely some of the impulse that drew viewers "to look in the pale faces of the dead" somehow "chained" by the "strange spell" of what was in their eyes was the same as the impulse that led thousands of Americans to visit séances or conduct them in their own homes. The association between death, trauma, and the ghostly, and their didactic function through the process of testimony seems also in evidence here.

The staging of war photographs, and even photographs of spirits, was much like that of postmortem photographs in which the dead would often be dressed in their finest clothing and posed at the center of groups of mourners, usually close family members. Though the codes were not identical to those of spirit photographs, they, too, were carefully composed. Specialists in the particular techniques needed for such photography passed information on to others within professional magazines. One such piece appeared in the *Philadelphia Photographer* in 1877 and gave a macabre account of how to place the corpse in a suitable position when it cannot be taken to the photographer's studio.

> [S]ecure sufficient help to do the lifting and handling, for it is no easy manner [sic] to bend a corpse that has been dead twenty-four hours. Place the body on a lounge or sofa, have the friends dress the head and shoulders as near as in life as possible, then politely request them to leave the room to you and your aides, that you may not feel the embarrassment incumbent should they witness some little mishap liable to befall the occasion. If the room be in the northeast or northwest corner of the house, you can almost always have a window at the right and left of a corner. Granting the case to be such, roll the lounge or sofa containing the body as near into the corner as possible, raise it to a sitting position, and bolster firmly, using for a background a drab shawl or some material suited to the position, circumstance, etc. . . . Place your camera in front of the body at the foot of the lounge, get your plate ready, and then comes the most important part of the operation (opening the eyes), this you can effect handily by using the handle of a teaspoon; put the upper lids down, they will stay; turn the eyeball round to its proper place, and you will have the face nearly as natural as life. Proper retouching will remove the blank expression and the stare of the eyes.[63]

The reanimation of the dead, complete with "retouching" of the eyes to make them seem lifelike, seems to have been the motive behind much postmortem photography. The mourning process that this material object was intended to assist in acknowledged that the beloved was dead, but represented them as if they were not—as if they were asleep, perhaps, or even just sitting in a chair or sofa waiting for a visitor. The eyes of the dead were not supposed to reveal the secrets that the eyes of Brady's soldiers seemed to promise. They should represent the dead as if they were still living—as if there were no death, to use a phrase spiritualists ritually enunciated.

This makes the subjects of postmortem photography closer to the spirits that appeared in séances than the soldiers of war photographs for they were more life-like, more alive, than the corpses of the soldiers. Crucially, too, their injuries or illnesses were disguised and they were often represented as if they were peacefully sleeping. When spirits appeared in séances they were frequently free of any disfigurements they may have had while alive. Spiritualist photographers produced images of spirits that aimed to make their spirit subjects life-like in many instances, often posed with a friend or family member as if they were still part of a domestic environment. The exceptions to these kinds of compositional details seem mainly to be associated with the spirits of spirit guides or nonfamiliar, nonfamily members, who could appear in quite a random way behind or next to the main sitter, disrupting the compositional stasis of a scene, of which in life they would never ordinarily have been part.

Later still, spirit photographers provided evidence of the production of ectoplasm. Professional spirit photographers knew that secrets such as the use of double exposures could produce successful images of blurry figures that had every attribute of the spectral. Photographers such as the pioneering William Mumler specialized in capturing the spirits of the dead who surrounded the bereaved living who came to their studios. Sitters who came to his studio were astounded to see the spirits of their loved ones standing beside or behind them, sometimes with a comforting hand upon their shoulders. Sometimes photographs of materialized spirits would reveal that they were surrounded by other spirits, invisible to the naked eye but visible to the lens of the camera.[64] This suggested that photography literally allowed for the invisible to be rendered visible. Technological innovation, available commercially, altered the desires of large numbers of people making them want, and even need, items and modes of recollection or communication that had previously been unavailable to them.

CHAPTER 1

CROSSING OVER: THE SPIRITUALIST ATLANTIC

HAUNTED CROSSINGS

There is a joke that claims spiritualists first crossed the water in order to get to the other side. Despite its obvious shortcomings, it does suggest a more serious imperative: investigating the significance of the Atlantic in both the historical and material origins of spiritualism and its rapid growth. Nineteenth-century spiritualism is routinely conceived of as a phenomenon that originated in the United States and spread across the Atlantic and then eventually worldwide. Given the concurrence of the emergence of spiritualism and the rapid development of faster and cheaper modes of transatlantic travel and communications, it is useful to ask to what extent, and how, the Atlantic affected the development of the aesthetic models spiritualists engaged with.[1] Did the Atlantic function as a divide to spiritualists on either side of it? Did the formal practices of spiritualists vary to any significant degree between the two sides? Is any variance determined by geographical specificity? Did the Atlantic have particular and specific meanings for spiritualists? Might the Atlantic itself, and the possibility of spirit travels across and beyond it, even be invoked as a source of proof of the truth of spiritualism's claims? In one of the examples examined later in this chapter this certainly seems to be the case.

In their pioneering works on spiritualism in nineteenth-century Britain, Logie Barrow, Janet Oppenheim, and Alex Owen all make passing, albeit differing, comments on the relation between the emergence of spiritualism in England and the transatlantic visits of key American women mediums.[2] Oppenheim argues that "As spiritualism steadily moved westward across the United States, expansion to the east, across the ocean, was only a matter of time. There was a virgin audience in Britain, primed by news of the American phenomena, and ready to be impressed."[3] This brief comment on what is represented as the inevitable expansion of spiritualism raises questions about what the transatlantic circulation of spiritualism might add to existing understandings of transatlantic and transcultural exchange.

Oppenheim's claims about the simultaneous western and eastern expansion of spiritualism conflates two different kinds of expansion. The first is associated with the settling of the frontier; the second involves cultural imperialism abroad. To some degree this destabilizes conventional understandings of U.S. imperialism, which have tended to support what Amy Kaplan has called "a central geographic bifurcation."[4] Oppenheim's comment is very brief; the focus of her work is elsewhere. Yet, perhaps inadvertently, she adapts language often used for Manifest Destiny to describe the spread of spiritualism. Instead of the "virgin land," which awaits the white settlers who will displace the native population and bring it civilization, usually associated with the frontier myth we have the "virgin audience" in Britain, "primed" and waiting for the arrival of spiritualist mediums.

The metaphor has profound ethical and political implications, as Donald Pease has recently argued,

> Virgin Land narratives placed the movement of the national people across the continent in opposition to the savagery attributed to the wilderness as well as the Native peoples who figured as indistinguishable from the wilderness, and, later, they fostered an understanding of the campaign of Indian Removal as nature's beneficent choice of the Anglo-American settlers over the Native inhabitants for its inhabitants for its cultivation.[5]

As we will see, spiritualism follows the trajectory of the simultaneous expansion of trade routes and internal markets with the development of connections to international ones. The fact that its myth of origin places it firmly in 1848 allows us to read it in the context of other events associated with what Michael Rogin has called "the American 1848."[6] These include pioneering women's rights statements, such as the Seneca Falls Declaration, which was prompted after Lucretia Mott was refused a seat at the World Anti-Slavery Convention in London. But they also include repressive rather than progressive social and political agendas. Recent critical work has documented the appearance of the structures and rhetoric of imperialism in the popular culture of that period. In addition it has teased out the complex relationship between continental and imperial expansion, as well as the domestic and foreign, reconfiguration of models of the imperial United States.[7] Rogin writes, "While bourgeois Europe faced social revolution, America fulfilled in the Mexican War the Manifest Destiny initiated on Indian soil. While European dreams of equal political rights foundered on the social question, American expansion, in Andrew Jackson's words, 'extend[ed] the area for freedom' to the West."[8] At the contested moment at which Manifest Destiny was coined as a way of describing both a process and an aspiration of U.S. expansion and settlement, spiritualism was spreading throughout the United States and beyond. This cannot be read as mere coincidence: spiritualism was developed from contemporary ideological beliefs. One recent critic has even argued that "spiritualism constructed its own manifest destiny within the psyche."[9]

Owen attributes the spread of spiritualism from the United States to England to the visits and proselytizing of American mediums, such as Mrs. Hayden and Mrs. Roberts. Both Hayden and Roberts crossed the Atlantic in the early 1850s and were, as Owen puts it, "the forerunners of a steady stream of transatlantic visitors who helped establish a pattern of close ties between spiritualists in both countries."[10] She notes that when Harriet Beecher Stowe visited Britain in 1853, after the massive success of *Uncle Tom's Cabin*, abolition and spiritualism were "among the foremost topics of the day."[11] As we will see, however, though many early spiritualists were also avowed abolitionists, some converts to spiritualism maintained and developed their radical interests and others tended toward a more conservative understanding of spiritualism. A figure such as Stowe represents an amalgam of these two different positions: white, Christian, middle class, and with reforming tendencies. One British observer wrote to her husband in 1853 that "'The great talk now is Mrs Stowe and spirit-rapping, both of which have arrived in England.'"[12] The notion of arrival is more fraught and problematic than this commentator suggests. Stowe had long ago "arrived" in England in the disembodied form of her writings and reputation. A

French cartoon of the period plays with the conflict that these simultaneous arrivals caused. It shows Stowe abandoned by her would-be admirers who are all frantically engaged in table rapping.[13] Here Stowe does not just represent an American celebrity. As the author of a novel that brought abolition out of pulpits and political meetings into many polite drawing rooms and to new audiences, she is an important symbol for how the political and domestic are complexly intermingled.

What this and later chapters reveal is that, as more people converted to spiritualism on both sides of the Atlantic, they adapted it to fit with their own belief systems. This could (and in many instances did) mean that its radical and racial content—chiefly its engagement with the politics of slavery—was filtered out. At the same moment, territorial expansion within the United States was revealing (and exacerbating) anxieties about the nation itself, slavery, and "the racial identity of citizenship," which helps to explain why white Americans chose to regulate the racial aspect of spiritualism.[14]

What is undisputed is that the story of nineteenth-century spiritualism is one that involves a crossing over from one nation to another, via the Atlantic. Though it spread outside of Britain and the United States, it is beyond the scope of this chapter to do more than consider the transatlantic spread of spiritualism in its narrowest sense.[15] That crossing over has usually been read as being one way— from the United States to Britain. However, it went in both directions. The case of Daniel Dunglas Home, one of the most famous of all mediums, is telling. Home was a Scottish-born migrant to the United States who had spent enough time there to be regarded by some as an American when he returned to England in 1855. Contemporaries were confused by his national identity (Was he Scottish or American?), just as they were bemused and delighted by his extraordinary feats that blended magic, showmanship, and spiritualism. Home was particularly interested in showing his talents to members of the European aristocracy—notably in France, Italy, and Russia, where he was presented to figures such as Pope Pius IX, Napoleon III, and the Empress Eugenie.

Though many American and British spiritualists were more interested in the site of the séance, and the revelations it might contain, rather than its cultural origins, the same cannot be said for many historians of spiritualism. U.S. spiritualism is usually read as a culturally specific form that arises from a number of local geographical, cultural,

and political factors.[16] Such an approach, however, does not suffi-
ciently account for the complexities of its inheritance. It does not,
for instance, consider in detail the heterogeneity of a movement that
draws from both sides of the Atlantic, from European traditions of
magic, the occult, and religious beliefs and practices as well as the
presence, impact, practices, and importance of Indians and Africans.
Furthermore, it seems out of line with recent cultural criticism,
which finds in transatlanticist and/or circum-Atlantic readings of
U.S. culture significant ways to account for the experience of being
"a unit comprised of a plurality," as James Dunkerley has recently
described the United States.[17]

One shared critical assumption of such approaches is that pursuing less nationalist readings of crucial periods of Euro-American
interactions, such as the late eighteenth century, allows for more
productive readings of the complex entanglements of that period.
So, W. R. Verhoeven argues in his introduction to a collection of
essays, which focus on transatlantic literary relations between 1775
and 1815, that the essays suggest

> that the many revolutions that produced the national ideologies, iden-
> tities, and ideas of state of present-day America and Europe were not
> in the first place part of a national but of a *transnational* and, more
> particularly, *transatlantic* dialogue (between Europe and America), or
> even trialogue (between France and Britain and America).[18]

The problematization of the idea of nation-state as a category for the
investigation of culture more generally is one that many writers on
the transatlantic have acknowledged. Paul Giles has noted that
"Transatlantic Studies might be said to situate itself at that awkward,
liminal place where the national meets the global. . . . [It] takes its
impetus from an uncomfortable, highly contested situation where
traditional identities find themselves traversed by the forces of
difference."[19] Throughout these pages the séance is itself conceived
of as a site of diverse contestations, which reveal juxtapositions not
just of class, gender, and ethnicity—or indeed life and death—but
rather place and time. Thinking about what is here called the "spiritualist Atlantic" involves recognition of the diversity and heterodoxy
of the intellectual, cultural, political, and religious influences that
have contributed to the formation of spiritualism and the impact and
significance of the Atlantic in producing them. At the same time it is

important to recognize its role in disseminating spiritualism and taking it beyond the borders of the United States by its more material significance as a transportation route. The account of the development of mesmeric discourses and practices within the United States, which is discussed in chapter 2, demonstrates the significance of the trialogue outlined above.

THE TRANSATLANTIC MARKET IN SPIRITS

Séances could fulfill a variety of entertainment functions, satisfying a wide range of emotional and entertainment needs. Since it was important to professional mediums who earned their livings through séances for their audiences to return, putting on a good show was essential. What is clear is that gradually, on both sides of the Atlantic, the private séances that characterized early spiritualism evolved into practices that were knowingly performed with levels of professionalism that turned them into ways of making a (sometimes lucrative) living. While these included placing advertisements in newspapers, charging admission fees, publicizing attractive young mediums by circulating their photographs (the medium Cora Hatch was celebrated for her beauty), they also included responding to other forms of entertainment that were rivals for the kinds of audiences mediums wanted to attract.

Many spiritualist mediums were attuned to a market that became increasingly international. Specialist journals and books and the interest of eminent individuals (including the involvement of the Fox sisters with Horace Greeley, the editor of the *New York Tribune*, and P. T. Barnum) all helped boost the public's interest and give them ways of pursuing it too. Mediums constantly evolved novel ways of engaging with the spirit world and this changing spiritualist culture kept audiences coming back to attend séances with great loyalty. The emphasis of innovation, on the one hand, and an unchanging message, on the other, was both reassuring and exciting. Mediums, as advertisers would do with increasing sophistication later in the century, found different ways of saying the same things. What amounted to subtle distinctions in the packaging of messages allowed mediums to retain aspects of séances that were proven to work well and to innovate, too. This aspect of spiritualism, its recognition of the role of markets and consumers in spreading its message and being appreciative audiences for it, was always a part of the way in which it operated on both sides of the Atlantic. To understand the close relationship between its methods and its spread let us turn to its emergence in New York State in 1848.

One key aspect of the Rochester rappings often noted by critics is their geographical and historical location. Strictly speaking, Margaret and Kate Fox's first encounter with spirits took place in a location about twenty miles from Rochester called Hydesville. But they were rapidly taken to Rochester by their mother to live with their married sister Leah when the huge interest created by the rappings severely disrupted their lives. The part of New York State in which the Fox sisters first started their extraordinary communications with spirits has had a significant significant role to play in the economic, political, and religious histories of that moment. The impact of the geographical and historical proximity of spiritualism, women's rights, abolition, and religious transformation is further suggested by the fact that key individuals were involved in spiritualism and abolition, spiritualism and women's rights (for example, the political activist Victoria Woodhull), or spiritualism and challenges to conventional religion, or a combination of these.[20] While Rochester had an important role to play in the development of religious and political discourse and activism, it was also (and not coincidentally) on an important trade route: the Erie Canal. In this way it contributed to the opening of the West to settlers and the development of international trading networks. It was a region that had a significant role as a place of transition. It was experiencing rapid growth and change. Finally, it had also been powerfully affected by the itinerant preachers of the Second Great Awakening.[21]

The Revolutionary War and the War of 1812 both made the strategic significance of gaining control of the rivers and lakes of eastern New York and developing and extending them by artificial waterways, such as canals, a pressing concern.[22] George Washington argued that such improvements would allow for extensive trading, leading to a greater volume of exports and a national cohesion that would bind "these people to us by a chain which can never be broken."[23] Christopher Colles, an Irish engineer who had previously worked on the improvement of the River Shannon, wrote in 1785 of envisaged developments that would lead to innovative trading possibilities. He argues that "internal trade will be increased—by this also, the foreign trade will be promoted—by this, the country will be settled—by this, the frontiers will be secured—by this, a variety of articles, as masts, yards, and ship timber may be brought to New York, which will not bear the expense of land carriage."[24] What Colles envisaged was nothing less than the emergence of a competitive trading nation building its status and wealth through international capitalist exchange. Making the natural waterways more navigable and developing an infrastructure based on the creation of artificial waterways would encourage the development of trading possibilities that could challenge those of the more established nations of Europe. The swift and efficient movement of peoples and goods would allow for military defenses where needed on the one hand, and the transportation of luxury goods associated with cosmopolitan standards on the other.[25]

Others echoed the ambitions of Colles. Gouverneur Morris, contributor to the U.S. Constitution and international statesman, wrote of the possibilities that navigable waterways would offer. In an 1800 letter to an overseas correspondent he noted, "As yet, my friend, we only crawl along the outer shell of our country. The interior excels the part we inhabit in soil, in climate, in every thing. The proudest empire in Europe is but a bauble compared to what America *will* be, *must* be, in the course of two centuries, perhaps of one."[26] The discourses of navigability, trade, warfare, nation, and empire are all perceivable here as part of a composite narrative of national expansion and consolidation. This, in miniature, echoes David Kazanjian's argument of the significance of mercantilism in creating a dominant United States within an international system of economic exchange. He cites William Earl Weeks's claim that "the home market cannot be understood apart from its international context . . . the development of the nation cannot be understood apart from the development of the empire."[27] Rochester's position within eastern New York made it ideal for development as a key settlement along the envisaged trade route.

The Erie Canal was opened in 1825 by the governor of New York, DeWitt Clinton, who sailed from the start of the canal to the point at which it joined the Hudson River and from there to New York and the Atlantic. The vessel he traveled on was called the *Seneca Chief*; its cabin contained a lithograph by George Catlin of Clinton draped in a Roman toga. Catlin was later more celebrated for his images of Indians, but he was also implicated in territorial expansion through the landscapes he produced on his 1832–1834 travels among Indians.[28] The image of Clinton suggests the complex imperial imaginings of that moment. On his arrival in New York he poured water from Lake Erie into the Atlantic, in a ceremony called the Wedding of the Waters, symbolizing the possibilities of the transformed connection between East and West and the potential this offered for international and transatlantic trade as well as cultural and economic exchanges. A part of the water was kept to one side to be given to the Marquis de Lafayette, who had traveled along the Grand Canal joining Buffalo and Albany as part of his celebratory tour of the United States the previous year.[29] As we will see, he had an important role in introducing animal magnetism to the United States from France. Animal magnetism, in a somewhat altered form, would subsequently become better known as mesmerism and finally as hypnotism, the term still used for it today. The gradual period during which its name altered also saw a change in the way it was believed to work, and the manner in which it was practiced. The popularity of animal magnetism played a significant part in preparing the way for the emergence of spiritualism, which had some close connections with it. Water from other major rivers, including the Nile, the Ganges, and the Rhine, was also symbolically poured into the ocean, suggesting a more expansive idea of transnational trade and commingling.

Rochester was well placed to contribute to the social, political, and economic formations of that moment. Its significance as a seminal point on a trade route linking East and West, the impact of its role in the challenges to religion that were taking place in the period, and its contribution to political and religious activism all suggest the ways in which it was a place of important contestations in the young Republic. The Fox sisters claimed that the spirit who first communicated with them was that of a peddler who had been murdered a few years earlier. Such a figure personifies mobility and flexibility and vividly suggests the significance of trade and commerce—the movement of capital and people. Jackson Lears has argued that the figure of the peddler was "an early carnivalizer of culture and purveyor of commodity fetishism."[30] Rootless and mysterious, the peddler, with his combination of goods, cures, esoteric knowledge, and ability to entertain, suggested access to widely variant other worlds, including that of the supernatural. No wonder, then, that peddlers were often characters in the popular ghost stories of the period.[31]

Spiritualism's emergence within the particular arena of activities and discourses that marked out that geographical area and temporal

moment suggests the need to read it alongside the important challenges to the political and social status quo that were taking place,
which include women's rights, the rights of African Americans and
Indians, and contestations over social positions and the appropriation of, and access to, culture and land. Many of these had important
transnational dimensions in which the Atlantic played a key role. The
most obvious example is abolition: in 1840, for example, London
hosted the world antislavery convention.[32] In 1848, when the Fox
sisters launched spiritualism on the world, the United States was still
reliant on a system of slavery that allowed it to prosper economically;
but alongside this, the country had experienced encounters with
indigenous peoples whose effect on U.S. culture was more profound
than white Americans were comfortable to admit.

U.S. AND BRITISH SPIRITUALISTS

U.S. spiritualism seemed, to those who believed in it, to be one way
of domesticating and containing the spirits of the dead, and keeping
them within the comforting confines of the familiar. Spiritualism
removed fear from encounters with the dead and replaced it with
tenderness, benevolence, and love. It turned these meetings into
events to be anticipated with pleasure rather than dread or fear.
Sentiment and melodrama became important formal modes for creating the rhetoric and models of behavior involved in encounters
with spirits. They even created a certain decorum that helped maintain the discipline of the séance. Spiritualism could make such
encounters into social occasions in which long-separated family
members came together again and exchanged news, public entertainments, and exercises in nostalgia, which were also about making
the extraordinary ordinary once more, through a process that was
itself extraordinary. The ways in which Americans came to engage
with their dead through spiritualism were profoundly attractive to
many but repugnant to others.

Wherever spiritualism spread, many of its adherents grappled with
the fact that it had its origins in the United States. Seen in this way,
it appeared to be a cultural import that was an early example of the
many other American imports that had affected the experience of
Europe from the colonial period onward. These included peoples
like the Indians, who had been brought to Europe since the sixteenth

century to mixed responses of awe and abhorrence; foodstuffs like potatoes; intoxicants such as tobacco; as well as literary and other cultural productions. To describe it in this way might seem exaggerated, but the history of spiritualism's spread across the Atlantic and the movement of spiritualists back and forth between the United States and Britain, carrying particular structural tropes and language with them, show the significance of its transnational and transatlantic expansion.[33]

Once spiritualism had crossed the ocean and "arrived" in England, its extraordinary spread on that side of the Atlantic rivaled even that of its remarkable explosion in the United States. Its growth within Britain sparked a good deal of anxiety among many observers who cast their anxiety not just as a fear about its unknown nature but specifically as one about a form of American cultural imperialism, and indeed contamination, which needed to be resisted. This strange fad, which had crossed the water, might be acceptable in the United States, but what place did it have in Britain? What kinds of challenges did it pose to the British way of life, and what kinds of contributions could it make? Contemporary British commentators on American life, such as Charles Dickens, Fanny Trollope, and Frederick Marryat, had shown to the British public that in many respects the New World and the Old were indeed very different.[34] In *American Notes* (1842), Dickens argues that with respect to religious practices there was less division between the two countries than might seem to be the case.

> I do not find in America any one form of religion with which we in Europe, or even in England, are unacquainted. Dissenters resort thither in great numbers, as other people do, simply because it is a land of resort; and great settlements of them are founded, because ground can be purchased, and towns and villages reared, where there were none of the human creation before. But even the Shakers emigrated from England; our country is not unknown to Mr Joseph Smith, the apostle of Mormonism, or to his benighted disciples; I have beheld religious scenes myself in some of our populous towns which can hardly be surpassed by an American camp-meeting; and I am not aware that any instance of superstitious imposture on the one hand, and superstitious credulity on the other, has had its origins in the U.S., which we cannot more than parallel by the precedents of Mrs Southcote, Mary Tofts the rabbit-breeder, or even Mr Thom of Canterbury: which latter case arose some time after the dark ages had passed away.[35]

This uneven catalogue of figures scarcely veils a contempt that had already been exposed explicitly elsewhere in the book in his account of his visit to a Shaker community. If he is correct, his claims have a use in explaining a reason why spiritualism captured the imagination in nineteenth-century Britain. Dickens suggests the contiguities between Britain and the United States that allowed for shared experiences. As Owen puts it, "Unconcerned by dire warnings that spiritualism was 'an especially American plot' concocted by those who sought to 'propagate their own religious and political views,' many were keen to give the spirits the benefit of the doubt."[36] More pointedly, perhaps, many converts simply were not interested in such interpretations, finding in spiritualism rather a set of practices that they found congenial, comforting, exciting, unconventional, spectacular, and ultimately available to them. In other words, many British spiritualists seem to have cared very little about whether spiritualism had come over from the United States, or what it implied even if had. For, the whole point about it to them was surely that by its very nature spiritualism, predicated on notions of boundary crossing, rendered the notion of boundaries and of crossing more complex than such attacks implied. Faced with the "evidence," as it was usually seen, that dead loved ones could communicate with the living even after crossing over, it made no sense that only dead Americans could perform this feat. Though a great deal in the world of spirits closely resembled the living world, national boundaries were largely absent from descriptions of the spirit world.[37] The dazzling array of figures from different cultures that regularly appeared in séances on both sides of the Atlantic seemed to offer pluralist possibilities that overcame mere human and national boundaries.

That is not to say, however, that many American attempts to describe the world of spirits did not borrow heavily from Republican sentiment, political theory, or rhetoric, as Bret Carroll has recently shown. Andrew Jackson Davis published a new version of the Declaration of Independence in *The Spirit Messenger* in 1851, emphasizing religious rather than political concerns.[38] What this suggests, then, is that British spiritualists were embracing a cultural movement without expressing great anxiety about its origins or source. They were less interested in a defensive, conservative reading of culture than in embracing novelty.[39] This account of cultural migration has implications for the great wave of American cultural exportation that is currently evident. It is as true today as it was in the nineteenth century that the circulation of American images, ideas, and even items (clothing, food, and so on) often takes place without a highly sophisticated analysis of what their meanings are. Conversely, of course, the opposite can also be true. British spiritualists embraced a cultural form that was an amalgam of a set of collisions that took place within a republic that had broken with Europe but still maintained close relations with it.

Why did spiritualism cross the water and establish itself as a popular and successful form in Britain and elsewhere as quickly as it did? Much existing work on nineteenth-century British spiritualism has resisted that question, though these are still early days in that particular area of investigation. Logie Barrow has questioned the established wisdom of the accepted account of origins in England propounded by some cultural historians. In his insistence on some of the shared characteristics between England and the United States—a profound interest in self-education, some shared religious groups or sects with belief systems that anticipated spiritualism (such as the Shakers)—he argues that the chronology and geography of early spiritualism and its spread have been misrepresented. He rightly insists on the complexity of the relation between a series of sometimes loosely related phenomena that seemed to focus, for a moment, upon spiritualism. As he writes, "very broadly, we should talk less in terms of lines of descent than of points of blur and tension between, say, Owenism, herbalism, Swedenborgianism, mesmerism, Methodism, Chartism and other isms."[40] His injunction to consider conjunctions blurs, and tensions opens up a hugely rich vein of investigation that has been probed by a number of scholars.[41]

One way of considering the significance of these "points of blur and tension" is, paradoxically, to pay close attention to the origins and forms of spiritualism and to trace contiguities and overlaps. This is to take issue, for a while in any case, with Daniel Cottom's argument that the meaning of spiritualism is more significant than its origins.[42] Instead, it seems the origins of spiritualism themselves help to elucidate its meaning, as well as the "experiences, discourses, and practices" that primarily interest Cottom in his work on spiritualism and surrealism.[43] Accounts of origins may well be highly significant in defining and suggesting the range of experiences that go into producing the discourses and practices of spiritualism. They may, to put it another way, be indistinguishable from each other in key areas. If this is true, then we ignore them at our peril.

Very early on, spiritualism was ethnically hybrid, and it appealed across ethnic lines. My focus here is largely on white subjects, but there were a number of black subjects who also investigated the spirit world. Spiritualism is crucially enmeshed within the abolitionist movement through the different kinds of involvement of a number of key abolitionists, both white and black—notably William Lloyd Garrison, Sojourner Truth (who converted late in life), William Cooper Nell, Amy and Isaac Post, and Harriet Tubman.[44] The black Shakers Rebecca Perot and Rebecca Cox Jackson converted to spiritualism and were active mediums. Too little is yet known about the activities of black mediums. Furthermore, spiritualism's appeal among abolitionists, and also those involved in the women's rights movement, suggests its movement from the margins into mainstream American culture—even literary culture—which needs to be investigated.

Geoffrey Nelson has described the spread of spiritualism from the North East to the rest of the United States and beyond, arguing that in its earliest period the strongest opposition to spiritualism came in the Southern states. Spiritualists in Memphis, who came to hear the celebrated medium and historian of spiritualism Emma Hardinge Britten preach, were threatened with lynching at one point. (She faced the same threat in South Carolina and cancelled her lecture as a result.) In Alabama, the State Legislature passed a bill that threatened a fine of $500 for anyone giving a demonstration of spiritualist manifestations.[45] Yet the hugely successful white medium Cora Hatch was "welcomed" into black churches in Washington, DC, even though she never experienced such invitations from white evangelists.[46]

Nelson and Braude both argue that one reason for the virulence of opposition to spiritualism in the south was the association between spiritualism and abolition. The kinds of religious syncretism that spiritualism always built upon were also more intimately connected to ethnicity in the South than they were in the rest of the United States. There are common elements between Africanist religious beliefs and practices and those of spiritualists (ideas of spirit possession in voodoo, the significance of ancestors, and so on), which, allied to spiritualism's avowed egalitarianism, made it attractive to African Americans. Given this, it is unsurprising that New Orleans seems to have been a center of Southern spiritualism with African American mediums and supporters alike. Creoles and Catholics were also more involved in spiritualism there than Protestants. In the Northeast, on the other hand, spiritualists tended to come from a Protestant background. Spiritualist periodicals were published (in French) in New Orleans by Francophone ex-Catholics.[47] Free Creoles of color produced narratives that recorded their communications with spirits. One medium, Henri Louis Rey, received messages from Jesus, President Lincoln, Montesquieu, Napoleon, Rousseau, Toussaint L'Ouverture, and Voltaire, among others.[48] More work needs to be done on the activities of black mediums working in the Southern states, which might alter existing histories of the subject.

Many white mediums acknowledged their presence, often in passing, in their writings. Emma Hardinge Britten mentioned meeting a number of black mediums, including slaves, on a visit to the South in 1859–1860, though she gave limited detail about what her experiences with them were.[49] New readings on the relations between such black mediums and diasporic religious belief systems might allow scholars to follow up possibilities of interaction between the activities of Northeastern white spiritualists and African American Southern spiritualists, who came from quite different religious, political, and ethnic backgrounds. In addition the spiritualist and spiritist practices of Haitians, Puerto Ricans, Mexicans, Cubans, and others who have become entangled in U.S. imperial ambitions have contributed to the heterodoxy of contemporary spiritualism.[50] These different types of spiritualism, or spiritualisms, might better be understood within a context of origins and also through less nation-based readings. The close connection between radical politics and the earliest manifestations of spiritualism is one of the aspects that do not remain constant over time. Yet at its earliest inception its radical roots are the most apparent, most particularly in relation to slavery, women's rights, sexual politics, and the franchise.

The transnational and transatlantic nature of the debates about abolition and women's rights, and the internationalism of their proponents in this period have had increasing recognition in recent years. Margaret McFadden has identified six main factors that contributed to what she calls "woman-to-woman international connectedness" in the nineteenth century.[51] They are: new possibilities in the realm of communications and travel and their publicization; the impact of the work of Protestant and Catholic religious figures (despite the conservatism of their ideologies); the impact of reform movements and their internationalism; the role of utopian movements; the extensive ideological and personal connections of revolutionaries, refugees, and others; the impact of the work; and personal example "female literary celebrities" (her examples are Harriet Beecher Stowe and George Sand).[52] British and American activists shared platforms on both sides of the Atlantic. They exchanged ideas, gave each other intellectual, personal, and political support and hospitality. The interest of a number of reformers in spiritualism and the networks that already existed between them also allowed for spiritualism's rapid spread.[53]

Given the connections between these forms of political engagement, it is not surprising that spiritualism, too, should have an international profile very early in its history. Central to this is the possibility of travel and its relation to communications technology. The increasing speed, safety, and commercial availability of systems of travel in the nineteenth century allowed mediums to travel within and between Britain and the United States—even as far as New Zealand—to demonstrate their skills and to publicize and market their writings. New technologies also, famously, provided metaphors by which supernatural occurrences could be described and understood. The medium John Murray Spear explained the significance of electricity and telegraphy within his spiritual cosmos in the following way: "Between the Grand Central Mind and all inferior minds there subsists a connection, a telegraphic communication, by means of what may be termed an Electric chain, composed of a greater or less number of intermediate links. The greater mind, being always positive to the lesser, can affect, impress, or *inspire* it."[54] The wide comprehension of the relevance of such a metaphor is suggested by the fact that the most significant American spiritualist periodical of the 1850s, edited by Samuel Brittan, was called *The Spiritual Telegraph*.[55] Spiritualists rapidly embraced photography, as we have seen. Many spiritualists embraced scientific innovations and looked to science for explanations for how the spirit world might be constructed. Many scientists were fascinated by their investigations of the spirit world.[56]

TWO SIDES OF SPIRITUALISM

We can explore what transatlantic connections meant to spiritualists by examining the experiences of two figures whose involvement in spiritualism took place on both sides of the Atlantic. Reading these through a transatlantic focus leads to an understanding of spiritualism's relation to modernity (in its broadest sense) and to complex meanings, as well as helping to think through issues of cultural contact and spread. In her seminal work *There Is No Death* (1891), the British novelist Florence Marryat describes an incognito visit she paid to a New York séance in 1884 that left her a firm believer in spiritualism. The visit took place while she was in transit to a professional engagement in Boston, having just traveled from England. She was already well known as a writer and a spiritualist, but also as the daughter of Captain Frederick Marryat whose novels, largely about the sea, had sold in huge numbers earlier in the century.

She writes that having arrived in New York with some time to spare before she left for Boston, she decided to attend a séance. Looking in the local newspaper, she found an advertisement for a meeting at which full body materializations of spirits were to take place. Such materializations were very popular among spiritualists; they seemed to bring the realities of the existence of spirits closer to them. Seeing the spirits of their dead loved ones before them in body form was of far greater comfort to many spiritualists than just hearing raps or receiving written messages could ever be. Marryat had attended many such séances in Britain already (a detail that is significant here) and had encountered the spirit of her dead daughter, Florence, a number of times. Florence had died shortly after her birth, but was readily recognizable to her mother by her cleft palate even when she appeared as a much older figure. Some spirits, especially the spirits of very young children, grew older in the spirit world. In a previous manifestation she had appeared in the form of a girl of about seventeen years. Marryat arrived at the New York séance keen to use the experience as a test of the facts of spiritualism and also, perhaps, to have an experience of what séances were like on the other side of the Atlantic. Might American spiritualism differ in some ways from British spiritualism or from the way American mediums operated in Britain? She was keen to find out.

In the New York séance she witnessed a series of materializations that impressed her so profoundly by their sheer quantity that she sought a physical explanation for them. She found it in the climate, suggesting that "the dry atmosphere of the United States" assisted whatever the process was that allowed for such transformations to take place.[57] She also noted that she found the number of spirits that materialized in the United States surprising. Female spirits tended to wear white clothing rather than white drapery, as she had experienced in Britain, while male spirits wore clothes that approximated those they appeared in while alive.[58] What struck her most, though, was the appearance of figures she had longed to see. The male conductor of the séance made the following announcement, which particularly interested her:

> "Here is a spirit who says she has come for a lady named 'Florence,' who has just crossed the sea. Do you answer to the description?" I was just about to say "Yes," when the curtains parted again and my daughter "Florence" ran across the room and fell into my arms. "Mother!" she exclaimed, "I said I would come with you and look after you—didn't I?"
>
> I looked at her. She was exactly the same in appearance as when she had come to me in England—the same luxuriant brown hair and features and figure, as I had seen under the different mediumships of Florence Cook, Arthur Colman, Charles Williams, and William Eglington; the same form which in England had been declared to be half a dozen different media dressed up to represent my daughter, stood before me there in New York, thousands of miles across the sea, and by the power of a person who did not even know who I was. If I had not been convinced before, how could I have helped being convinced then?"[59]

The appearance of Florence convinced her mother through her resemblance to the spirit she had seen in numerous séances in England, despite all that skeptics had told her about how she was being duped. Further, as the extract above shows, it is the fact that Marryat believed herself unknown in New York that convinced her. How could what she had seen possibly be fraudulent? As the séance continued, and the spirit of a friend appeared, providing her with additional proof (though by this time she was already persuaded), she found her conviction strengthened by the conductor of the séance. She continues,

> I was more deeply affected than I had ever been under such circumstances before, and more deeply thankful. "Florence" made great friends with our American cousins even on her first appearance. Mrs. William's conductor told me he thought he had never heard anything

more beautiful than the idea of the spirit-child crossing the ocean to guard its mother in a strange country, and particularly, as he could feel by her influence, what a pure and beautiful spirit she was. When I told him she had left this world at ten days old, he said that accounted for it, but he could see there was nothing earthly about her."[60]

This experience of a séance on the other side of the Atlantic was clearly seminal for Marryat, particularly given the path that had taken her to it. When she was younger she had thought of contact with a world beyond this one as something unmediated by others— in other words, as something individuals experienced for themselves through seeing spirits or ghosts as they might call them, or having heightened spiritual awareness. This form of belief was one she claimed for her father; she gave an example of it in *There Is No Death* when she described his account of seeing the spirit of his brother while he was anchored off the coast of Burma.[61] The spirit told Frederick Marryat that he had died, and Marryat then recorded the exact moment this happened in his log. Later he claimed that this was indeed the time at which his death took place.

Florence Marryat gave an account of seeing spirits in the years before she became a convert to spiritualism. While living in India with her first husband, she saw figures draped in white, which she initially mistook for Indians and then recognized, she said, as spirits. While such experiences were geographically varied, as these examples show, her experience of visiting séances and consulting mediums had often been associated with the United States. It was, for example, when she visited an American medium in London in 1873 that her investigations into the spirit world became systematized and started to involve professional mediums. Though she consulted a number of British mediums while in London, she also went to the séances of American mediums based there and entered into a transatlantic correspondence with an American medium in the late 1880s. Such transatlantic links were a characteristic of spiritualism from its very earliest days as accounts by Marryat and others show. Spiritualism was often characterized not just by social mobility but by geographical mobility too, as the case of Emma Hardinge Britten demonstrates.

Britten spent many years of her life in the United States, marrying the American spiritualist William Britten there. Her most celebrated piece of work, *Modern American Spiritualism* (1870), is a seminal account of the emergence and spread of spiritualism within the United States. From any perspective, she is an important figure; from a transatlantic one, she is crucial. Her autobiography attests to a life of significant mobility and activity, and an involvement in substantial development of spiritualism on both sides of the ocean. She is a figure who can be cast as a notable transatlanticist in terms of her travels across the Atlantic and her Anglo-American perspective.

Like Marryat she had a strong feeling for the sea. Some of her most dramatic narratives, clearly intended as being proofs of her mediumship, tell of shipping disasters predicted and narrowly avoided by her. Like Marryat, who found considerable comfort (as well as evidence of spiritualism) in spirit messages from her sailor stepson and sailor brother, sailors played a part in Britten's life. Her spiritual beliefs were underpinned by the superstitions traditionally associated with sailors and the sea. Certainly, magic and the occult, which were folklorized throughout the eighteenth century, continued to play a part in the lives of seafarers beyond the point at which they was significant to the general population.[62] Her father was a sea captain, like Marryat's, and she wrote that her dead sailor brother (later a spirit guide for her) sent her the first message from the spirit world that convinced her of spiritualism.[63] Her brother's message, rapped out to her as she pointed a pencil at the letters of the alphabet, provided a proof to her that only she could have recognized. She laboriously spelled out a message that represented both her brother's last words to her while still alive, and his first to her from the spirit world: "*Darling Emma, find a great sea snake for Tom.*" The message is a cryptic reference to two sea songs that he had particularly liked, and a reminder of the traveling life he had led.[64]

In making reference to that sort of a traveling life, it can also be read as a refutation of boundaries and fixities, including that of national identity itself. This confusion of national identity is also a key element of the story she tells about her own life. Paul Gilroy has famously argued that the trope of the ship is especially important to the theorization of the Black Atlantic.[65] In the cases of Marryat and Britten, the invocation of dead sailor brothers and their connection with sea travel, mercantilism, and colonial endeavor suggests that the trope of the ship is significant to theorizing about the "spiritualist Atlantic." The longstanding and indisputable association between sailors and the world of the supernatural and superstitious, and the multiethnic makeup of ships' crews suggests connections between the black Atlantic in the origins of spiritualism itself and then of its subsequent practices and performances.

Marryat cites her father's experience of the supernatural (in an imperialist context) as being significant to the development of her own interest in spiritualism. Frederick Marryat's connection to the United States, to the West Indies sugar trade, and to slavery should be noted. His grandfather, Thomas Marryat, a medic, had spent several years in the 1760s traveling and picking up work in North America. His son Joseph, Frederick's father, was a member of Parliament for Sandwich and a colonial agent for Grenada, and owned a significant amount of property in the West Indies that depended on slave labor. He married an American woman, Charlotte Von Geyer, whose loyalist family had lost a great deal of money after the Revolution. Joseph Marryat was actively involved in the bill for the abolition of the trade in slave-grown sugar. Frederick Marryat's comments on the relative merits of free African Americans in Philadelphia and the Afro-Caribbeans of "our West India Islands" in his *A Diary in America* (1839) caused outrage in Grenada. A pamphlet containing strong refutation of his remarks was published in London. It was substantially comprised of a series of letters published in Grenada in the *Saint George's Chronicle*.[66]

One writer makes the claim that Marryat should be more circumspect in his comments since "it is generally reported and believed, that Capt. Marryat is descended from a coloured ancestor of no very remote date, or exalted rank." Whether this is correct or not (and by its nature, such a claim is difficult to prove), it is certainly true that others raised questions about his ancestry periodically, too, even after his death.[67] There was a significant black presence in the navy at this point. Paul Gilroy writes, "it has been estimated that at the end of the eighteenth century a quarter of the British navy was composed of Africans for whom the experience of slavery was a powerful orientation to the ideologies of liberty and justice."[68] Marryat served on the Impérieuse, which was involved in the defense of the castle of Trinidad against the French in 1808 and spent several years in ships in the West Indies, along the coast of the United States, and around Burma. The family's history was, then, profoundly enmeshed within the history of the black Atlantic, the politics and practices of slavery and also British imperialism. Florence Marryat lived in India for some period as the wife of an officer in the British army. The legacy of that period often broke out within séances: she claimed on a

number of occasions to have seen Indian spirits, dressed in traditional clothes, materialize in front of her. As we have already seen,
she mistook Indian "spirits" for living Indians when she was in the
subcontinent with her husband. The uncanny presence of living and
spirit Indians is remarkably consistent.

Marryat claimed to have seen spirits of subcontinental Indians,
yet Emma Hardinge Britten's encounters with American Indian spirits were striking too. Marryat also wrote of her encounters with such
spirits while she was in the United States. The appearance of
American Indian spirits in the séances of British mediums needs to
be read within the context of the politics of the representation and
reception of key American Indians who visited Britain from the
period of the early sixteenth century onward. The most famous of
these figures was Pocahontas, who converted to Christianity, married an Englishman, and died and was buried in England.[69]
Pocahontas is one of the American Indian spirits who recurs
throughout the nineteenth century on both sides of the Atlantic. A
well-documented scene of nineteenth-century British spiritualism,
involving a moment of exposure, provides a fascinating example
about how American Indian spirits could be used by white mediums.
Here, questions of impersonation and theatre, belief and disbelief,
race and gender, converge.

In 1882 a spiritualist wrote to the British spiritualist periodical
Light claiming that a young medium, C. E. Wood, had been exposed
as a fraud while performing in his own home. The exposure echoed a
number of other scandals that had taken place in the 1870s and, to
some degree, simply replicates many cases involving the revelation of
fraud, including an earlier exposure of Wood, which had taken place
in Blackburn in 1877.

Wood was a celebrated plebeian medium specializing in the full
body materialization of spirits. Wood had a "small company of
favourite spirits" included Meggie, Benny, and Pocahontas an
American Indian child usually known as Pocha or Pocka.[70] Pocha
(the name's closeness to that of the mischievous Puck would probably
not have been lost to her audience) was a particularly popular spirit
among her séance regulars. She was lively, playful—and of course
exotic. The spirit was seized during materialization "and found to be
Miss Wood, on her knees, partially undressed, and attempting to hide
a quantity of muslin." It was indeed not the first occasion on which
the spirit and her medium had been exposed in such a manner.[71] On

each occasion the inevitable attacks on her were met by the counter-arguments of her supporters. She was able to survive exposure, though eventually succumbed to alcohol just like Margaret and Kate Fox and other women mediums who found that spiritualism could be a precarious way of earning a living.

The 1882 seizing of Pocha was an event that already had established precedents and might legitimately be read as another exposure of a medium—whose theatricality and execution was beginning to seem clumsy—to a spiritualist audience with increasingly sophisticated expectations, as Alex Owen has done. But it also reveals key questions about the origin and spread of spiritualism by revealing the spread across the Atlantic of certain familiar tropes of spiritualism that have more obvious connections with the United States than with Britain. One simple question raised by this incident is what is the relationship between a British medium such as C. E. Wood, from the Northeast of England and an Indian spirit?

Pocha's appearance in England might invite unwelcome complications since the historical Pocahontas has key connections with England. Yet the way in which Pocha and the historical Pocahontas are connected is here largely mnemonic. Pocha was only one of a wide number of Indians to act as spirit guides, or to appear in manifestations, to white American and British mediums who had at their disposal a wide retinue of available spirits, male and female, adult and child, some of whom acted as spirit guides to their mediums. The appearance of Indian spirits to British mediums, with no obvious connection to or context for them, suggests one way in which it is possible to read spiritualism's spread from the United States, bringing with it signs of its origins, which were then molded and utilized by a difference set of practitioners in front of foreign audiences.

From the earliest moments of spiritualist historiography and autobiography, the presence of Indian spirits and religious beliefs have been acknowledged as being significant to the formation and practices of spiritualism. Emma Hardinge Britten raised the centrality of Indians to spiritualist experience on a number of occasions in her autobiography. The most striking of which is a bizarre, apocalyptic vision she had on her final journey across the Atlantic to retire in England, when the ship she is traveling on was just outside Liverpool. The encounter she witnessed while in a trance between Indian spirits (especially her own spirit guide, Arrowhead) and the inhabitants of her birthplace in "every town, city, village, and street of England"[72] suggests the radical juxtaposition of the American life she chose for much of her adulthood and the English life she eventually returned to.

Yet the vision also has its roots in a Protestant tradition of religious mysticism, millenarianism, and iconoclasm, which marks it out as borrowing from both sides of the Atlantic. It bears a relation to British radical plebeian spiritualism, which could, at times, invoke the United States as a counter to European imperialism. John Henry Brown, a Nottingham-based crystal-seer medium, published an 1857 pamphlet warning of an invasion of England by Russia and her allies, which would lead to Armageddon. Then, a successful counterattack would be launched by the British and Americans and would lead to the flying of the U.S. flag "from every nation's public building."[73] In this reading the United States becomes part of a revolutionary set of millennial possibilities. Britten's vision assumes that such radicalism needs to take place within the kind of counternationalism that Indian spirits might represent. Her long account of it, quoted in full, is as follows:

> It was the night previous to our expected landing at Liverpool that one of these "visions" which has always formed a marked phase of my mediumship, was presented to me. I thought I saw an immense ship, bound, like our own, for England. On board this ship were tens of thousands of Spirit people of all ranks and classes, amongst whom were scattered numerous North American Indians. The entire throng was marshalled by the only Red Indian Spirit that has ever controlled me, "Arrowhead," a glorious being of gigantic proportions, and whom I have good reason to believe has exercised his beneficent protecting power over me on many occasions of imminent peril.
>
> Presently I saw our ship sail into port, its visionary hosts landing and stretching out under the direction of their Indian leader, until they filled every town, city, village, and street of England. As they passed on their way, I saw that, though so plain and life like to me, they were assuredly Spirits, and invisible to the people whom they encountered.
>
> None saw them, but all felt their passage. The rush of the mighty hosts stirred all things around them as in a resistless wind. Added to this, they struck right and left at all the people they passed, and these, not beholding their invisible assailants, turned angrily upon each other, until the entire land was a scene of discord and contention. The invisible hosts struck at the grandest palaces and the tallest buildings, until some fell, and the foundations of others were shaken. They

struck at the churches wherein the wondering people sought refuge, but the tottering walls and crumbling columns, the broken images, and ruined ornaments, compelled the refugees to fly into the woods and fields, where all was peaceful and quiet.

At length the mighty iconoclasts ranged themselves before St. Paul's Cathedral, which I at once perceived to be representative of the National State Church. Here the work of demolition proceeded with such force and speed that I soon expected to see the great edifice become a shapeless ruin. When, however, the huge dome fell, and the cross that surmounted it was sinking amidst the ruins, "Arrowhead" snatched it up, and for the first time I heard him speak and say: "This emblem has been held dear to the human heart, and is the visible symbol of such religion as the people alone can understand. It is too sacred to be lost amidst the ruins. Take it then," he cried, as he lifted it towards the heavens, "and keep it until the people of earth know better how to use it, than to fall down and worship it." As he spoke, a luminous cloud in the sky opened, and countless little white hands stretching down to receive it, he tossed it up towards them. They caught it and carried it away, and disappeared behind the clouds.

Then for the first time, turning to me, "Arrowhead" said: "Behold! The soldiers of the new Reformation! Amidst the unrest, discord, and contention caused by these invisible warriors, all things are coming into judgment. Mourn not that we strike down or uproot the old, the effete, and the idolatrous. Before the soul of man can enter the new heaven, it must grow into manhood on the new earth, and the Lord and Master of life Himself cannot lay the foundations of the new, the true and the beautiful, as long as the ground is occupied with the worn out ashes of the dead past. When the clamour of war and the voice of strife is in thine ear, child, look aloft, and the dawning light of the new Reformation shall assure thee 'The morning cometh.'"[74]

Britten's millennial fantasy shows the destruction of the past by agents of the present comprised of spirits "of all ranks and classes" led by the spirits of Indian "warriors." They are represented as being at the center of a religious, cultural, and political transformation of England, and from there, presumably, the rest of the world. Crediting Indians with having particular access to spiritual truths as well as occult and magical knowledge had long been part of the way in which they were culturally constructed. This anticlerical, anti-ecclesiastical dream prophecy places an ethnic group, whose access to power had radically diminished in the years before her dream, at the center of a religious and social revolution as the instigators of a new social order on the other side of the Atlantic. What is crucial to her vision is that the spirits are invisible and that they are Indian. Whatever threat they might represent to a society they were literally turning upside down, their immateriality showed that threat to be devoid of the kind of embodied presence that might take the dream beyond allegory and into a call for, perhaps violent, action.

Time and time again the crucial combination of Indianness and immateriality allowed spiritualists to invoke qualities of a spiritual transcendence that they believed characterized a group that was repeatedly imagined as being in the process of vanishing. It is impossible to imagine Britten's dream having the same meaning if her ethnic subjects were African American. Indian spirits allowed spiritualists to invoke fantasies of a new social order arrived at with a minimum of violence in a way that African American spirits could not. The ongoing political repercussions of slavery and its aftermath, and the highly visible presence of a black population ensured that this could not be the case. While Toussaint L'Ouverture was a model for successful black revolutionary and militaristic heroism (as he would be for Jacob Lawrence whose 1937–1938 *Toussaint L'Ouverture* series marked his dramatic public debut as an artist), Indian leaders like Black Hawk (whose very popular *Autobiography* was published in 1833) or Metacomet could be represented as the last revolt of a dying race. Similarly, the imaginative and revolutionary possibilities represented by Nat Turner, whose visionary beliefs were well-known and feared by many whites, could be powerfully meaningful for African Americans.

In many ways the stories of Florence Marryat and Emma Hardinge Britten remind us that transatlantic travel was easier and more readily undertaken than is sometimes acknowledged today. Spiritualism can be read as an enabling principle: it gave women a community, as well as contacts and possibilities, within which they could find a functioning place wherever they were. What particularly concerns the argument of this chapter, and this book as a whole, are the many ways in which notions of crossing have been imagined: both by critics and historians of spiritualism, and by nineteenth-century spiritualists. The words "crossing" or "crossing over" may be read as peculiarly apt suggestions of the many modes of impersonations and performances, gender, racial, and class transgressions that took place within the boundaries of the spiritualist séance. Crossing over suggests not just a movement from one place to another, but also a mode of transformation, assumed or simply possible, that might and often did take place within the arena of actions with which spiritualism is associated. Crossing over suggests itself as a useful metaphor, as well as an actual description of a series of activities or acts. It signifies a challenge to divides of geography, class, race, and gender, but it also suggests ways in which the self-descriptions and justifications spiritualists gave of themselves and their practices utilized discourses from religion, science, and material culture. Crossing over implies an ability to adapt and utilize, to make a narrative from a series of disparate, often transatlantic, sources.

In this way, spiritualism allowed for the crossing of boundaries in ways that were genuinely radical and enabling as several scholars, notably Ann Braude, have shown. Yet, in addition to the suggestion of linguistic inventiveness, there are many other ways in which the terms might be read or considered. In this chapter and in the rest of the book, the notion of crossing over will be conceived of in two broad senses: as a form of movement from one world to another (the spirit world to the material one) and as from one side of the Atlantic to the other and back again. To put it another way, it will be thought of as crisscrossing, but it will also be considered as a mode of transformation of subjectivity that could and did take place through the complex nexus of suggestions and willed imaginings within the séance.

CHAPTER 2

REVOLUTIONARY SPIRITS: THE PERSISTENCE OF THE OCCULT

HAUNTED AMERICANS

T. S. Eliot's "Whispers of Immortality" (1920) starts, famously, with a reflection on literary representations of death in revenge tragedy:

> Webster was much possessed by death
> And saw the skull beneath the skin;
> And breastless creatures under ground
> Leaned backward with a lipless grin.[1]

His depiction of Webster's fascination for death bears an interesting relation to readings of the canonical writers of the early to mid-nineteenth century that were the staple of his education in American literature. A preoccupation with death, its processes, consequences, symbolic possibilities, and aftermath in the form of haunting is also at the heart of much of this writing. This chapter will show the ways in which motifs of haunting and the practices of magic and the occult recur in literary texts written in the revolutionary period and the early Republic. They provide metaphors for explaining the changes taking place within the United States as well as an explanation for the emergence and popularity of spiritualism. The literature produced in the earlier period of the Republic suggests that there was a considerable belief still persisting in a range of ghostly and occult possibilities.

By examining some of the metaphorical uses of ideas of the supernatural in a number of texts from the period of the early Republic to the 1850s, this pattern will be revealed. There are analogies to be made between the transmission of ideas about mesmerism and spiritualism, their relation to popular culture, and to their representation in literary texts. Exploring those will be one part of the work done here. Ideas about magic and other beliefs that seemingly transcended nature were remarkably resilient. One way of articulating one of this book's key assumptions is to use a metaphor of haunting. The idea of haunting might be used to articulate the ways in which the dead are invoked, aestheticized, feared, and loved by the living and also a process by which certain cultural forms linger within mainstream culture (sometimes on the margins, sometimes more centrally) in a manner that resembles the liminality associated with the spirits of the dead. As Nathaniel Hawthorne puts it in "The Custom-House," "But the past was not dead. Once in a great while, the thoughts, that had seemed so vital and so active, yet had been put to rest so quietly, revived again."[2]

Foundational arguments about the significance of death in American literary culture include Leslie Fiedler's *Love and Death in the American Novel* (1960). Fiedler famously argues that U.S. literature is unable to deal with the responsibilities of adult sexuality (indeed heterosexuality) and retreats from this into violence and death. He writes that "American literature likes to pretend, of course, that its bugaboos are all finally jokes: the headless horseman a hoax, every manifestation of the supernatural capable of rational explanation on the last page—but we are never quite convinced."[3] More recent critics have certainly been unconvinced by the attempt to trivialize such "bugaboos," instead finding, in the depiction of the gothic, profound anxieties about the possibilities of the new nation. Julia Stern has argued that the literature of the early Republic challenges the promise the revolution seemed to offer, revealing the social and political cost of freedom. She writes that the literature of the late eighteenth and early nineteenth centuries "suggests that the foundation of the republic is in fact a crypt, that the nation's noncitizens—women, the poor, Native Americans, African Americans, and aliens—lie socially dead and inadequately buried, the casualties of post-Revolutionary political foreclosure."[4]

The idea of social or political death is one that has been repeatedly invoked by other critics in recent years. Stern writes of the "invisible Americans, prematurely interred beneath the great national edifice whose erection they actually enable."[5] Russ Castronovo argues that while the United States prefers its citizens to be in a quiescent state, the "unruly bodies" of women, slaves, and others who were denied full citizenship had a great deal of subversive power. He writes that the

> deathly logic of citizenship that sentenced women and slaves to excessive and lethal embodiment also conceives these subjects as bodies who necessarily reanimate the lifeless citizen, hinting that *his* abstract identity and legal authority always rests on memories, corporeal residues, and other material contexts, no matter how completely disavowed or forgotten they seem.[6]

The notion of the persistence of memory is one that has famously been appropriated by Toni Morrison to consider the consequences of slavery. Writing of the literature of the early republic she notes in a frequently repeated remark that "For a people who made much of their 'newness'—their potential, freedom, and innocence—it is striking how dour, how troubled, how frightened and haunted our early and founding literature truly is."[7]

Morrison's focus is on the haunting power of an Africanist presence within American literary culture, which shapes cultural productions even as their writers try to avoid and efface it. Like Stern, she suggests that the United States' refusal of equal rights to all its citizens produced a profound unease that was articulated in the new nation's cultural productions. The texts that form the basis of this chapter demonstrate that a typology of haunting was established in this period. Haunting could be experienced as a form of pleasure, as something that could be enjoyed and even be deliberately sought out. But it was also a reflection of a more troubled sense of what it was to be American, especially to be a white American. In this second sense it was not actively looked for by Americans, rather it came to them, unsought and unwanted, and was difficult to exorcise. Other recent work has argued that because the foundation of the United States was in a "historical trinity of U.S. imperialism—war, slavery, and territorial expansion," the "supposedly aberrant gothic effects" characterizing American cultural production are in fact "realistic representations of the smooth functioning of American constitutionalism."[8]

In this argument, then, the gothic preoccupations of American writers do not expose "cultural contradictions," since the "fugitive imperial state" that has often evaded critique has been built on just such a foundation.[9]

However U.S. imperialism is theorized (and increasingly the argument that empire is central to the inception of the nation is accruing more persuasive evidence), the representation and treatment of Indians is central to understanding it. As many critics have noted, one frequent way of considering the processes by which the new Republic was developing and settling the land was by reflecting on the conditions of Indians. This was frequently not done through real political engagement with their situation and rights; rather it was simply argued that they were in the process of vanishing. By perceiving them as being in the process of disappearing, white Americans were able to distance themselves from their responsibility towards the plight experienced by Indians.

We have already seen that Indians came to play a part in the séances of white mediums. White writers had earlier found Indian subjects central to the establishment of the new nation. Margaret Fuller and Nathaniel Hawthorne, for instance, represented the settling of the United States as an expansionist project that carried with it the "ghosting" of Indians. If the process of colonization created images of Indians as ghostly, haunting the margins of lands claimed by new settlers, then it could also carry with it an imaginative figuring of Indians as a nonspecific or indeterminate generic group. David Kazanjian argues that the use of the Iroquois as "the figure for racialized particularity" in Kant's *The Critique of Judgment* (1790) corresponds to a colonial construction of the Indian, which elided tribal and other differences. He writes that, "Iroquois played an important role in the imaginations of the colonial Dutch, French, British, and independent Americans, as each constructed their colonizing projects around fantasmatic understandings of the individual tribes and the collective alliance."[10] Indians, then, were often known in phantasmal terms with "fantasmatic"—that is to say both fanciful and insubstantial—notions of their particularities. They were thought of, and represented, as being in the process of becoming ghostly. Hawthorne argues that they would appear as "misty phantoms" in the future, having left no monuments behind them.[11]

The desire not to share the fate of the vanishing Indians prompted Americans, including Hawthorne, to produce works that would attest to their own presence and impact in North America. As part of the ambition to create such a culture, a shift in the notion of what constituted indigeneity transformed white colonizers into indigenous peoples and Indians into "obstacles or backdrops."[12] One obvious example of this is in the work of the Hudson River School whose landscapes reduced Indians into tiny figures while celebrating the transformation of the land by white settlers who often loom far larger. As Tim Barringer puts it, "Paintings of landscape documented the territories of empire, but were most effective as a medium for expressing the latent fantasies, aspirations and emotions generated by imperialism."[13] The need to exorcise the dead white men whose overwhelming influence and status dominated the new Republic was experienced at the very same time as white Americans experienced themselves as being haunted by a so-called dying race.

The guilt and anxiety created by such a process also led to the production of a haunted consciousness. The imagination was disturbed by recollections of the cost of the foundation of the Republic: slavery, warfare, and the dispossession of native peoples. No wonder, then, that ghostly rhetoric and motifs persisted in the writings of Americans well into the nineteenth century, where they could be associated with the very processes of nation-building and expansion. In addition to this, though, occult and magical beliefs and practices, or groupings and organizations that borrowed from ideas derived from ancient sources of one kind of another, also persisted in a range of forms right through the period of the Revolution and beyond.[14] Two brief examples demonstrate this point.

Charles Brockden Brown's engagement with the power that an individual who has the ability to impersonate the voices of others can have is the subject of his extraordinary novel *Wieland* (1798) and its unfinished sequel *Memoirs of Carwin the Biloquist*. Carwin's experiments in biloquism, the eighteenth-century term for ventriloquism, lead to calamitous consequences for his unfortunate victims. *Wieland*'s preoccupation with the troubled relationship between Europe and the new Republic, the rights of individuals and the extent of civic duties, and the contact between different religious and philosophical ideas are all subjects that had continuing consequences for later U.S. writers. Many of these writers saw themselves as emerging from a tradition in which Brown was an important figure.

Washington Irving was one of the key U.S. writers to develop Brown's work. The idea of haunted landscapes was one that Irving made his own with the publication of "Rip Van Winkle" in 1819–1920. This combines European folk myths, including ideas of magic, with his interpretation of Indian superstitions to make a striking hybrid and transatlantic narrative. The persistence of haunting comes through his synthesis of these two different oral cultures. In addition, his use of the picturesque, a form that Larry Kutchen has argued is deeply embedded in U.S. imperialist ambitions, allows for a reading of the ways in which a preoccupation with the ghostly and occult within American texts of this period—one which often used the picturesque as a way of producing a sense of haunting—often has significant political implications.[15]

A HAUNTED LANDSCAPE

The language of haunting and death permeates the opening paragraph of Emerson's seminal 1836 essay "Nature." Emerson chooses the language of the crypt to articulate white Americans' relation both to their ancestors and to the culture and landscape they sought to mould in their new nation. The passage has been rightly celebrated and often dissected, yet it remains important to repeat it here. Emerson writes,

> Our age is retrospective. It builds the sepulchres of the fathers. It writes biographies, histories, and criticism. The foregoing generations beheld God and nature face to face; we, through their eyes. Why should not we also enjoy an original relation to the universe? Why should not we have a poetry and philosophy of insight and not tradition, and a religion by revelation to us, and not the history of theirs? . . . [W]hy should we grope among the dry bones of the past, or put the living generation into masquerade out of its faded wardrobe? The sun shines to-day also. There is more wool and flax in the fields. There are new lands, new men, new thoughts. Let us demand our own works and laws and worship.[16]

The gothic tenor of Emerson's vocabulary—"sepulchres of the fathers," "dry bones of the past"—suggests his frustration with a backward-looking culture that constantly invokes the significance of its dead white men. Emerson's focus on the possibilities of a "national rebirth, in opposition to mourning" is central to his work and highly evident in the language of this passage.[17] Yet even in his search for a subject that might provide a new topic for Americans' intellectual interrogations ("There are new lands, new men, new thoughts"), he seems compelled to use the rhetoric of haunting. Why does he choose a word so loaded with implications of past history, insubstantiality, and death at the very moment that he wishes to invoke newness, life, the potential suggested by the future rather than the limitations of the past?

The last two lines of the second paragraph set out the limits of the rest of his introduction: "Let us interrogate the great apparition that shines so peacefully around us. Let us inquire, to what end is nature?"[18] The invocation of apparitionality within the context of the natural world (the proximity of the natural to the supernatural) is a fascinating one. Though one definition of the term limits its meaning to the natural world—the *Oxford English Dictionary* gives one meaning of the word "apparition" as, "The first appearance of a star or other celestial body after disappearance or occultation"—when used in conjunction with the language of bodily decay, it seems closer to its most common meaning: the "action of appearing or becoming visible," whose chief manifestation is the appearance of ghosts, angels, demons, and spirits. The word might apply to people then, yet equally it might be used for things that occur in the world of nature.

Such a problematic usage by Emerson, rather than being simply perverse, is entirely in keeping with the intellectual focus and representational modes of his historical moment. His anxiety about the new republic, the weight of history, and the troubling imbalance in the political and social rights and responsibilities of its inhabitants, both citizens and noncitizens, remains visible. His invocation of an idea of nature that drew from his profound engagement with Romantic thought is a far cry from the terrifying forceful nature that Herman Melville would delineate within a few years. What is fearful about Melville's nature is not so much any notion of apparitionality, but its very materiality and substantiality, its sheer power. Melville's description of a proto-imperialist nation, expanding its frontiers through capitalist expansion and bloodshed, explicitly articulates the fearful imaginings of an earlier period.

Twelve years after Emerson's essay appeared, another highly influential document invoked the idea of haunting to explain a process that the writer hoped would transform the world in which he lived and provide new ways of engaging with the present and construct future citizens. The resonant language of Samuel Moore's 1888 translation of the 1848 *Communist Manifesto* represents communism as being conceived of as a sort of ghost. "A spectre is haunting Europe—the Spectre of Communism. All the powers of old Europe have entered into a holy alliance to exorcize this spectre: Pope and Tsar, Metternich and Guizot, French radicals and German police spies."[19] Marx's ironically pejorative use of spectrality, explored in detail by Derrida in his *Specters of Marx* (1994) suggests "old" Europe's terror at the ideas not just of communism but also of the continuing power of ghosts.[20] As such its use as a trope is only partially like that of Emerson's "apparition," which seems to have had any sense of fear at its appearance stripped away from it, at least on the surface. When Emerson links the idea of apparitionality to that of nature he does not bring with it the kind of anxieties that Marx associates with old Europe's response to communism. Emerson's apparition does not need exorcism; instead, it requires investigation and the application and pursuit of reason by citizens of the new Republic. To some degree the way in which both men invoke the idea of the spectral seems partially distinct from each other: Marx stresses a residual anxiety about the spectral, experienced by the ruling class, which is applied to a phenomenon associated with the horrors attendant on the ghostly. Emerson is more engaged by harnessing the transformative possibilities of becoming apparitional.

A sense of a much darker understanding of the meaning of the ghostly can be found in the work of Hawthorne. Of all the canonical nineteenth-century U.S. writers it is Hawthorne who seems most engaged by the ways in which magic and the supernatural might lend themselves to an investigation of the present as well as the past. His writing is full of figures who are variously ethereal, insubstantial, or diabolic: his oeuvre is saturated by confrontations between good and evil, light and dark, with battles between Puritan "saints" and satanic others. The figure of Pearl in *The Scarlet Letter* (1850)— sprite, imp, goblin, and arabesque embodiment of her mother's adultery—seems to hover between material and immaterial worlds. Roger Chillingworth's knowledge of folklore and herbal medicine, and his habitual lingering in the dark forests with the Indians who have taught him some of their lore, suggests a belief in the proximity of occult practice and herbal remedies that is characteristic of the pre-nineteenth-century period.[21]

In "The Custom-House," which is set in Salem, Massachusetts, Hawthorne links this interest to his own family's history (one of his ancestors was a judge) and to that of the nation. While the narrative insists on the centrality of Salem itself to the events that unfold, it also repeatedly links Salem (and the romance) to a changing national history dominated by transcultural and commodity exchanges made possible through maritime mercantilism and slavery. The narrative opens with a description of the port of Salem at a moment in which it was flourishing, with ships arriving or departing from Europe, Africa, and South America. He writes, "Here, too, comes his owner, cheerful or sombre, gracious or in the sulks, accordingly as his scheme of the now accomplished voyage has been realized in merchandise that will readily be turned into gold, or has buried him under a bulk of incommodities, such as nobody will care to rid him of."[22] The process of commodity exchange is compared with the alchemical process: base metals (the bodies of Africans and raw materials) can be transformed into gold in a mysterious and magical procedure characterized by secrets and ancient lore.

Invoking a magical metaphor of this kind to describe commodity exchange (particularly the process by which black bodies are transformed into gold) was scarcely outlandish. Marx himself invoked table-turning or the movement of tables during séances to describe the transformation that turns a simple wooden table into a commodity fetish.[23] Magic and fortune-telling, to use just two examples, continued to be pervasive into the nineteenth century, as Jon Butler has shown, demonstrating that these beliefs may have shifted into a different realm, but they had not been banished altogether.[24] While magical beliefs were molded into ways of explaining the possibilities offered by the market, by the turn of the century, economists sought out psychical rationale to explain financial crises and panics.[25]

Jackson Lears has argued that not just magical rhetoric, but magical practices continued well into the nineteenth century in a form closely allied to economic advancement. Not only would individuals use "the materialistic magic" inherited from Europe to seek out hidden treasure, but gamblers looked to dream books to interpret the relation between their nocturnal reveries and the numbers they should bet on.[26] Central to this was the idea of transformation, which, incidentally, was the English title for Hawthorne's 1860 romance *The Marble Faun*. Lears writes that

> By the 1840s and 1850s, a crucial dimension of consumer goods'
> emotional pull in American culture involved a carnivalization of the
> psyche—a brief entry into a world brimming with possibilities for
> self-transformation. . . . [I]t suited a mobile, market, society: the
> sense of personal identity was loosening; social distinctions were
> increasingly based on fungible assets and movable goods rather than
> land and livestock.[27]

Such a transformation of identity was, of course, the dynamizing
feature of Hawthorne's *The House of the Seven Gables* (1851), which
opens with Hepzibah Pyncheon's transition from lady to shop-
keeper and centers on disputes over Indian land, magic, and
inheritance; a preoccupation with treasure seeking resulted in his
tale "The Great Carbuncle."

In *The House of the Seven Gables* Hawthorne links technology,
witchcraft, and the occult through the figure of Matthew Maule,
whose fascination with the daguerreotype (seen by some contemporaries as a form of magic, witchcraft, or even spiritist in itself) is
suggestively intimated to be a form of seeing what is invisible to less
sensitive figures. Ann Douglas has provocatively argued that "In
America, technology and magic were synonymous: one and the same
thing."[28] The significance of the portrait, including the daguerreotype picture as a trope within Hawthorne's oeuvre, is suggested by
his use of it in an 1837 story "The Prophetic Pictures." For him, and
for many of his contemporaries, the possibility that portraiture
(particularly one made possible by new technologies) may offer a
way of seeing past the surface into a private self was very powerful.[29]

Poe's necrophiliac fantasizing about being buried alive and the
consequences of revivification (echoed to some degree in Washington
Irving's work) and Hawthorne's concern with his own and his
nation's Puritan past and its own fascination with the transposition
of witchcraft, spells, and religious iconography into an American set-
ting are celebrated examples of the power of different kinds of
haunting within canonical U.S. literature. Hawthorne's anxieties
about the political and social consequences of the past are brilliantly
exemplified in Holgrave's furious outburst in *The House of the Seven
Gables*. His language echoes that of Emerson,

> Shall we never, never, get rid of this Past! . . . It lies upon the Present
> like a giant's dead body! In fact, the case is just as if a young giant
> were compelled to waste all his strength in carrying about the corpse

of the old giant, his grandfather, who died a long while ago, and only needs to be decently buried. Just think, a moment; and it will startle you to see what slaves we are to by-gone times—to Death, if we give the matter the right word! . . . a Dead Man, if he happens to have made a will, disposes of wealth no longer his own; or, if he dies intestate, it is distributed in accordance with the notions of men much longer dead than he. A Dead Man sits on all our judgement-seats; and living judges do but search out and repeat his decisions. We read in Dead Men's books! We laugh at Dead Men's jokes, and cry at Dead Men's pathos! We are sick of Dead Men's diseases, physical and moral, and die of the same remedies with which dead doctors killed their patients! We worship the living Deity, according to Dead Men's forms and creeds! Whatever we may seek to do, of our own free motion, a Dead Man's icy hand obstructs us! Turn your eyes to what point we may, a Dead Man's white, immitigable face encounters them, and freezes our very heart! And we must be dead ourselves before we can begin to have our proper influence on our own world, but the world of another generation, with which we shall have no shadow of a right to interfere.[30]

Holgrave is the ancestor of a reputed wizard, a Fourierist visionary, and a daguerreotypist whose images (including a postmortem daguerreotype) see beyond the social faces of his subjects and seem to read their dark thoughts. In this passage he articulates the anxiety that infuses all of Hawthorne's works. This centers on the power of dead white men who seem physically to intervene and enslave new Americans who desire to change the world they find themselves in. *The House of the Seven Gables* is pervaded by the irrefutable fact of death and presence of dead men but also of the power of inheritances to bring the past into unavoidable conflict with the present. The secret of the house itself, revealed at the end of the romance, is that of the location of claims to Indian lands that have been falsely taken from Matthew Maule (and, of course, unnamed Indians themselves) at the very start of the narrative. The troubling legacy of violent colonial encounters persists throughout his work.[31]

Haunting also pervades Margaret Fuller's *Summer on the Lakes, in 1843*. Her account of her tour of the Great Lakes is an amalgam of descriptions of places, peoples, and introspection. It is clear that she regards her text as being in part an investigation of a region that will soon be transformed by the waves of settlers who travel with her, a tourist, to the new West "where the clash of material interests is so noisy."[32] Her anxiety about the meanings and consequences of the replacement of Indians by what she calls "these immigrants who were to be fathers of a new race" is strikingly articulated on the first occasion she encounters Indians when she is a steamboat passenger. Fuller writes,

> Coming up the river St. Clair, we saw Indians for the first time. They were camped out on the bank. It was twilight, and their blanketed forms, in listless groups or stealing along the bank, with a lounge and a stride so different in its wildness from the rudeness of the white set-tler, gave me the first feeling that I really approached the West.[33]

This first encounter with Indians marks them as alien, allied to the land rather than to the urban and, certainly, ghostly. A number of features help to develop this form of representation: the twilight scene, the lack of definition of body shape caused by the blankets, and the distinctiveness of their movements, which are closer to that of the natural environment (already specifically delineated as being haunted by Fuller) to that of "the rudeness of the white settler."[34] Immediately after this description of the Indians, Fuller turns instead to a more comprehensive, and negative, account of her fellow travel-ers, whose lack of spirituality and preoccupation with material pos-sessions is particularly commented on. Their concentration on what they might "get" rather than "do" in the West is represented as being highly distinct from the mentality of the Indians she has just described, whose lack of materialism is suggested by the temporary nature of their habitations. The go-getting new white migrants to the West are displacing a group that, for Fuller and for many of her contemporaries, are inevitably moving toward extinction.

Fuller sees the Indians as already ghostlike, and as inhabiting a landscape that is passing into history. She describes her first encoun-ters with Niagara Falls as having been already been prepared for by her familiarity with a variety of representational forms that had led to what she believed was an already-existing familiarity with the landscape and, as it becomes evident, its inhabitants. She writes that "When I first came here I felt nothing but a quiet satisfaction. I found that drawings, the panorama, &c. had given me a clear notion of the position and proportions of all objects here; I knew where to look for everything, and everything looked as I thought it would."[35] Fuller's interpretation of the landscape comes ready made for her through the eyes of those articulating what has been called the "'dreamwork' of imperialism": landscape art.[36] Her notion of what the meaning of the West was had already been formed by seeing it through an imperializing gaze.

Gradually, though, this apparent familiarity was challenged by the experience of seeing the landscape for herself rather than through the interpretations of others. First she experienced the kind of dread associated with the sublime, but this was rapidly transformed into an acute anxiety about the noise of the water and the fact that this made hearing other noises impossible. She describes this as follows:

> I realized the identity of that mood of nature in which these waters were poured down with such absorbing force, with that in which the Indian was shaped on the same soil. For continually on my mind came, unsought and unwelcome, images, such as never haunted it before, of naked savages stealing behind me with uplifted tomahawks; again and again this illusion recurred, and ever after I had thought it over, and tried to shake it off, I could not help starting and looking behind me.[37]

Her anxiety about the presence of the Indians and the way in which the natural world is able to shelter them and form them is rapidly transformed into the fear that they are likely to attack her. With her immersion in the wilderness comes the emergence of a new array of experiences, which bring with them novel terrors. Previously her sophisticated aesthetic understanding of her new environment had brought her a sense of cosmopolitan pleasure. But with her rapid understanding that experience transforms subjectivity, it leads her to a new understanding of the inadequacy of experience mediated through aesthetic and commercial forms: paintings, panoramas, books. An important part of this transformation of experience is described through using a motif of being haunted. To Fuller, it is not just that the Indians are like ghosts, and that the landscape seems haunted by the memories of what has taken place there and the traces of the past, but that the correlation between desire and the imagination is akin to that of being haunted.

Fuller uses the idea of haunting in two ways: to describe the presence of the Indians and their physicality and to comprehend experiencing and satisfying desire. She writes that having seen Niagara Falls she feels replete. As she puts it, "Our desires, once realized, haunt us again less readily."[38] This metaphor is repeated, as has already been described, when she finds that she cannot shake off a terror, which was never previously experienced, of being attacked by Indians.[39] Quite rapidly, though, the idea of haunting is replaced by one of a somewhat mystical apparitionality associated with the landscape itself. The falls have "magical effects," the river seems "to whisper mysteries," and finally the experience of seeing the falls by moonlight effected a transformation in what she experienced turning it into a "misty apparition."[40] Though this is to some degree a Romantic commonplace by this time, its Wordsworthian element should not occlude what is specifically American here: the presence of the Indian, which disrupts Fuller's aesthetic pleasure and produces fear instead. While the experience of the sublime of necessity includes the experience of fear, Fuller's initial anxiety is not produced by or through the experience of sublime nature: rather it is constituted through an understanding that the natural world is not empty of other human inhabitants.

This preoccupation with the idea of a haunted landscape develops later into her celebrated account of the Seeress of Prevorst, which forms a large part of chapter 5. Her description of the Seeress is taken directly from Justinus Kerner's book *Revelations Concerning the Inward Life of Man, and the Projection of a World of Spirits into Ours*, which she read in German. This was a work that spiritualists were also fascinated by.[41] She called it "a biography, mental and physical, of one of the most remarkable cases of high nervous excitement that the age, so interested in such, yet affords, with all its phenomena of clairvoyance and susceptibility of magnetic influences."[42] She claimed that her descriptions of it were prompted by the request of others. It sits oddly with the text that surrounds it.

She read the book while spending a couple of days resting in Milwaukee after a busy period of traveling and visiting Indian encampments and the homes of new immigrants to the West. She writes, "Very strange was this vision of an exalted and sensitive existence, which seemed to invade the next sphere, in contrast with the spontaneous, instinctive life, so healthy and so near the ground I had been surveying."[43] But this "spontaneous" and "instinctive" life seems to refer to the lives of only some immigrants rather than Western settlers in general or Indians. Each description of Indians that immediately precedes this focuses on qualities of melancholy, dejection, and despair, creating a highly picturesque, but not "healthy," depiction of what she encounters. They confirm the belief she repeats later that "this race is fated to perish" given the onslaught of new Americans. She writes, "I have no hope of liberalizing the missionary, of humanizing the sharks of trade, of infusing the conscientious drop into the flinty bosom of policy, of saving the Indian from immediate degradation, and speedy death."[44]

Although *Summer on the Lakes* contains many descriptions and anecdotes of the lives of individuals throughout, her account of the Seeress is unusual because it focuses on a young German woman who had no connection with the United States. (Many of her comparable anecdotes are of Indians or of Western settlers.) What is the function of the lengthy section on the Seeress and how does it relate to a book that centers on considering the expansion and landscape of the West? Arguably, it is the narrative's focus on the idea of haunting that allows these disparate parts of the texts to work together. Fuller's book envisages the landscape as haunted by past history, violence, and the figures of Indians whose debilitated physicality is repeatedly delineated. Just as Fuller's West is haunted by Indians whose presences cannot be ignored, the section on the Seeress represents the part of Germany where she lives as haunted too.

In addition to a preoccupation with hauntings that makes a connection between the narrative of the Seeress and the experiences of settling the West, it is the Seeress's ethnicity that allows Fuller to see a connection between narratives. In a significant moment in her text, Fuller reflects upon her lengthy discussion of the Seeress and makes a form of apology. She writes,

> Do not blame me that I have written so much about Germany and Hades, while you were looking for news of the West. Here, on the pier, I see disembarking the Germans, the Norwegians, the Swedes, the Swiss. Who knows how much of old legendary lore, of modern wonder, they have already planted amid the Wisconsin forests? Soon, soon their tales of the origin of things, and the Providence which rules them, will be so mingled with those of the Indian, that the very oak trees will not know them apart,—will not know whether itself be a Runic, a Druid, or a Winnebago oak.[45]

It is this prospect of cultural commingling that the narratives seem most to envisage. The story of the Seeress needs to be read, then, as a narrative that allows Fuller to respond elliptically to some of the major preoccupations of her time in the West: the fate of the Indians, the meanings of Westward migration, and the transformation of the landscape itself.[46] The processes by which European folklore and Indian legend come to be transformed into American narratives are one part of what Fuller anticipates in *Summer on the Lakes*.

MESMERISM AND THE TECHNOLOGY OF THE SPECTRAL

In his seminal work *Mesmerism and the End of the Enlightenment in France* (1968), Robert Darnton argues that the Marquis de Lafayette, one of the most celebrated heroes of the American Revolution, was also one of the earliest disciples of animal magnetism. The Austrian-born Franz Anton Mesmer was both its pioneer and its most flamboyant early exponent. It was directly through him that Lafayette first encountered such beliefs. The animal magnetism familiar to Mesmer and his disciples involved a belief in an invisible fluid surrounding and penetrating bodies. Obstacles could inhibit the fluid's flow through the body, and a skilled practitioner could manipulate this by massaging the body's poles (the analogy of magnetism was frequently used) and in this way overcome the problem and restore the body to health. Mesmer's treatment was famous for its utilization of tubs of iron filings and mesmerized water from which iron rods protruded. Patients formed linked circles around the tubs or bacquet and applied the rods to the affected parts of their anatomies. Fashionable Parisians flocked to the new cure. Mesmer had many adherents and imitators, some of whom modified or adapted his cure.

One important stage in the development of animal magnetism was in its movement away from a particular preoccupation with the physical to the psychological. The special interest in physical fluids was replaced by an emphasis on the rapport between mesmerist and subject. One follower of Mesmer, the Marquis de Puységur, found that his mesmerized patients "spontaneously performed feats of telepathy, clairvoyance, and precognition."[47] As mesmerism developed and was practiced by an ever-wider range of individuals, it attracted the attention of assorted occultists, mystics, Rosicrucians, and others who saw in mesmerism the possibility of encountering spiritual, even philosophical, truths.[48]

Later, when doctors such as James Esdaile pioneered the use of mesmerism for surgical procedures within his Mesmeric Hospital in Calcutta, it moved further into the domain of medicine. Later still, when Charcot, Freud and others made hypnotism a key component of the talking cure, it is clear that a long process had been going on in which "mesmerism gradually, almost imperceptibly, merged into the burgeoning field of dynamic psychiatry."[49] During this slow transformation, proponents were so anxious to develop and maintain a respectable name for psychiatry that they distanced themselves from aspects of mesmerism, and trances, which might associate it with the "supranormal."[50]

In its movement through this nomenclature the modifications that took place reflect stages of an evolution. Animal magnetism changed from an encounter in which subjects could report states of clairvoyance and trances, to one in which what was emphasized was the bond between the subject and practitioner, and especially the hypnotist's privileges and powerful control over the subject rather than the subject's own—occasionally supernatural—performance. This became the subject of a great deal of investigation within popular newspapers and was explored by many writers on both sides of the Atlantic.

Among the most celebrated explorations of the manipulative association between sinister (often foreign) mesmerist and female victim is the British writer George Du Maurier's 1894 novel *Trilby*, which was set in the 1850s. Its success on both sides of the Atlantic spawned innumerable articles of merchandise based on Du Maurier's characters, as well as a stage adaptation and many skits. A town in Florida even named its streets after characters in the novel.[51] Mesmerism emerged in Europe and was brought to the United States, where it achieved great popularity both as a form of healing and as a popular spectacle. It was one of the key antecedents to spiritualism. Its journey from Europe to the United States and its transformation from a secretive practice carried out by elite and entitled individuals in specially prepared venues, to one that was taken from place to place by traveling showmen practitioners, is an example of the important transatlantic cultural connections that were being laid out.

Lafayette and Mesmer had encountered each other in Paris, where Mesmer had arrived from Vienna in 1778. Lafayette had joined a select group called the Society of Universal Harmony as its ninety-first disciple. The Society was established with one hundred founding members each paying one hundred louis d'or for the privilege.[52] The group was dedicated to protecting Mesmer and his doctrine from attacks by the government and academics and was bound by rites and ceremonies that borrowed from occultism (though Mesmer officially repudiated the occult) and freemasonry, which obscured its scientific respectability.[53] They received training and when qualified they were to be awarded diplomas that would allow them to practice what they had learned.[54]

Lafayette was a keen member of the society and a freemason. Many Parisians shared his enthusiasm for mesmerism. Between 1783 and 1784 Parisian fervor over mesmerism was at its height, dominating journals and conversations within fashionable circles and being the source of debate within the academies, cafés, and salons alike but also attacked in songs, doggerel, and cartoons. Alan Gauld has speculated on the reasons for the receptiveness of Paris to Mesmer's ideas, identifying as one factor what Baronne d'Oberkirch called "the love of the marvellous," encompassing ritual magic, prophecy, and the occult, a love which found an object in mesmerism.[55]

Lafayette was a proselytizer for mesmerism, particularly during this period. He became so enthused by the possibilities it offered that he wrote to George Washington on May 14, 1784,

> A German doctor named Mesmer, having made the greatest discovery about animal magnetism, has trained some pupils, among whom your humble servant is considered one of the most enthusiastic.—I know as much about it as any sorcerer ever did. . . . Before leaving I will obtain permission to let you into Mesmer's secret, which, you can count on it, is a great, philosophical discovery.[56]

His register shifts between the magical and the philosophical. In this manner he seems to imply that Mesmer's system could in some manner be interpreted within a rational frame. By calling it a "discovery" he incorporates it into a discourse that includes other discoveries, such as those that might be opened up by scientific or mathematical investigations. He allies himself, with his esoteric knowledge, to a sorcerer, while simultaneously claiming Mesmer's discovery for the Enlightenment and rational discourses. This subtle movement between two differing positions is characteristic of animal magnetism's liminal location at this moment.

The prospect of his being able to "obtain permission" to reveal the secrets of animal magnetism to Washington seemed highly improbable.

All the founding subscribers to the Society of Harmony were obliged to sign a contract that restricted their abilities to pass the secrets of animal magnetism on. His contract, signed just five weeks previously, made a series of stipulations. Among other things it said,

1. He will not instruct any pupil, nor transmit directly or indirectly to anyone, either the whole nor the least part of the doctrine of Animal Magnetism, without my written consent.
2. He will not enter into any negotiation, treaty, or agreement relative to Animal Magnetism with any prince, government or community, this right being exclusively mine.
3. Without my express written permission, he will not establish any public clinic or bring patients together in order to treat them in a group by my method; he is permitted only to see and treat patients individually and in private.[57]

When Lafayette wrote to Washington with the promise of initiating him into the mysteries of Mesmer's secret, he was on the verge of departing for the United States. He left Paris about a month after writing this letter, around June 18, and ten days later set sail for his third trip across the Atlantic, which would provide the occasion for his investigations into what he thought of as American versions of animal magnetism.

Lafayette had already demonstrated his interest in popular science the previous year. He made a substantial donation to what turned out to be an elaborate hoax involving the claim that a Parisian watchmaker had discovered how to walk on water using a pair of "elastic shoes" in which he proposed to cross the Seine on New Year's Day.[58] He was by no means the only figure who donated money to the hoax, though he did promise one of the largest amounts. While this reflected the opportunities brought by his considerable wealth, it also suggests the excitement he felt at the wondrous possibilities that Parisians felt they were on the verge of witnessing.

The incident has been cited by Darnton as one proof of the enthusiasm for science and the chance it offered to understand in late eighteenth-century France, one that embraced balloon flights, theories about cosmology, flying machines, and other discoveries and which was demonstrated by the large numbers of people who flocked to public lectures and who read popular journals and news-papers in which debates flourished. As he puts it,

> In the eighteenth century, the view of literate Frenchmen opened upon a splendid, baroque universe, where their gaze rode on waves of invisible fluid into realms of infinite speculation.[59]

Within this atmosphere of excitement about what science might offer, Lafayette was a keen participant. But others were made more anxious about what the implications of his interest in animal mag-netism might be. Thomas Jefferson, currently the U.S. representative in France, was particularly worried about what might happen if an enthusiastic Lafayette preached about the subject to his adoring American fans. The consequence of such a craze was one Jefferson and others wished to avoid. Such ideas were outside of the pantheon of the register of a Republic based on a classical model. They were potentially powerfully disruptive then.

It may be that Jefferson was conscious of, and concerned about, what Robert Fuller has called Americans' "congenital susceptibility to a wide assortment of religious sects and utopian social move-ments."[60] How might Americans respond to this irrational new fad when a figure like Lafayette introduced them to it? Though it is somewhat crude to suggest the susceptibility of Americans was "con-genital" it is true, as we will see, that Americans found themselves to be particularly adept at adapting new ideas to their own situations and needs. Lafayette had already had a county in Pennsylvania named after him. The State of Virginia had presented him with a bust of himself. The revised edition of Hector St. Jean de Crèvecoeur's *Letters of an American Farmer* (1782) was dedicated to him. All these details suggest the huge esteem in which he was held, and the likely impact of his proselytizing among Americans about the Parisian craze.

Faced with this potential crisis, Jefferson was quick to act. On April 24, 1784, a royal commission was appointed in Paris to inves-tigate animal magnetism. Among the prestigious commissioners were the chemist Antoine Lavoisier and Benjamin Franklin. After experimenting with animal magnetism themselves, the commission came to a negative conclusion: the imaginations of the mesmerists were responsible for the effects they claimed for the cures.[61] Knowing of this conclusion—which was commemorated by a cartoon that depicted Franklin showing the commission to the vanquished mesmerists—Jefferson distributed copies of the commission.[62] The following year after the huge success of a burlesque of Mesmer that ran for twenty-one performances in Paris, Jefferson noted that animal magnetism was "an imputation of so grave a nature as would bear an action at law in America" and wrote in a journal of letters on February 5, 1785, "Animal magnetism dead, ridiculed."[63]

This was, however, a premature judgment. At the point at which Jefferson wrote this, animal magnetism had spread throughout France and beyond, though increasingly its practitioners were moving away from an interest in curing illness and toward communication with the spirit world and making connections with occult ideas. While Swedenborgians in Stockholm wrote to mesmerists in Strasbourg suggesting the connections between the two sets of beliefs, the mesmerists of the Lyons-based society, La Concorde, "blossomed with Rosicrucians, Swedenborgians, alchemists cabalists, and assorted theosophists recruited largely from the Masonic Order des Chevaliers Bienfaisants de la Cité Sainte."[64] In the very few years in which mesmeric practices had existed within France they were already being adapted and appropriated by figures with very different interests. Such a transformation would continue with some rapidity once they began to be practiced in the United States. What was added to the way in which it spread in the United States was more showmanship than had previously been experienced, and a closer sense of the relationship between mesmerism and popular culture.

Meanwhile Lafayette's campaign continued and seemed only to be enhanced by an incident that took place while he was at sea in 1784. While crossing the Atlantic, an opportunity arose to test his practical application of the cure he was so excited about. A cabin boy fell off a rope and was badly injured. He apparently healed the boy using the techniques he had boasted about to Washington. This cure took an added significance when he arrived in the United States. In August 1784 he gave a lecture to a special meeting, held in his honor, of the American Philosophical Society. His subject was animal magnetism and he cited his successful cure of the young sailor as evidence of the remarkable possibilities of the new discoveries being explored in Paris.

His explicit avowal of a possible relation between what was happening in Paris and what its consequence might be for the United States suggests the extent to which he was keen to pursue

Franco-American alliances. The following month he visited the Shaker village near Watervliet that would figure sensationally in the period of the Era of Manifestations in the 1830s and 1840s. To Lafayette, Shakers allowed for the possibility of seeing a form of animal magnetism at work, since he believed there were connections between their healing practices and those he was learning. He even tried to mesmerize a Shaker. On September 30, while part of a peace-making commission, he witnessed a group of Oneida Indians dance and even saw in this something akin to animal magnetism. He suggested he might write an "'Essay on savage dances' to be read to the Union of Harmony."[65]

Paris was also the source of a piece of powerful visual technology with links to spiritualism. The premier there of Etienne Gaspard Robertson's phantasmagoria show in 1799 was an important moment for the popular production of ghosts. From there it spread to Britain and then to the United States. It was wildly successful there from about 1803 to 1839.[66] In such shows, that took place in darkened rooms with ghostly props—as séances would do later—ghosts mingled freely with celebrities and historical figures.[67] The original of such performances was in the magic lantern shows that had used ghostly elements to great effect for many years.[68] These often reproduced images of specters and skeletons. They also might show scenes from places such as the Holy Land, perhaps pyramids and oriental figures to make up a panoply of difference in which the exotic imagery of the foreign and the exoticism of the spirit world could be produced together.

Again this suggests a shared otherness in which the unknown contours of foreign lands and the dramatic scenes of past events could be read alongside one another and with the outlines of spirits, specters, skeletons, and other thrilling and frightening images of the unknown. It also implies the continuing interest in the relation between traditions of magic and the occult (often associated with ancient lore and magicians from the Middle East) and contemporary engagement with spirits. The transatlantic movement of such technologies has a long history. For example, four Iroquois sachems visiting London in 1710 took a magic lantern back with them when they returned to America.[69] Robertson's show mixed the new technology with effects that seemed to be associated with older traditions. He claimed to have moved beyond pre-Enlightenment superstitions to a more rational, even scientific, understanding of spirit production.

Robertson, and the other showmen who imitated his successes, liked to stress rational and technological accounts of their performances, unlike Lafayette. Instead of willing their audiences to believe in ghosts they aimed at dispelling belief. At the end of his shows he would announce that "I have shown you the most occult things natural philosophy has to offer, effects that seem supernatural to the ages of credulity . . . but now see the only real horror . . . see what is in store for each of you, what each of you will become one day: remember the phantasmagoria."[70] At that point the skeleton of a young woman in a crypt would be illuminated. This emphasis on the steady bodily progression to the grave may have developed a focus on the rational and explicable, but the performance element itself still encouraged precisely what Robertson claimed he was attempting to dispel—a belief in the supernatural. This was particularly the case at moments in the show in which he deliberately invoked magical practices apparently in order to produce the spirits of the dead. The vivid theatricality of his performance and the ways in which it appeared to emulate—albeit in a comical and slightly subversive mode—the activities of magicians, played upon the existing beliefs of his intended audience.

During the performance Robertson would announce that he would produce the spirits of the dead. The following description of an event that took place in France, cited in his own memoirs, described the extraordinary, and comical, scene:

> A moment of silence ensued; then an Arlesian-looking man in great disorder, with bristling hair and sad wild eyes, said: "Since I wasn't able . . . to reestablish the cult of Marat, I would like at least to see his face."
>
> Then Robertson poured on a lighted brazier two glasses of blood, a bottle of vitriol, twelve drops of aqua fortis, and two numbers of the journal *Hommes-Libres*. Immediately, little by little, a small, livid, hideous phantom made a frightful grimace and disappeared.[71]

The brilliant comic details here suggest a satire aimed at the credulous and providing all the details that might be needed to render this into a clever miniature satire of audience, practitioner, and recent events. It is not surprising that the phantasmagoria shows, effectively a form of early horror film of the kind that would come into its own in the twentieth century, were hugely popular forms of mass entertainment. Such shows, which flourished during the late eighteenth and early nineteenth centuries on both sides of the Atlantic, included historical figures (Thomas Jefferson, Napoleon, and George Washington, to name just three) alongside representations of ghosts, skeletons, and other images. This commingling of celebrity and the ghostly (or indeed celebrity spirits) is further suggested by the fact that Paul de Philipsthal, the German who first brought the phantasmagoria to Britain from the Continent in 1801, exhibited with Madame Tussaud, who came to Britain from France with her waxworks in 1802. They toured together for two years.[72] De Philipsthal's phantasmagoria was described in the following terms:

> All the lights of the small theatre of exhibition were removed, except one hanging lamp, which could be drawn up so that its flame should be perfectly enveloped in a cylindrical chimney, or opake shade. In this gloomy and wavering light the curtain was drawn up, and presented to the spectator a cave or place exhibiting skeletons, and other figures of terror, in relief, and painted on the sides or walls. After a short interval the lamp was drawn up, and the audience were [sic] in total darkness, succeeded by thunder and lightning; which last appearance was formed by the magic lanthorn upon a thin cloth or screen, let down after the disappearance of the light, and consequently unknown to most of the spectators. These appearances were followed by figures of departed men, ghosts, skeletons, transmutations, &tc. . . . Several figures of celebrated men were thus exhibited with some transformations; such as the head of Dr Franklin being converted into a skull, and these were succeeded by phantoms, skeletons, and various terrific figures, which instead of seeming to recede and then vanish, were (by enlargement) made suddenly to advance; to the surprise and astonishment of the audience, and then disappear by seeming to sink into the ground.[73]

The juxtaposition of eminent dead men with ghosts is a detail that is reiterated with regularity in the early history of spiritualism, while disappearing through sinking into the ground was something that spiritualists eventually managed to achieve within séances only some years after 1848. Franklin, a figure who was internationally known both as the American author of a defining American document, his 1791 *Autobiography* (published just a year after his death), his involvement with the Declaration of Independence, and as a scientist, was held in particular regard by spiritualists. Similar performances toured within the United States to substantial audiences. In many cases, performers found that the huge successes they met with in one country could be followed up in another. The quality of such performances could vary considerably. An example of one showman's introductory talk, published in the *European Magazine* in 1803, tells how the show will even produce the audiences' friends and relatives. He claims,

> Ladies and gentlemen, hin the hurly hages of hignorance, there wasn't no such thing as a Phantastigrorium; it is a quite spick span new invention, never invented before. Here you will see, Ladies and Gentlemen, your friends and relations, dead and alive, present or absent, above or below. You'll excuse my descending into particulars. Never mind; we'll put ye in spirits, I warrant ye, and keep ye in them too; proof spirits for the Ladies, and choice spirits for the Gentlemen. I should have no objection to a drop of brandy myself.[74]

The puns, wordplay, and teasing of this showman's language and the tantalizing suggestion of seeing familiar faces (whether those of the dead or the living) must have had a great appeal. The juxtaposition of the famous and the familial is certainly one that makes its way into spiritualist séances.

The phantasmagoria shows that flourished in the United States borrowed substantially from their European antecedents, relying on advertising techniques that stressed their relationships to showmen like Robertson. These could come from close professional associations. For instance, a show that ran from December 1806 to January the following year in the Columbian Museum in Boston was organized by Martin Aubée who had, with his brother, assisted Robertson in France. They toured in Europe before crossing the Atlantic. Martin's show, heavily reminiscent of Robertson's, was also performed in New York, Philadelphia, and Baltimore.[75] It included spectacular storms, figures from Shakespeare (the dying Romeo and Juliet), and also for its new audience, "the Apotheosis of Washington."[76] As time went on the shows moved away from figures associated with the macabre and ghostly. The second act of a show performed in New York in 1808 included "the Vision of the Night Mare; an American Rattlesnake; the Cock of France; the Beggar's Petition; Fifteen Likenesses of Distinguished Persons, such as Washington, Jefferson, Adams, Hancock, Robert Morris, Frederick III of Prussia, and Mrs. Jones, late of the New York theatre; and a Song."[77]

The American dimension or innovation of these shows seems to have been in the specific, local, additions suggested above. They would have been very recognizable on either side of the Atlantic, for the most part. Clearly the terrifying spectacle that the phantasmagoria once specialized in was changing. Indeed, one 1818 phantasmagoria show in Boston admitted children for half price, suggesting that the subject matter of such performances had certainly evolved.[78] Still, the shows were significant models for other kinds of performances of ghosts, even in their less frightening transmogrifications. Their popularity was partly due to their mobility. By moving about they were able to reach large audiences and come to have a more profound impact than might otherwise be the case. Again, we see a precursor to spiritualism.

Evidence of the popularity, visibility, and legibility of the phantasmagoria can be adduced from the ways, and frequency, with which the word was invoked within writing from that period onwards. The word was used to describe the dancing of the Modernist Loïe Fuller, who was herself an important transatlanticist into the twentieth century.[79] Castle has argued that the phantasmagoria became "a kind of master trope in nineteenth-century romantic writing," tracing its usage by Honoré de Balzac, Victor Hugo, Byron, Walter Scott, Henry Lemoine, and Thomas De Quincey, among others.[80] She shows that in some instances it was used in referential ways, but elsewhere its usage was largely metaphorical. Both forms of usage appear in the work of Edgar Allan Poe. In readings of "The Fall of the House of Usher" and "Ligeia" she argues that Poe used the special effects of the phantasmagoria as models for the revivification of Ligeia and the return of Madeline Usher from her grave.[81] Many of Poe's stories bring the dead, notably women, back to life articulating a necrophiliac desire of communion between the bereaved living and the dead beloved.[82] Poe is the outstanding example of the manner in which popular discoveries could be incorporated into literary texts.

Many of the new discoveries of the era, and those of the previous one, were used as subjects in Poe's writing. Stories on ballooning and mesmerism, for example, showed his fascination with their possibilities. He was also intellectually engaged by the many scientific and pseudoscientific discoveries of the period and the opportunities the plethora of new knowledge gave of duping the public. Harold Beaver's pithy summary of his movement between different domains and discourses remains an acute description of the sources and effects of his writing in this period:

Poe too—quite self-consciously, of course—was working in this gothic vein. Within his husk of mathematics, as often as not, lurks an old-fashioned kernel of magic. In a sense, he recreated all the traditional feats of magic in pseudo-scientific terms (of galvanism and mesmerism). Alchemy became the synthetic manufacture of "Von Kempelen and His Discovery"; resurrection of the dead, the time travel of "Some Words with a Mummy"; demonic possession, the hypnotic or "magnetic relation" of "A Tale of the Ragged Mountains"; apocalyptic vision, the cataclysmic fire of "The Conversation of Eiros and Charmion." Just as the pseudo-scholarship (in antiquarian statutes and genealogies) of Scott, or gothic elaboration of Hawthorne, was part of an attempt to make the imaginative spell more potent, more binding, so Poe's detailed and mathematical science intensifies his imaginative fusion with the occult.[83]

He was the subject of intense interest to spiritualist poets, notably Lizzie Doten and Sarah Helen Whitman, who believed that they communicated with him beyond the grave.[84]

The movement of the showmen who put on the ghost shows, which so captivated Poe and others, paralleled that of those who made mesmerism into a popular performance that was, and could be, demonstrated before audiences in towns and cities. While mesmerism in Europe had been particularly attractive to the wealthy, especially the aristocracy, in the United States it was taken up by the middle classes. Robert Fuller has argued that "Parlor-room and stage demonstrations were . . . mesmerism's only laboratories; its theories were advanced in public lecture halls and small metaphysical clubs."[85] Mesmerism was subject to particular investigations after 1836, when a French mesmerist, Charles Poyen, went on a lecture tour of New England. The great success he met with seems largely prompted by his audience's fascination for the somnambulic state that he put his subjects in, and the "feats of clairvoyance" they performed while entranced.[86]

Poyen left the United States in 1839 to return to France. At that point an Englishman, Robert Collyer, started an extensive lecture tour of the Eastern seaboard, initially focusing on phrenology, but rapidly with mesmerism central instead.[87] While these were the most celebrated early exponents of such subjects there were many other lesser-known public speakers and healers who also carried news of mesmerism and its potential into cities, towns, and villages, often following routes already taken by evangelists. This was a pattern that would be repeated by spiritualist mediums and lecturers within a very few years. Crucially, too, the popularity of mesmerism was also due to its availability to be harnessed into discourses of perfectibility and Manifest Destiny, to utopianism and to nationalism.[88]

While a number of writers considered mesmerism a subject well worth fictional exploration, Hawthorne's *The Blithedale Romance* (1852) investigates the significance of mesmeric trances and the novelistic possibilities of supernatural symbolism in perhaps the most detail.[89] He takes on the subject of mesmerism, socialist experiments and gender relations in the 1840s and finds in them a metaphor for dangerous vulnerabilities and potential moral instability. The novel is full of spectral and supernatural metaphors that continually suggest the insubstantiality of characters, motivations, and political sympathies. It opens with Miles Coverdale returning home after watching "the wonderful exhibition of the Veiled Lady" a clairvoyant sensitive purportedly in contact with the spirit world who turns out to be the ethereal Priscilla.[90] Within a few lines Hawthorne delineates the transformations that such performances have undergone within the last decade or so, making it clear that for all Coverdale's purported desire to live within a utopian community, he is anchored to a life in which this kind of entertainment, and the materialism it implies, are inescapable, as the end of the novel so damningly reveals. Hawthorne represents the young United States as being caught up in a struggle between conflicting possible futures. The legacy of its past, and the violence of its present, are palpable reminders of the nation's problematic and inescapable heritage.

CHAPTER 3

SACRED THEATRES: THE SPIRITIST PERFORMANCES OF SHAKERISM IN THE 1830S AND 1840S

STAGING SPIRITS

Emma Hardinge Britten frequently put on stage performances with other spiritualists. The potential difficulties these might involve were described in her autobiography, notably in an account of an incident at the New York Athenaeum. After an enthusiastic theatre-going helper had seen the effects that colored fires might produce, Britten began to use them. She had been an actress before becoming a spiritualist and clearly had a quite sophisticated understanding about the possibilities of lighting. Key scenes were lit by burning materials in fire pans that then cast the required color onto the stage. Yet the lighting also occasionally went quite wrong, turning a "jolly gipsy encampment" that she had envisaged being lit up "à la 'Guy Mannering,'" into "a company of ghastly phantoms" on one occasion, through the unexpected production of "a sickly glare of green fire."[1] Likewise, a tableau vivant of Britten dressed as Saint Cecilia, draped in white and lit by white lighting was particularly successful at producing a heavenly aspect, as she noted, for "the white fire gave us . . . an angelic appearance."[2] On the second encore, the men producing the colored lights became confused and when the curtain was raised again disaster struck. She writes, oh horror! from one wing appeared the lurid glow of a crimson fire, from the other shone the dismal hue of the green light, and as if to make confusion worse confounded, the two poor gentlemen who held the pans had got so choked and blinded with the fire smoke they thrust the pans full on the stage in sight of the audience, whilst they turned their half-suffocated heads the other way.[3]

Clearly, such lighting could be a hazardous business and could produce precisely the wrong effects. But if done correctly, it could help to create an impressive spectacle for a paying audience. Here the transformation of St. Cecilia's brilliant whiteness to "lurid" crimson and "dismal" green suggests a movement from the celestial to the diabolic, whereas the reverse transformation of the "gypsy" scene from red to green suggests a movement to the phantasmal. St. Cecilia's white drapery, formerly enhanced by white lighting, is first effaced and then transfigured by the commingling effects of the colored lights and the smoke from the pans.

This disastrous experience provides a useful illustration of the preoccupations of this chapter, which is about the processes of effacement and transformation within the theatrical contexts of séances and of Shaker manifestations. The performativity of spiritualism is considered in relation to a series of events that took place within a more strictly codified religious arena than that of the séance—a series of stylized, sacral performances, or "sacred theater," that took place in the late 1830s and early 1840s within Shaker communities.[4] Such occasions explicitly sought to situate themselves outside of commercial culture. They differed in form from the practices of some spiritualists who (as previous chapters have shown) relied on systems of advertising and niche publications to popularize their activities. These will be interpreted within the context of what has been called "playing Indian"—dressing up (usually by whites) as Indians—and considered in relation to the later practices of the spiritualist séance.[5]

Garrett has argued that spirit possession may usefully be seen as a form of theatrical performance by individuals performing in a "socially sanctioned" manner.[6] The implication of this is that there are social codes for reading such scenes of possession that can be knowable to the historian and indeed that there are codes for the participants that enable them to act out these performances in recognizable ways. He writes, spirit possession, interpreted as sacred theater, can provide . . . a price-less resource for historians of popular religion. One can examine and describe the "performance," try to ascertain how it was under-stood by its audience, and ask what kinds of cultural and theological expectations the performance and its interpretation by the audience implied.[7]

These are key methodological issues about how to decipher not just the Shaker manifestations, but also spiritualist séances. In this read-ing of Shaker events I follow this model of investigation by looking at the responses of individuals who witnessed the performances and wrote first-hand accounts of what they saw. I also make a case for the relation between these events and recurring tropes within spiritualist séances and manifestations in order to suggest a way of reconstructing what Garrett calls "the lost world of popular belief," one part of what is being mapped throughout this work.[8]

Séances are highly performative phenomena. The drama of initia-tion, discovery, and revelation is manifest through details of pacing and production.[9] Special effects utilized within some séances, such as the use of phosphorescence and colored lights, allowed spirits to appear and disappear in startling and dramatic ways, convincing séance goers that what they were seeing could not be produced by trickery and must be real. Some could be so persuaded by this that even when the séance did not go smoothly and the medium risked exposure, people attending séances might still find explana-tions that exonerated the medium.[10]

The use of such techniques certainly bears a strong resemblance to aspects of staging known more familiarly in the theatre. Scholars of spiritualism have recognized for some time that there are a num-ber of pronounced connections between spiritualism and theatre. The staging of some séances relies on theatricality in explicit ways. There are many shared elements between the theatre and the séance, including lowered lighting, a key performer (the medium) and a number of other supporting actors (embodied spirits), and audience participation. Further, there are accompanying noises that give great dramatic effect such as rapping or knocking, props, and even stylized speeches. In addition there are often contiguities between the arrangements of the participants (spectators/audience) in relation to the activity of the medium. This might be exemplified by the plans sometimes included in descriptions of séances, which act in some ways like stage directions, indicating where the audience should be seated in relation to the medium and to the cabinet (if there is one) and so on.[11]

In conjunction with these details about performance and space, other intriguing connections can be explored, such as the theatrical experiences of mediums themselves. Alex Owen has discussed the numbers of young women mediums in nineteenth-century Britain who had some sort of theatrical training prior to their involvement with spiritualism, and the same could be said of American mediums.[12] It is not surprising that such experience might be useful for mediums, since the sort of work they were engaged in often required impersonations and negotiations that were certainly dramatic and, in some cases, highly melodramatic.

Many women learned oratorical techniques such as speech projection from the stage, which they then transferred to their experiences within the séance, or public trance lectures. They often dazzled audiences with a wide range of topics, most frequently women's rights. The relationship between acting and public oratory has been noted in the area of political activism.[13] This, too, has implications for spiritualism, since many of its advocates were also involved in abolition, women's rights, and other political campaigns.[14] These sorts of political and spiritual performances were so familiar to nineteenth-century American audiences that Henry James made them the center of his novel *The Bostonians* (1886), which for him captured a peculiarly apt aspect of American social, political, and cultural life in the period.

The moment at which Verena Tarrant begins to speak while in trance is brilliantly captured by James. He writes,

> She began incoherently, almost inaudibly, as if she were talking in a dream. . . . She proceeded slowly, cautiously, as if she were listening for the prompter, catching, one by one, certain phrases that were whispered to her a great distance off, behind the scenes of the world. Then memory, or inspiration, returned to her, and presently she was in possession of her part. She played it with extraordinary simplicity and grace; at the end of ten minutes Ransom became aware that the whole audience—Mrs Farrinder, Miss Chancellor, and the tough subject from Mississippi— were under the charm. I speak of ten minutes, but to tell the truth the young man lost all sense of time. He wondered afterwards how long she had spoken; then he counted that her strange, sweet, crude, absurd, enchanting improvisation must have lasted half an hour.[15]

Verena's trance speaking is described using the language of the stage, indeed James's description reads at times exactly like a review of an improvised piece of theatre, which in some ways is just what it is. It is an elaborate display that, so to speak, entrances her audience. Verena's speech is represented as being like a theatrical monologue that she initially has difficulty remembering or being inspired to reproduce. Once this period of uncertainty is over she is described as shifting into a different mode, she "was in possession of her part," which she then plays with great skill. What James is capturing is the way in which the performance itself is not always dependent on language. A significant aspect of what intrigues Verena's audience about her impassioned plea for the rights of women, is her sexual attractiveness and youth, a combination notoriously associated with young spiritualist mediums and the older men often linked with them. Ransom's hostility leads him to characterize her as a performer who has been given a poor role to play in a badly written piece, yet who still carries it off with charm. He reconciles himself to the political content of her speech by dismissing her capacity for invention or origination.

Opponents of spiritualism could also resort to theatricality on occasions. Critical work has shown the ways in which interesting exposures of fraudulent mediums have relied on a striking level of theatricality and performance. The public debunking of spiritualism has been associated with theatrical performers who include consummate entertainers of very different sorts and in varied periods such as Harry Houdini in the United States and Henry Irving in Great Britain. If the enactment of spiritualism was sometimes raised to the level of an art form, then so was the staging of public exposures of fraudulence. Houdini was a brilliant performer. His early interest in spiritualism was in what it offered to him as way of making money. This developed into a profound distrust of it and a desire to reveal what he saw as fakery and clumsiness. He showed, in gripping ways, that even a skeptic like him could produce the effects that spiritualism claimed as its special domain. Through this, he built on his earlier reputation as a skilled entertainer with a shrewd understanding of what his audience wanted.[16]

In short, the séance borrowed from a number of differing theatrical forms and moved from melodrama (lachrymose meetings between long-parted—and departed—loved ones) to high farce (exposures of fake mediums in highly undignified positions) without ever reaching what might truly be described as tragedy. Indeed the only truly tragic aspect of spiritualism, in this respect, is the fate of some key women mediums who found the pressures of mediumship within a competitive and often skeptical environment so terrible that they lapsed into alcoholism and, eventually, poverty.[17]

SHAKER PERFORMERS

In his seminal work *The Communistic Societies of the United States* (1875) (republished in 1993 as *American Utopias*), Charles Nordhoff argues confidently that the Shakers are largely English speaking and American-born, "industrious, peaceful, honest, highly ingenious, patient of toil, and extraordinarily cleanly," and that they are "pronounced Spiritualists" who regularly interact with the spirit world.[18] In a fairly lengthy description of the habits and practices of Shakers, he repeatedly alludes to the relationship between spiritualism and Shakerism. He notes, for example, that

> At a Shaker funeral I have heard what purported to be a message from the spirit whose body was lying in the coffin in the adjoining hall. In one of the societies it is believed that a magnificent spiritual city, densely inhabited, and filled with palaces and fine residences, lies upon their domain, and at but a little distance from the terrestrial buildings of the Church family; and frequent communications come from this spirit city to their neighbors.[19]

These beliefs—in hearing the voices of dear departed ones and in the idea of a hereafter that is close by and in some way reachable—are recognizable tropes about death and the afterlife. They have their equivalents within literary culture notably the appearance of ghosts—or of messages from ghosts—that warn, implore, or punish.

In the United States of the late eighteenth and early nineteenth century, one of the most famous of such figures was the ghost of Hamlet's father, who reveals the treachery of Claudius and Gertrude. His status and political and symbolic power as monarch are features of significance in terms of the structure of what the returning dead mean within a cultural context. The appearance of dead leaders (monarchs, presidents, and religious leaders, for example) is a common feature in cultural memory and representation.

The ghost in Hamlet has another function in the literary culture of the early republic too. The parable of the relationship between political and social power and incestuous familial relations is implic-itly alluded to in *Wieland* in which the warnings come not from the ghost of a dead father (though the novel starts with his mysterious death through spontaneous combustion) but the ventriloquist Wieland. Stern has argued that the fiction of the early republic "con-joins the efforts of individuals blending their voices *with* each other—whose experiences of identification become a form of fellow feeling . . . with the practices of those who would speak *for* each other—whose acts of representation degenerate into tyrannical usurpation."[20] This distinction between the joining or "blending" of voices and the substitution of voices might interestingly be applied to the politics of the Shaker performances, which have themselves been seen as part of a power struggle between elders and those expe-riencing visions and gifts, many of whom were young and female, like many mediums.[21] It is the particular conjunctions of belief and performance, and the meanings given to such phenomena that ally these practices to those that spiritualists would adopt after 1848.

One part of the prehistory of spiritualism is the period of extraor-dinary religious upheaval within Shakerism that was known as Mother Ann's Work or the Era of Manifestations. It is a specific moment within Shaker history, characterized by spiritual manifesta-tions, spiritual gifts of songs, hymns and beautiful imaginary objects, and mimed performances of "eating, drinking, washing, planting, harvesting, fighting, and countless other ritual actions" that has pro-vided a key focus for Shaker historians.[22] It also needs to be seen within the context of the history of Shakerism that preceded it so that its significance is not misunderstood. For, as Stephen J. Stein has elegantly argued, the Era of Manifestations should be inter-preted as part of a continuum of spiritist experiences that always characterized Shaker religious consciousness rather than as an episode that had no precedent within the history of Shakerism.[23]

But another part of what the moment demonstrates—and that the narrative of *Wieland* with its invocation of dreams, ventrilo-quism, and religious fervor also indicates—is the complex intertwin-ing of what Jon Butler has called "a dramatic American religious syncretism that wedded popular supernaturalism with Christianity and found expression in antebellum Methodism, Mormonism, Afro-American Christianity, and spiritualism."[24] The ethnic performances of Shakers need to be examined within a rich nineteenth-century context that ranges on the one hand, from traditions of the occult and supernatural (some already alluded to), and on the other, to patterns of theatrical representation to suggest the range of sources available to Shakers who wanted to demonstrate their spiritual gifts.

The appearance of the spirits of Indians within spiritualist séances has been thought of as perhaps originating in these Shaker manifestations, though there were other sources too.[25] But where did these Indian spirits within Shaker manifestations come from? What part did they have in the rituals of a radical Protestant sect that originated in the Northwest of England? It was the effect of moving across the Atlantic and living within a new and alien landscape that created the circumstances in which Indian (and sometimes African) spirits could play a part in the practices of Shakers. This, in turn, went on to contribute to the patterns of spiritualist séances along with modes of ethnic performance from the theatre and stage. These spiritist performances of the 1830s and 1840s need to be read within a transatlantic context.

It says a good deal about the fascination that has been generated by a celibate, peace-loving group of people that the history of the Shakers is so widely known, albeit often in a highly romanticized way.[26] The most important of the early Shaker figures, its founder Ann Lee, was born in Manchester, baptized in 1742 and left England with a group of fellow believers in 1774 to start a new life in North America. Though there is no definitive agreement on the intellectual and religious origins of Shaker beliefs, it seems likely that the influence of the French Prophets who arrived in England from France in the early eighteenth century, the Quakers, and even the Methodists all contributed to the formation of Shaker ideology.[27] The Shakers merged traditions of prophetic speaking and divine inspiration with ecstatic dancing and singing. Like the Quakers, they were anti-ecclesiastical.[28]

The first currents of the Era of Manifestations were felt in Watervliet, New York, in 1837. News of the events taking place soon spread throughout the society by personal correspondence, letters from the ministry, and personal visits. The striking displays included singing, dancing, and speaking, while apparently under the influence of spirits. As time went on the experiences within Shaker societies there and elsewhere expanded to include more complex trance speaking and visions, which included encounters with Jesus, Mother Ann and other founders of the society, deceased family members, and angels. Again there was a precedent within Shaker tradition for conversing with "notable spirit figures" and this pattern would emerge within spiritualism too.[29]

There are many different and fascinating accounts of the appearance of the spirits who made themselves known during this period. A Shaker publication of 1874, for example, describes a series of extraordinary events that took place in the North Union Society of Shakers in Ohio. Elder James S. Prescott wrote that at that time a letter had informed him that "there was a marvelous work going on in some of the Eastern societies, especially at Mt. Lebanon, New York, and at Watervliet, near Albany." He continued:

> when it reached us in the West we should all know it, and we did know it; in the progress of the work, every individual, from the least to the greatest, did know that there was a heart-searching God in Israel, who ruled in the armies of heaven, and will yet rule among the inhabitants of earth.[30]

This work would prove the existence of God without doubt. Mount Lebanon and Watervliet are both places close to Rochester, New York—which is significant in its relation to American spiritualism's foundational narrative and its historical role as a center for political and religious activism in the early nineteenth century.

What Prescott describes is a sometimes bizarre moment of theatrical ethnic impersonation, which may well have its roots in the sorts of politicized political performances of "Indianness" by whites that, as Philip Deloria has shown, have taken place from the earliest days of the Republic to the present.[31] Prescott's description of events is unusually clear. He writes that the first experience his society had of these events, in 1838, was when a group of young women heard "beautiful singing" above their heads when they were out walking. Later some of these young women became what he called—using vocabulary today (and already in 1874) very familiar through spiritualism—spirit mediums. His writing suggests familiarity with the Rochester rappings: he is keen to portray the events he describes as antecedents to them.[32]

While the first experience was that of young women, girls were the chief protagonists of the second. He was at worship on the Sabbath and was interrupted by an excited messenger who told the elders "that there was something uncommon going on in the girls' department." Closing their worship, the elders "'went over to witness this strange phenomenon." In the room there was a great

deal of rapid activity going on, and the girls "were under the influence of a power not their own." A group of girls

> were hurried round the room, back and forth as swiftly as if driven by
> the wind—and no one could stop them. If any attempts were made in
> that direction, it was found impossible, showing conclusively that they
> were under a controlling influence that was irresistible.

The language used here—"irresistible," "controlling," "influence"—
suggests externality. The narrative reveals, albeit in a virtually imper-
ceptible way, a drama of rapid movement and alarmed response, of
activity and of attempts to prevent it. The girls finally fell into trances
and lay prostrate with their bodies stiffened. They were lifted up and
placed on beds. They then

> began holding converse with their guardian spirits and others, some
> of whom they once knew in the form, making graceful motions with
> their hands—talking audibly, so that all in the room could hear and
> understand, and form some idea of their whereabouts in the spiritual
> realms they were exploring in the land of souls. This was only the
> beginning of a series of "spirit manifestations," the most remarkable
> we ever expected to witness on the earth.

The use of quotation marks around "spirit manifestations" shows
that he is aware of using what was already a borrowed vocabulary.
But there is a further borrowing going on here too. The language
used to describe the events being witnessed recalls accounts of
earlier scenes of possession, such as in seventeenth century Salem.

One such account can be found in Cotton Mather's description
of the possession of the twelve-year-old Abigail Williams. She "was
at first hurried with violence to and fro in the Room (though Mrs.
Ingersol endeavoured to hold her) sometimes making as if she would
fly, stretching up her Arms as high as she could, and crying *Whish,
Whish, Whish*, several times; presently after she said, there was
Goodw. *N.* and said, *Do you not see her? Why there she stands!*"[33] The
rapid physical activity combined with the impossibility of preventing
Williams's movement, the gesticulations, the vocalization, and the
belief in a vision that only the main protagonist experiences are all
common features of both scenes. Yet they are not simply specific to
both, for they follow a common pattern familiar from scenes of
possession. Within these Shaker examples the frenetic activity that

preceded the trances seems to be replaced by a sense of an emerging
rationality. The hand gestures and speech of the girls suggest the end
of a particularly physical crisis, which has led from a form of
movement that seems involuntary and hysterical to something that
can be read as rationalized and controlled. In place of a dramatized
excess of movement, there is a return to "converse," to harmony,
and to discourse, which can be represented and interpreted by commentators and viewers.

Prescott notes that a particular characteristic of these manifestations was what is known as "gifts," particularly those of songs and
hymns. The first of these, called "The Song of a Herald" was sung
by "one of the young sisters, while in vision, with great power and
demonstration of the spirit." He goes on to quote it and notes that
it was "Given by inspiration, at North Union, August, 1838, ten
years prior to the 'Rochester Rappings.'" Though such gifts have
roots in a tradition of religious mysticism and utterance, they would
also find their equivalent in later literary products of poet mediums,
such as Achsa Sprague and Lizzie Doten.[34]

The gifts continued and led to further scenes of apparent travel
in which those possessed attempted to give some idea of what the
spirit world was like. It seems as if an elaborate pantomimic performance was witnessed and performed by the Shakers, with the
older men providing the audience for the young female actors. Such
a scene of acting/audience is familiar from the early iconography of
Shaker history.[35] Similar instances were described as taking place
within the boys' department, where not just boys, but also girls and
adults had started to experience gifts.

They claimed to have visited the Blue City, a place inhabited by
the spirits of Indians. This city was the first they reached "after crossing the river," meaning that it was the most easily accessible to the
mediums. "Crossing the river" of course carries connotations of
crossing over to the other side, to a spirit world, a life after death.
Equally, it augments a notion of geographical location and of travel
and is particularly associated with the Indian removals going on in
this period. Prescott records a series of questions and answers that
took place between observers and the instruments. In form it
resembles a dialogue hymn, such as the one published in Watervliet
in 1833, which urges a confession of sins.[36] However, this conversation might be interpreted as an exercise in information gathering.

Question—What city is this? Answer—The Blue City. Question—
Who lives here? Answer—The Indians. Question—What Indians?
Answer—The American Indians. Question—Why are they the first
city we come to in the spirit-land, on the plane, and most accessible?
Answer—Because the Indians lived more in accordance with the law
of nature in their earth life, according to their knowledge, and were
the most abused class by the whites except the slaves, and many of
them are now in advance of the whites in "spirituality," and are the
most powerful ministering spirits sent forth to minister to those who
shall be the heirs of salvation.

This answer is perfectly consistent with the belief of some spiritualists.
There seems also to have been a complex identification both of
attraction and repudiation going on between Shakers and Indians.
Like these fantasy Indians, Shakers lived more symbiotically with
nature than their more urban counterparts; like them, they experienced persecution; like them, they were engaged in a process of
vanishing through their chosen policy of celibacy.

Some Shakers had preached or undertaken missions to Indians,
and Shaker tradition asserted that it was an Indian who first recognized the "saintliness" of Ann Lee.[37] On still another occasion, a
group of fifteen Shakers of both sexes felt themselves possessed by
the spirits of Indians from the Blue City, "then followed the Indian
songs and dancing, and speaking in the Indian tongue, which was
wholly unintelligible to us except by spiritual interpreters." The use
of the definite article here implies a wholesale categorization of
Indianness that makes no distinction between tribes, languages,
rituals, and so on. The idea of the Indian being invoked is a composite cultural and linguistic category. A progression is going on
here. The young Shakers who claimed to be possessed seem to be
moving by degrees to a wholesale performance of ethnicity, which
involved acting out "Indian" dances and songs, and speaking in
"Indian" languages that required interpretation. This would be particularly well demonstrated a few years later in Watervliet.

The relevance of these and other Shaker manifestations is
twofold. First, these two separate series of events (both of which are
claimed as having a certain primacy) the Shaker manifestations and
the experiences of the Fox sisters both emerge from a shared geography. Second, the Shaker manifestations help to construct a history
of spiritualism that suggests the value of new fields of investigation.
These include a consideration of the complexity of spiritualism's ethnic

history and inheritance. There are points of contact between Indian religious practices and those of spiritualists, as both spiritualists and scholars have noted. It is hardly surprising that the identity formations of both the colonizers and the colonized were altered by the experience of contact.

This was certainly the case in terms of religious encounter.[38] The presence of the spirits of the dead and the importance of shamanism within Indian belief systems are the two most obvious examples of shared practice.[39] Britten gives a lengthy account of witnessing a series of manifestations, produced by an Indian from a tent, that bear a very close relation to descriptions of séances.[40] Later, figures such as Annette Leevier, from mixed French Canadian and Ojibbeway-Mohawk ancestry, became active spiritualist mediums, drawing on both sides of their spiritual origins.[41]

Visiting Shaker villages was as fashionable at that period as collecting Shaker furniture is today. In 1843 Rebecca Cox Jackson visited Watervliet and was converted to Shakerism. She later became increasingly interested in spiritualism and attended a number of séances. During the period of the Era of Manifestations, she was an "active visionist" and recorded a series of messages from the spirit world.[42]

Many others wrote dramas and fictions about the Shaker community that frequently included scenes of communal dancing and other features of Shaker life. These include Catharine Maria Sedgwick's novel *Redwood* (1824), Nathaniel Hawthorne's story "The Shaker Bridal" (1842), and Samuel D. Johnson's play *The Shaker Lovers* (1857).[43] Shakers, like Indians, were the subjects of wide-ranging representations in newspapers and fictional and other literary works that they probably never encountered firsthand. The juxtaposition of the silence and order of daily life with the synchronized movement or whirling and spinning of ritualized dancing produce a sometimes striking degree of theatricality in the representation of Shakers.

Around the time Jackson first visited Watervliet a bewildering series of spirits of all ethnicities and political perspectives and persuasions appeared and disappeared (with great rapidity) among the Shakers. In an 1869 publication, *A Revelation of the Extraordinary Visitation of Departed Spirits,* a narrator who describes himself as a "guest" of the Watervliet community wrote expressly to consider the relation between spiritualism and the Shaker manifestations.[44] The anonymous writer went to the Watervliet community in the winter of 1843 while on a visit to Troy. His visit appeared to be in line with the popular habits of other inquisitive outsiders, but once he arrived in Watervliet and heard of "the *visitation of disembodied Spirits,* who came to the nightly meetings of the Society, taking temporary possession of the bodies of the brethren and sisters engaged in worship" he became "much excited" and "expressed his desire to be present and witness the strange manifestations."[45] He claims to have attended a number of meetings at which these manifestations took place and made notes of what took place at that time, "presenting, as near as was possible, the language and ideas uttered by the various *Spirits* that spoke through the brethren and sisters."[46] Taking him at his word, it seems that this work will give a reliable and accurate account of what took place at these meetings.

Certainly that is what his readership is invited to do. On reading his account it is clear that his material has been crafted carefully throughout. Despite his claim that he wrote down what he heard at the point at which he heard and saw it, there is a 26 year gap between his visit and the publication dates. The work, he acknowledges, was only published in 1869 because there was a new market for it brought about by the great interest in spiritualism. Indeed, in this period spiritualism and Shakerism were so closely connected that within two years of the book's publication Elder Frederick W Evans made two missionary trips to England along with his friend James M. Peebles, a spiritualist speaker and writer. They lectured together to politicians, journalists, and others.[47]

Shakers believed that a new spiritual age was imminent, heralded by the events experienced during the period of Mother Ann's Work and reinscribed through the emergence of spiritualism a decade later. For them, the two were connected in important ways. The Shaker historian Anna White gave a lecture called "True Spiritualism, " which made an explicit connection between Shakerism and spiritualism. She was inspired to do this after reading an article about a clairvoyant and clairaudient medium in the spiritualist journal *Banner of Light.* Many Shakers saw a clear relation between their beliefs and those of Millerites, spiritualists, and other newly emerging religious groups.[48]

Quite apart from the way in which the Watervliet guest of 1843 presents this material for his reading audience, there is another issue: the way in which the Shaker participants in the manifestations he describes shaped their performances for him. He presents himself as a neutral and accurate recorder of events, yet the double performances of the Shakers and his involvement in the creation of this record are each of interest. Like the spirits who the Shakers believed were manifesting themselves through their bodies, this narrator was a visitor and his account needs to be treated with a degree of caution. Rather than reading the events simply as he presents them and would wish readers to interpret them (as genuine and fairly precise descriptions of a set of extraordinary experiences), the book must be read as a retrospective account of a fascinating occasion that is shaped and created by contemporary cultural and marketing practices. Placing spiritualism and Shakerism together was aimed at a wide audience, fascinated by both subjects and certainly by the conjunction of the two.

A final ambiguity about the guest's retrospective description should also be noted. By 1842 the Shakers suspended the public meetings at which outside spectators could observe their worship. This meant that, to take a celebrated example, when Charles Dickens expressed a "great desire" to visit New Lebanon in June of that year, an encounter that led to an excoriating description of Shakers, he found himself barred from meetings.[49] When he arrived there he met an elder ("a sort of calm goblin") who showed him a piece in a newspaper dated a few days earlier saying that "in consequence of certain unseemly interruptions which their worship had received from strangers, their chapel was closed to the public for the space of one year."[50] Finding that protest was useless, instead he wandered off to "make some trifling purchases of Shaker goods" and observed that Shaker buildings "were chiefly of wood, painted a dark red like English barns, and composed of many stories like English factories."[51] In the period following the closure, "great numbers" of Indian spirits were manifested.[52] Given Dickens's somewhat acid, but acute, remarks on the little he did see of the Shakers, it is a great shame that he did not witness such an event.

The guest's account of the events leading up to the first manifestation he saw is overtly theatrical and sets the tone for later manifestations. He describes the seating arrangements of the Shakers who, segregated by gender, faced each other across a room with two Elders and two Eldresses standing at the head of each group. He does not mention where he sat, though it would have been customary for him to sit separately. They sang a number of hymns and then danced. The leading Elder "delivered an extempore exhortation."[53] After this, first a male and then a female Shaker whirled and shook for some time. He noted that "such a performance the writer never witnessed upon the theatrical stage, or anywhere outside of those Shaker assemblages."[54] It was at this point that the manifestations started to take place in earnest:

> Several were discoursing in what were termed "unknown tongues." Some were whirling, and others gesticulating violently, when, on a sudden, loud, simultaneous yells were given, and several of the brethren and sisters sprang into the center of the room.
>
> The Elders advanced towards those thus *possessed*, and questioned them. They jabbered away in a curious, monotonous sort of dialect, until one of them said that they were a party of
>
> INDIANS
>
> of the Mohawk tribe, who had long ago left their wigwams and hunting grounds upon the earth.[55]

Here, the possession and speaking in tongues is interrupted by the yell that announces the arrival of the Indian spirits. They first jabber "in a curious, monotonous sort of dialect," before explaining who they are in speech that is never directly reported but that comes across as being highly stylized. It relies on words and phrases intelligible and recognizable to contemporary audiences interspersed with fragments of what remains unknowable. The interpreter calls himself the spirit of "a great chief" and a number of the female Shakers represent themselves as "squaws and Indian maidens" and "jabbered away apparently in their native languages, as used by them when living in the body."[56]

This performance is, by definition, dependent on being enacted in front of, and probably by, individuals for whom Indian languages were strange and unknown. At no point was any attempt at transcription made and across the whole range of Indian performances the tendency is toward description and miming rather than transcription or translation. So though the narrator claims to try to reproduce the utterances of the spirits, when it comes to languages other than English (and this included speaking in tongues), he does not reproduce them. Part of what is striking here is the sheer number of Indian spirits that appear. Of about sixty Shakers present in the room, apparently half of them received Indian spirits into their bodies and seemed "entirely changed, excepting in dress and complexion, and, so far as their language and actions were concerned, appeared in verity to be the *Spirits of the Red Men of the Past*."[57] They spoke of their "happy condition" and the pleasure taken in "occasionally wandering about their old hunting grounds." When, in contrast, the spirit of William Penn appeared among this group of "Indians" he spoke "in forcible words of great eloquence" about his continued interest in the welfare of Indian peoples both in the West and in Pennsylvania.[58]

It is quite clear, in this example and elsewhere, that the codes of performance for white spirits and nonwhite spirits are not the same. The nonwhite spirits tend toward a hyperbolic enactment of racial stereotype that relies on exaggerated gesture, movement, and mime. This tableau of an early encounter uses the Indians who appear in it as picturesque counterparts to William Penn whose ideological message is supported by his careful, rational, and comprehensible speech. The different emphasis on the verbal and the visual is a significant marker of ethnic difference. The juxtaposition of the group of Indians with an individualized white subject, William Penn, is crucial to the process of othering repeatedly to be seen within these Shaker performances. Such methods are used within frontier novels, as Dana Nelson has shown, to diminish individuality and instead suggest a generic set of group characteristics, which, in many novels, are represented in highly pejorative ways.[59] Nelson cites Mary Louise Pratt to demonstrate the way in which such a process relies on assumptions of essentialist and timeless identities. Pratt writes that

> The people to be othered are homogenized into a collective "they" which is distilled even further into a collective "he" (the standard adult male specimen). The abstracted "he"/ "they" is the subject of verbs in a timeless present tense, which characterizes anything "he" is or does not as a particular historical event but as an instance of a pregiven custom or trait. . . . Through this discourse, encounters with an Other can be textualized or processed as enumerations of such traits.'[60]

Such a process is amply demonstrated within the Shaker performances.

In a series of chapters the narrator goes on to describe the way in which a number of further manifestations took place. The abbreviated list includes: William Penn, a Negro Slave, an Irishman, Saint Patrick, Charles the First, Oliver Cromwell, The Arabs, Indian Chiefs, Cicero, Julius Caesar, Alexander, George Washington, Lafayette, Robespierre, Mirabeau, Dr. Benjamin Franklin and Wife,

Indian Tribes, The Esquimaux, The Signers of the Declaration of Independence, Henry VIII, Catharine of Aragon, Cardinal Wolsey, Ann Boleyn, The Chinese, Gladiators, The Druids, Robert Burns, Napoleon, Louis XVI, Marie Antoinette, Shakespeare, an Egyptian Mummy, Queen Elizabeth, Raleigh, Essex, George III, Queen Charlotte, Shelley, Lord Nelson, The Indians, John Wesley, George Whitefield, Pocahontas, Charles II, Rochester, William Penn, The Indians (again), Robert Emmett, Byron, George Fox, and Ben Jonson. In addition to these figures listed explicitly, further groups of Indians appear. There are precedents for the appearance of celebrated spirits within Shakerism, as has been shown earlier.

Three particular points emerge from reading this list, however. First, the sheer variety of figures, as well as their numbers, is striking. It would be fascinating to have more detail about how the audience recognized the figures, or how they made themselves known to them. Since this was not done through costume changes, lighting, or scenery (common visual signifiers of difference), it must have relied both on charade-like visual displays and self-disclosure. It seems that in many cases spirits actually introduced themselves and that they exhibited enough recognizable characteristics to allow for this character designation to be accepted by their audience, much as it might be in a theatrical performance in which a single actor plays multiple roles. Once such spirits began to appear with some regularity, the compact between audience and actor became more reliable and the Shakers who were being possessed could rely on ready identifications being made by their audiences.

Second, it is a list that, with some alterations, is consistent with figures who frequently appeared in spiritualist séances (such as those recorded by Isaac Post) later in the century.[61] These individuals were all famous in a variety of different arenas, in politics, art, or history or as representative of ethnic groups largely represented not as individual members but as collections or examples, in a manner that suggests an anthropological study.

Third, it shows that there is one consistent abiding presence here, that of Indians, principal among them and individualized: Pocahontas. Her appearance is described as follows,

> The Indian princess, in the person of a comely-looking sister, now manifested herself, and held a conversation with one of the Elders, at the same time that the Spirits of King
> CHARLES THE SECOND

of England, and the
EARL OF ROCHESTER
made themselves known through the brethren.[62]

Pocahontas is not described as jabbering or chattering in the manner that the speech of the other Indians is represented. Indeed she converses with a male Elder on what seems like equal terms. She occupies a place closer to that of other white and mainly male historical figures than to that of the groups of Indians who appear, one characterized by coherence and rationality. Within the performances of the egalitarian Shakers, the "he" of Pratt's argument becomes a "she." Yet this "iconic" figure—rational, attractive, and engaged in conversation rather than yelling—is not quite any representative figure. Her transatlantic story—involving self-sacrifice, conversion to Christianity, and a visit to England—was one repeatedly invoked within U.S. culture for a range of reasons, as we will see.

These figures appeared to and among the Shakers in part because they already knew them. A factor common to séances and Shaker manifestation is that spirits are usually known to the people they appear in front of, which makes validation and belief easier. The ways in which they are known is varied. Some are the spirits of individuals already personally known by the mediums or audience, and others are familiar from popular biographies, histories, and other narratives. Some of these contexts will be explained shortly, and some have been touched on briefly already. But it should be noted that the historical figures that appear here are not like the key generic group "The Indians" that is repeatedly invoked, though they need to be read in relation to them.

Furthermore, there are differences between the specificity of Pocahontas and the generic "Indians" as they appear here. These have a complicated cultural history that reveals a great deal about the nexus of debates around the past and future of the Republic and ideas of nationhood, and their relation to spirituality, ethnicity, and gender. Once read in the context of spiritualism, their meaning transcends national discourses and enters a different symbolic realm that (in the present moment, for instance) extends into New Age beliefs that valorize the spirituality and spiritual practices of native peoples. Pocahontas is, very early on, a hugely overdetermined figure with great symbolic significance.[63]

The series of manifestations draw upon a history of representation that emerges from traditions of melodrama and pathos and is associated with the stage as well as with fiction, poetry, and the visual arts.

Figures like these Indians form an important connection between the Shaker manifestations and spiritualism. Even if the Shakers who acted out the roles of Indians had not actually seen any of the Indian dramas that were so popular in the period, read the poetry and fiction, or seen the engravings and paintings and magazine illustrations that showed romantic images of Indians, they may have come across Pocahontas as part of their earliest educational experiences. Noah Webster included the story of Pocahontas in his hugely popular reader.[64] A brief outline of the historical representations of Indians by whites in the period leading up to the Shaker manifestations, and in the period between the manifestations and the accounts of them described here, will help to demonstrate the contiguity between them.

REPRESENTING THE INDIAN

Since the earliest encounter narratives, white colonists described and detailed the appearance and customs of the native peoples they came across. Not content with bringing home artifacts or written or visual accounts of the native peoples of the Americas, explorers and colonists brought native peoples back as early as about 1501, when three native men were presented at the court of Henry VII. Some of the individuals who made the journey over the Atlantic in the next few decades appear to have traveled voluntarily, while others were captured and taken against their will. An unnamed Brazilian king was brought to the court of Henry VIII some years later, a voluntary traveler. He died at sea on his way back to Brazil, establishing a pattern that would become horribly familiar.

In the 1570s four Inuits were brought from Canada to England. They were captured by Martin Frobisher who was searching for a northwest passage to China. The first, whose name has not passed into the record, was the subject of more than a dozen portraits that were later copied and reproduced. He died a few weeks after arriving in England. On a return journey to Canada, Frobisher captured a man called Kalicho at one location as well as a woman and her son— Arnaq and Nutaaq—at another. Like the first Inuit captive, they caused a great sensation and achieved celebrity—Kalicho's skill at hunting and using a boat "dazzled onlookers."[65] But neither of the adults reached London, their intended destination. Kalicho and

Arnaq both died in Bristol and were buried there. Nutaaq did reach London, but he died a week later.[66]

Many scholars have noted that the manner in which native peoples were represented and exhibited in the colonial period was closely tied to the array of meanings that colonists wished to find in them. Some were important in terms of what they could teach colonizers about their languages. In this way they were less important in themselves than as figures who could pass on the sort of information that would make settling the new land easier for the colonizers. So their significance was at once personal, political, and symbolic.

This earlier pattern of representation certainly continued into the Shaker manifestations. The Indian spirits who manifested themselves through the Shakers enacted their cultural and ethnic difference through the use of strange "languages," dances, and actions, thus dramatizing the parallel relationship constructed out of both the sameness and the difference between living Shakers and vanishing Indians. Indians were envisaged as being in the process of being effaced through the enactment of ideological and political campaigns against them in the name of Manifest Destiny. The Shakers who represented them were constructing for themselves identities that were contingent upon vanishing or disappearing—the inevitable outcome of the sect's required celibacy, but also an aspect of their culture of retreat from what they called the "world" into enclosed communities. This was reinforced by the terminology they adopted toward outsiders who were often referred to as the "world's people."

The most famous of these visitors was undoubtedly Pocahontas, who arrived in London in 1616. Her well-documented visit included meetings with Ben Jonson and (perhaps) Walter Raleigh, both important historical and literary figures who also appear in the Shaker manifestations.[67] She attended Jonson's masque *The Vision of Delight* at the Jacobean court and sat for a famous and much reproduced engraving by Simon van de Passe. She died in Gravesend in Kent, in January 1617, and was buried there.

One striking feature about the manner in which she was received in England was the shifting way in which she was seen both as an Indian princess and as the Christianized wife of John Rolfe. The van de Passe engraving shows her in clothing that, according to Karen Robertson, marks her out as the wife of an English gentleman rather than as a princess who is the daughter of an Indian king. By representing her as wearing the clothing neither of an Indian nor an

English aristocrat, the portrait suggests that her chief role is that of a wife. The subscript to the portrait notes that she is both: "Matoaks als Rebecka daughter to the mighty Prince Powhatan Emperour of Attanoughskomouck als virginia converted and baptized in the Christian faith, and wife to the worth. Mr Joh Rolff." Robertson writes that

> [the] exposure of Pocahontas's secret familial or tribal name [Matoaka] asserts English verbal dominance through their possession and exposure. The makers of the portrait define her status and label her as property: daughter of a king, trophy of conversion, and, finally, wife of an Englishman. The words insist on the success of the conversion narrative: Matoaka has been transformed; yet the tensions of the portrait—in perspective, posture, eyes and clothing—resist the smooth assertions of that conversion narrative.[68]

Robertson's interesting reading of these "tensions" suggests that the portrait at once disguises Pocahontas's Indianness, indeed seems to efface it altogether, while at the same time encodes it within a frame-work of masculinity.[69] The coding of racial difference within this famous portrait, the only image of her made within her lifetime, is particularly interesting since overtly the portrait resists the familiar tropes of savagery that dominate contemporary representations of other Indians who visit England.

As we will see, whites who dressed as or pretended to be Indians were usually not as subtle as this. These reversed performances (of whites as Indians) often used far less sophisticated methods to suggest ethnic difference. Although the van de Passe portrait was widely copied and reproduced, it did not establish a dominating pattern for the way in which Pocahontas was visually represented.[70] Instead, depictions of Pocahontas and other Indians responded to the particular contemporary cultural and political preoccupations of the dominant culture.

By the period of the Shaker manifestations the figure of the Indian was being represented within a highly romanticized context. In the American literature of the period, from the late eighteenth century to the 1830s, the Indian was constructed as tragic and romantic. The Indian as noble savage, proud, brave—and defeated, indeed vanishing—was frequently represented in literary and visual cultural forms. Some of the most famous examples come from the novels of James Fenimore Cooper, and more recently the novels of

Catherine Maria Sedgwick and Lydia Maria Child have received renewed critical attention. Scores of poems, plays, novels, and histories of the period showed the Indian as an essential part of U.S. history who could be viewed nostalgically, often fondly, and could take on a variety of meanings.[71]

The history of Pocahontas made an interesting transition in the two centuries between the portrait described above and the Shaker manifestations. Robert Tilton writes that

> By the early nineteenth century, Pocahontas had become an American historical personage, one who was in the ambiguous position of being both "other"—in that she was by birth a "savage"—and also (at least in spirit) an American—for her display of compassion that saved John Smith and with him the Jamestown colony. . . . The Rescue comes to be seen as part of a greater pattern of history that ultimately led to the Revolution and American nationhood.[72]

To see her as a significant historical figure associated with the birth of the new nation helps to make sense of her appearance among other historical personages in the Shaker manifestations—especially those associated with U.S. history such as Washington, Lafayette, Franklin (and wife), and the signers of the Declaration of Independence. If we add to this the fact that by the 1830s Pocahontas was seen increasingly in terms of the self-sacrificing nature of her rescue of John Smith, the nobility of her character, and her personal beauty, we may see why the Shakers separated her from other Indians.

Unlike the generic Indians who jabber in a strange tongue, Pocahontas holds a conversation with one of the Elders (presumably in English), while clearly impressing the narrator by her beauty. By the Era of Manifestations, then, the Pocahontas story—albeit one that was crafted according to current preoccupations and interests—was one that was instituted within U.S. culture. Further, as Rosemarie Bank has shown, the spectacle of Indians putting on their own theatrical performances of ceremonial presentations to whites were well established and "appear to have been the earliest red-white cultural interaction of the performer/audience type." She goes on to note that "white staging of 'Indian' ceremonies" followed on from these early interactions and dated from about 1804 or earlier.[73] It is likely that such occasions, which created a great deal of newspaper coverage (subsequently copied to local papers across the nation), would have been known to the Shakers. Charles Nordhoff claimed that the library at Watervliet contained about 400 volumes and that the society there took "a number of newspapers."[74]

The circulation of images of George Catlin's remarkable collection of portraits published as *The Manners, Customs and Condition of the North American Indian* (1841) suggests a taxonomy that celebrates (among other things) what he interprets as the theatricality of Indian dress, hairstyle, and paint. His detailed descriptions of the cultural meanings and significance of clothing, and so on, act as interpretative guides for his intended audience. He sets himself up as a mediator between white American culture and that of the vanishing Indian. However, after the success of the exhibition of his paintings of Indians and his collections of artifacts in the United States culminated in a disappointing failure to sell them to the U.S. government, Catlin instead took the exhibition to London. Here it achieved great success, and one particularly popular feature was his "Tableaux Vivants Indiennes" in which a group of white Londoners performed as if they were Indians, complete with authentic clothing.

When a group of Ojibbeway Indians turned up in Manchester where he had taken his show in 1843, he found them far better performers than his London recruits. After a ten-day stint in Manchester they left for London and their triumphs included performing for the Queen in a private show at Windsor Castle.[75] The six-year-old Thomas Moran, who would himself achieve fame for his images of the American West, saw the Manchester show a year before his parents emigrated to the United States.[76] The slippage between different kinds of performance here and contested notions of authority suggest the flimsiness of genuine understandings of Indian culture. What audiences wanted was partly just a good show.[77] Yet that show was never wholly innocent and was typically intertwined with imperialist designs.[78]

The vogue for Indian dramas is said to have started with George Washington Parke Custis's play *Indian Prophecy* (1828) and to have been continued by his hugely popular play *Pocahontas: or, The Settlers of Virginia* (1830).[79] Custis portrays Pocahontas as a figure representing the process of assimilation, and through her, seeks to legitimate the processes of Manifest Destiny. Though much might be said about these and other dramas of the period, a few words about one particular performance of *Pocahontas* will demonstrate the complexity of Indian/white interactions within a theatrical context.

In February 1836, the performance run of *Pocahontas* in Washington, DC, coincided with a delegation of Cherokees who were protesting at Indian removals. Bank argues that the proximity of the performance of the play and the arrival of the Cherokees "stimulated a competition for authenticity at a number of levels." The white actors, for example, wore dress donated by the Director of the Indian Bureau and a private collector.[80] The National Theatre, cashing in on the juxtaposition, announced that a group of Cherokee chiefs had offered to join in the performance and stage a war dance complete with ceremonial (rather than actual) scalping. Two days later a news item reported that this had indeed taken place. The group had "performed their real Indian war dance, exhibiting hate, triumph, revenge, etc., and went through the agreeable ceremony of scalping, all of which seemed to give great satisfaction to a crowded house."[81]

When the delegation protested that they had been too busy undertaking a far more important task, which had profound implications for their tribe, to perform at the theatre, the National invited them to attend the final performance of the play. This, as Bank succinctly puts it, is "an insistence upon a bi-racial theatre culture at the very moment when political pronouncements sought to legislate monoculturality."[82] Contrary to the newspaper report, the Cherokee delegates had not attended the earlier performance at all, let alone performed their "real" dances. Yet the National initially insisted that they had and then capitalized on the fact that they had not by publicly inviting them to see the show—an invitation which many of them accepted.[83] Nearly 200 years earlier, when Pocahontas attended a masque at the Jacobean court in 1616, she did not, of course, take part in the performance.[84] She did, however, like the Cherokee chiefs in Washington, DC, witness a performance that centered upon power, the possession of land, and "the subordination and erasure of those who are different."[85]

On a number of other occasions the spectacle of Indians at theatrical performances created a key moment of cultural cachet for the dominant culture, though occasionally it produced a moment of tension too. An example of this took place on June 6, 1833, when the presence of both Black Hawk—a prisoner of war who was forced to undertake a six-week tour of eastern cities and military sites designed to demonstrate the unstoppable might of white power—and Andrew Jackson at the same performance of a play in Baltimore resulted in "the attention of the house [being] . . . very equally divided between them."[86] Such occasions raise questions about the stability of the boundaries between the actors, the audience, and the overall performance.

But they raise questions of political and territorial boundaries, too. The Indian Removal Act was signed by Jackson in 1830. Within a little over a decade Arizona, California, Nevada, New Mexico, Oregon, Texas, and Utah would be added to the rapidly expanding United States. By 1838 the forced removal of Cherokees from Georgia led to the Trail of Tears despite the political and legislative efforts of Cherokees and their supporters. The question of how to produce theatrical legitimacy was one fraught with difficulties. How could white actors convince their audiences that they were like real Indians without losing the audience's sympathy?

In the case of the Shaker manifestations the sympathy was produced by a focus on the Indian as marginal, vanishing, romantic figures whose simple lives (like those of the Shakers) was threatened by a hostile world. A particularly interesting performance in this respect was that of the popular actor Edwin Forrest. John Augustus Stone's play *Metamora, or The Last of the Wampanoags* (1829) was written specifically for Forrest who toured with the play to great success appearing in Boston, New York, and Philadelphia.[87] Forrest's performance of "Indianness" was especially celebrated. Writing in 1837, a reviewer in the New York *Morning Herald* noted that Forrest's Metamora was "an excellent representative of the Indian of poetry," an extraordinarily circular compliment that he developed tellingly in a few more sentences.

> He has a large fund of that *sang froid* and self-sufficiency requisite to portray the stoicism of the red man. Endowed with a few set phrases about revenge, truth, lying, friendship, liberty, and the Manitou; the Indian carries us back to the heroic ages of Greece. . . . He is truly the impersonation of the Indian of romance. The Indian in his *true* character *can* never find a representative among the whites. Disgust, rather than admiration, would ensue, but if the author made him successful, our prejudices would revolt at the scene.[88]

This is a crucial definition of the way in which whites should play Indians if they wanted to avoid alienating their white audiences. The critic calls for a portrayal of those Indian characteristics that were being developed by white writers within the romantic narratives of the period—heroism and the power of oratory both contained within a primitivist frame—and not to depart from them. A focus on vanishing is crucial. This is the kind of performance that takes place in the Shaker manifestations. In this way figures such as Forrest could encourage audiences to sympathize with figures for whom in other circumstances they would have felt unease, perhaps even, to use the term of the critic, "disgust."

Here is the figure of the Indian produced by, and made palatable for, dominant American culture. Indeed, Stone's rewriting of history creates a more melodramatic, sentimental, and heroic scenario than would have been produced by strictly adhering to the facts. In a key moment of the play, Metamora exhorts his warriors in words that suggest aspects of interpretations of Indian religious belief that particularly interested whites and were especially the subject of white appropriation and imitation.

> If ye love the silent spots where the bones of your kindred repose, sing the dread song of war and follow me! . . . Call on the happy spirits of the warriors dead and cry, "Our lands! Our nation's freedom! Or the grave!"[89]

As this suggests, a further and crucial context for the appearance of this play was that of the Indian removals taking place in this period. Forrest's hero produced contradictory responses in his audiences. Paul Gilmore argues that Metamora, like the Indians of James Fenimore Cooper, was used "to represent a nostalgic vision of masculine wholeness and authenticity" through which audiences "could mourn the passing of the Indian, even as they supported Andrew Jackson and his policies designed to make sure the Indian did disappear from the United States."[90] Yet, between the 1820s and the 1840s, Forrest's protagonist came to have a different set of meanings, responding to changes in the economy, social and political institutions, class formations, and an emerging middle-class culture.[91]

When the Shaker manifestations are read within the context of the production of literary "Indianness" during the same period, it is clear that there are significant models for the appearance, the manner of speech, and the sentiments of these Indian spirits. Such complex identities that mixed ethnic and other identifications were also taking place within the cities of the North in the decade that preceded this, and they continued into the 1830s. Eric Lott has described an event in Philadelphia in 1834 in which "one hundred men in intentionally makeshift uniforms conducted elaborate sham maneuvers, accompanied, one newspaper said, by a masked band of 'Indians, hunters, Falstaffs, Jim Crows and non-descripts.'"[92] What were these final categories of nonspecific masked figures? Perhaps the kind of identificatory slippages implied here are also what was going on in the Shaker performances.

At moments, language and images, which are intended to be distinctive, break down into generalized locutions of difference. Yet if the ethnic boundaries manifested were never as clear as the performers may have wished, or if at times the policing of such boundaries was less significant than at other times, one detail about what the Indians who appeared was clear. Being possessed by Indian spirits seems to offer Shakers the opportunity to combine the highest potential for disruptive behavior with the most pronounced spiritual significance.[93] This might be read as a parallel to the entire Shaker project that deliberately situated itself outside of mainstream society in order to maintain a spiritual purity and a ritualized way of life that did not sit easily with the lives of those outside of it.

Indians were explicitly seen as having access to a level of spirituality other ethnic groups could only hope (and pray) for.[94] Certainly the Shakers' performances of ethnicity, particularly Indian ethnicity, demonstrated to some degree "identificatory desire," which Lott sees as being one part of blackface minstrelsy, just as they share with minstrelsy "an unstable or even contradictory power, linked to social and political conflicts, that issues from the weak, the uncanny, the outside."[95]

The genealogy of the Shaker's Indian spirits is complex. While some of the iconography and language of the Indian spirits that are manifested in this period is on the one hand rooted in traditional, classical ideas of death (going to the other side or over the river), it is on the other intimately related to with the forced movement of native peoples (including the movement of Indians to land west of the Mississippi.) Further, it is extended by the romantic belief that these figures represent the last of the Indians. Famous figures like the historical Metacomet, who were passing into literary mythologies, were also being reproduced in other popular forms such as magic lantern shows. Faced with the question of how to mimic Indian language or speech patterns, Shakers often spoke nonsense or gibberish (possibly combined with genuine words) or in other cases spoke in very crude, stereotyped, heavily accented English. These speech patterns—drawing from a range of sources including popular theatrical performance, Indian oratory (and bastardized forms of it), and fiction—influence how Indians were represented in other arenas.

Countless examples might be given of the reproduction and continuation of this pattern within later spiritualist séances. The following speech given by the spirit of Logan, reproduced in the *Spiritual Telegraph* in 1854, is fairly typical of the sort of language associated with Indian chiefs:

> I am permitted by the Great Spirit to leave the happy hunting grounds of the red men, who have passed away, that I might visit you to-night at your council fires, and bring the calumet of peace, that its fragrance may ascend as an offering of peace and good-will to all on this earthly sphere, where I dwelt in the form.[96]

Another piece in the same volume tells of a séance in Iowa in which two (presumably white) mediums who were possessed by Indian spirits debated together and then completed their performance in song with words initially "in some Indian dialect, then in the English language." The use of the indefinite and definite articles indicate an unabashedly hierarchical description.[97]

For the most part, the Shaker performers avoided the use of specific costumes, so facial and stylized bodily gestures became especially important as a way of signaling "Indianness." Such behavior also continued into spiritualist séances in which costume changes were problematic for mediums. Instead of relying on clothes as a way of signaling ethnicity, spiritualists sometimes tried to give other explanations for the ways in which spirits could be recognized. A series of trance speeches by Mrs. Conant at the *Banner of Light* circle, which spanned nearly two decades, for example, resulted in the publication of messages from a wide range of sources including Indians, rabbis, and celebrated American preachers and writers.

The collator of their speeches, which were published in 1876, suggested that it is "intuition" rather than "reason" that governs readers accurately to interpret and identify the voices they encounter.[98] What they are engaging with, he suggests, is the approximation of a certain style of speech. That style then becomes evidence of the origin of the voice. This suggests a suspension of disbelief and a willingness to have faith, which is often a part of religious discourse. In order to recognize the spirits, the audience must

already be in the state of mind in which it might be possible to identify them—one that resembles the state of the medium herself.

The Indian spirits who manifested themselves through the
Shakers enacted their cultural and ethnic difference through the use
of strange "languages," dances, and actions, and through this, they
dramatized the parallel relationship constructed both out of difference and out of sameness between living Shakers and Indian spirits. The "wild actions" of the Shakers while possessed by Indian
spirits were seen as a "special test" for them.[99] While Shakers might
go into trances and even speak in tongues while manifesting a variety
of spirits, the kinds of extremes of boisterous and uninhibited
dancing that sometimes characterized the Indian spirits extended
the degree to which they usually enacted their spiritist tableaux.
Behaving like an Indian spirit seemed to allow an ecstatic loss of
control beyond that offered by other spirits, which may explain why
it was often younger Shakers who experienced Indians manifesting
themselves through them rather than older Shakers who could
distrust what was going on within the performances.

Enacting "Indianness" allowed for kinds of transgressions that
were highly problematic in any other context: Shaker women might
tear their caps from their heads when possessed, as if throwing off a
repressive symbol of their religious faith and of their gender. The
Shakers performers correspond particularly to the categories of mis-
rule, appropriated from European traditions, which Philip Deloria
associates with Indian performance in New England.[100] Indian spirits
might speak in unknown languages which could then be translated
into crude forms of English that at times seemed an amalgam of
Indian imagery and the language of minstrelsy, with occasional
Shaker doctrine thrown in. This is exemplified by the lines of one
translated song "In me canoe me will go to Mudder Dare me will
sing lobe lobe lobe."[101] Here the reference to the "canoe" signifies
that the spirit is that of an Indian, and the reference to "Mudder"
(Mother) suggests Shaker beliefs. But though the repetition of "me
will go . . . me will sing'" replicates the verbal formulations of stage
Indians the final "lobe lobe lobe" (love love love) reads more like the
speech patterns familiar from minstrelsy.[102]

Outsiders sometimes saw connections between them that
included their positions within a panoply of possibilities, including
that of the supernatural. One final example shows how this could
be constructed within a literary text. In an early and unflattering

description of Shakers in Catharine Maria Child's *Redwood*, there is a blurring of language that suggests contiguities between Shakers, Indians, and supernatural beliefs that certainly existed and linked socially marginal groups in the antebellum period. The sudden eruption into loud singing and dancing by an unscrupulous Shaker, Reuben—who is later revealed to be involved with an equally shady Indian figure in a bid to abduct a young woman—is met by a demand to "Stop your dumb pow-wow!"[103]

The furious response to his noisy activity suggests the novel's anxiety about the range of peoples and beliefs that exist within the early Republic. Reuben's swarthy physicality and "cunning" expression both point to his untrustworthiness. But the word "cunning" also suggests his role as the possessor of knowledge that can only be acquired through unconventional practices that lie outside the boundaries of conventional Christianity. The *OED* gives one meaning of "cunning" as "Possessing magical knowledge or skill: in *cunning man, cunning woman*, a fortune-teller, conjurer, 'wise man,' 'wise woman,' wizard or witch."[104] His dancing and singing with its uncertain meanings and alien movements takes place next to the dead body of a young man and seems to suggest, within the novel, ritual practice that alarmingly displaces more conventional ways of dealing with the dead. Instead, his form of Shakerism is allied to the foreignness of Indian rituals that are themselves in this period being co-opted within magical and supernatural texts and lore.[105] The apparent strangeness of Shaker and Indian practices allows both groups to be represented as allies outside the frame of mainstream culture.

CHAPTER 4

SPIRITED AWAY: THE DEATH OF LITTLE EVA AND THE FAREWELL PERFORMANCES OF KATIE KING

SENTIMENTAL SPIRITS

Depictions of deathbed scenes are commonplace within mid- to late nineteenth-century U.S. literary culture, particularly sentimental fiction. They serve a variety of ideological and aesthetic functions and have rightly received a good deal of critical attention. One aspect of their importance and broad impact that has not yet been included within revisionist assessments of the aesthetic and political strategies of sentimentalism is the primary focus here.[1] The stylized representational modes that characterize the dying of many characters in literary texts, magazine illustrations, paintings, and other cultural productions were appropriated by nineteenth-century spiritualists to perform farewells between spirits and the living within the many séances that proliferated on both sides of the Atlantic from the late 1840s onward. The conventional structure of such partings, predicated on the imminent death of at least one of its participants, focused on an exemplary death in which tearful goodbyes and final words were significant features and followed formal patterns.

Yet when spiritualists appropriated the formulae of such scenes it was within a set of practices that explicitly denied the fact of death. Since for spiritualists death was a chimera, the adoption of the symbolism of the deathbed scene as a model for how to facilitate different kinds of departures—not always those that took place between the soon to be dead and those they leave behind—took the rhetoric and practices of dying and transformed them. Spiritualist séances frequently used tropes and models from existing literary forms, notably from melodramatic stage performances and sentimental novels. What went on within nineteenth-century séances was to some degree ritualistic—certain patterns were repeated, becoming new tropes that were soon recognizable to séance-goers. Soon, what many spirits most sounded like was each other. More specifically, they often sounded quite highly repetitious and acted in ways that seemed to echo each other, too. What governed these ritualized models of greetings, messages, and departures? Are there certain patterns that can be described or outlined? How can they be accounted for? In other words, how do we—and how did contemporaries of the period—read them?

Establishing a language and a set of practices for how to perform the kinds of farewells that might take place within séances was a problem that mediums had to overcome. The farewell performances that spirits sometimes enacted, though modeled on deathbed scenes within literary culture, were always finally distinct from such scenes because spirits cannot die. A key site for the production and projection of grief and mourning for nineteenth-century readers on both sides of the Atlantic was the dying and the death of Evangeline St. Clare in one of the best-selling novels of the nineteenth century, Harriet Beecher Stowe's *Uncle Tom's Cabin* (1852). This has been the subject of a great deal of critical attention that confirms its status as a formative moment within nineteenth-century U.S. literary culture that is revealing about the configuration of taste and of divides between high and popular culture in the period.[2]

Examining the effective transposition of the lengthy farewells that precede Eva's death into two series of séances in London and Philadelphia helps to trace a transatlantic circulation of images between the stage, visual culture, novels and popular culture, and séances. Some of these images borrow from the sentimental tradition (though not exclusively) and help contribute to its continuation and proliferation within a culture of popular performance and impersonation that is the basis for the full-body materialization characteristic of some, though not all, séances.[3] While Eva's death, and the manner of it, found its way into such performances, the impact of Stowe's private investigation of spiritualism, her visits to séances and correspondence on the subject—which followed the deaths of two of her sons, Samuel and Henry, and has been extensively examined by biographers—also helped to mold the manner in which she wrote about death in her later novels, notably *My Wife and I* (1871). This circularity is reflected in a pattern of influence in which the inflected readings of Eva's death, which produced the departure of spirits in séances, went on to produce a shift in the kinds of representation of death that Stowe herself was influenced by. Her complex and contradictory responses to spiritualism have been recounted in detail elsewhere, but the ways in which she contributed to a pattern of representation that assisted its success has not yet been explored. Seeing the relationship between Stowe's novel and the séances this chapter will investigate allows us to develop an understanding of how some patterns of transatlantic mourning were constructed.

A crucial element is that the focus on the death of Eva effectively effaces the deaths of the black characters in the novel. Spiritualist mediums, many of whom were white women, appropriated the aesthetic features of Eva's death and largely ignored the novel's engagement with abolition. As spiritualism spread across the Atlantic and back again, its engagement with the politics of abolition, women's rights, and other reforms diminished. Eva's death became a model of a kind of beautiful parting that could easily be reproduced within séances. As mediums became increasingly aware of the need for the séance to be an attractive (even lucrative) event, careful crafting of the proceedings needed to be managed. Those elements of transatlantic exchange that were the most politically problematic, chiefly slavery, were filtered out. The uses made of *Uncle Tom's Cabin* are a good example of this. Whereas the most gothic or supernatural elements of the novel concern the haunting of Simon Legree by his mistress Cassy as a form of revenge for his involvement in slavery and, crucially, his sexual exploitation of her, these do not seem to have formed a part of what was reproduced within séances. Instead, mediums drew on a parting scene which itself had innumerable precedents within the popular literature of the period that substantially influenced it.

Eva's death was by no means innovative in terms of its structure and tropes; part of its appeal was due to an already-existing familiarity with what it reproduced. But crucially, it exceeded the popularity even of some of the texts it invoked. Many of them sold well: but not as well as *Uncle Tom's Cabin*, which exceeded and eclipsed them due to its market success, availability, and reach. Furthermore the way in which its original readership was expanded by the marketing of the commercial products its success spawned was a highly significant aspect of its impact. Stowe molded existing strategies of writing about death, then, to produce a telling combination of grief and remembrance that would become part of a ritualized pattern for many. She synthesized them into a new and iconic scene of dying.[4]

The fantastic literary and financial success of *Uncle Tom's Cabin* and its many diverse spin-offs (plays, poems, illustrated song sheets, ballads, card games, stationery, jigsaws, clothing, foodstuffs, and so on) helped make Eva's death internationally known and its author a public celebrity.[5] This model certainly had as its basis a wide variety of precedents on which it drew and enlarged, but it is Eva's death that still remains familiar to readers today even when other popular works have been forgotten. It is not surprising, then, that her death—both a synthesis and apotheosis—became one significant moment that spiritualists drew upon when dealing with the difficult issue of how spirits should say goodbye within séances.

The development of belief in the possibility of communication with the spirit world had developed rapidly in the 1850s. Writers, who had themselves experienced personal losses, were quick to recognize this new interest in speaking to the spirit world. In 1868 Stowe wrote to the editor of the *Atlantic Monthly*, James Fields, that she had noticed increasing numbers of articles on planchette and offered to write one based on the case of a woman she knew.[6] The article does not appear to have been written, but her offer suggests her canny recognition of the available market for such pieces (one that parallels the market for postmortem daguerreotypes produced by the new desires such technologies made possible) as well as her understanding of a shift in practices of mourning and remembrance that might make investigations into the world of spirits increasingly mainstream.[7]

Such acumen was also demonstrated by the fact that she made sure that her writing was advertised in spiritualist publications to boost sales. When she wrote to her publisher suggesting that her 1869 novel *Oldtown Folks* be advertised in the spiritualist newspaper *The Banner of Light*, the aspect of the novel that she must have anticipated as having the greatest appeal to the journal's readership was the representation of the protagonist's supernatural visions—which were based on the experiences of her husband, Calvin Stowe, who claimed to have long-standing experience of seeing the spirits of the dead that started when he was a boy.[8] The protagonist, Horace, told of the experiences he has as a sensitive boy when he believed that he encountered spirits on a nightly basis. Horace's visions need to be read within a triad of possibilities, which Stowe saw as being connected in important ways. First, to biblical traditions of prophecy, trance states, and visions; second, to Calvin Stowe's experiences; and finally, to the new experiences she was encountering at this point through spiritualism. Certainly when she tried to explain her spiritual experiences she was keen to place them within a Christian context and not to see them as emerging in any simple way from what was merely fashionable at that time. One chapter of the novel, called "My Spirit Wife," explicitly uses a lexicon shared by spiritualists who used the term to suggest idealized sexual partnerships between kindred spirits (who were often very much alive) that cut across conventional beliefs. (These included current husbands and wives who indignantly opposed the claims of spirit unions.) Such beliefs were invoked explicitly in books such as William H. Dixon's *Spiritual Wives* (1868).

Stowe's position here represents a combination of tentative belief and shrewd commercialism that recognizes the way in which the emergence of spiritualism might extend her readership. It is interesting to note in this context that George Aiken's celebrated 1852 stage adaptation of *Uncle Tom's Cabin* incorporated an unflattering reference to spiritualism through a character created especially for the dramatic purposes of his production: Gumption Cute. This figure is one of the stock comedy characters within the play who represents some of the topical issues of the moment—which in that period included spiritualism—while being a vehicle for a useful subplot that involves Cute being the witness to the murder of Augustine St. Clare, the father of Little Eva. Cute reveals that he has led an itinerant life, which includes an unsuccessful period as a traveling medium, and his punning dialogue and audacious name reveal him to be a humbug and fraud.

Stowe would certainly have known about the existence of Aiken's lowlife character and his unflattering involvement in the more overt humbuggery of spiritualism. But it did not stop her continued and growing interest in the subject, one that was shared by many of her serious-minded peers on both sides of the Atlantic: she corresponded with George Eliot who remained skeptical, for instance, and Elizabeth Barrett Browning, who did not. She attended séances in the United

States and was a visitor at health resorts, taking cures in which encounters with spirits were part of the process of returning the patient to health. Many spiritualists had been engaged with the reform of medicine and of health regimes from its first appearance.[9] The novel's use of haunting and spectral vengeance tropes partly comes from a gothic tradition that was well established in U.S. literature. Yet it also emerges from motifs of haunting that were a persistent aspect of Beecher religious rhetoric, drawing significantly from Calvinist traditions, as Karen Halttunen has argued.[10] The dominance of a Calvinist-influenced language, in the Northeast in particular, had a profound effect on the rhetoric and ideology of many of the writers listed here, especially Stowe.

Members of her family, notably her sister Isabella Beecher Hooker, were also fascinated by spiritualism and attended séances and spiritualist lectures on a regular basis. Hooker's admiration for Victoria Woodhull (whose early advocacy of spiritualism was largely opportunistic, as a vehicle for her political ambitions) and Beecher Stowe's antagonistic distaste for her fed into her novel *My Wife and I: or, Harry Henderson's History* (1871), a work clearly influenced by spiritualist thought and language. Yet it is clear that Stowe was aware how far her need to believe in a world of spirits was triggering her investigations. She noted, in a letter to Elizabeth Barrett Browning, whom she visited while in Rome in the winter following the death of her son Henry that, "I don't know how people can keep up their prejudices against spiritualism with tears in their eyes—how they are not, at least, thrown on the 'wish that it might be true,' and the investigation of the phenomena, by that abrupt shutting in the faces of the door of death which shuts them out from the sight of their beloved. My tendency is to beat up against it like a crying child. Not that this emotional impulse is the best for turning the key and obtaining safe conclusions—no."[11]

The kinds of borrowings that spiritualists made from popular culture can be exemplified by a further detail. A spirit called "Topsy" appeared in séances in the 1930s, almost a century after the publication of *Uncle Tom's Cabin*, which suggests the extent to which the novel's diffusion into popular culture (which Marcus Wood has traced) was far more than just a passing phenomenon.[12] She was known for her "good humor, her quaint choice of phrase and her happy disposition" and was said to have died in 1851, the year the serialization of the novel started. Her real name was said to be Lili Alani, and she was described as ethnically Samoan, though she later became a slave in the United States.[13] Figures by the same name appeared in minstrel shows on both sides of the Atlantic regularly too, another way in which she remained within the public domain. Yet, as W. T. Lhamon has argued, Stowe's Topsy "came chiefly from the minstrel show, which was a main producer and conduit in Atlantic communities for the problem of conflicted selves."[14] She came from, and returned to, the minstrel shows of the nineteenth century.

Slavery did not altogether drop out of the patterns of transatlantic mourning appropriated and promulgated by spiritualists. But it was sanitized and depoliticized: figures like Topsy were happy and content, humorous, and not dangerous or in danger. The extent to which they or other ethnically marked figures disrupted séances, as they sometimes did, could be largely contained and managed by mediums. The plantation was now a place of music, dancing, and harmony. Indeed, it was so happy, it seems, that Topsy's medium explained that she had been given that name by "the plantation workers" and that "it is easy to understand how her fellow slaves, kindly and good natured, rather than frighten the child by continued questioning, christened her the commonplace 'Topsy'—and the name remained with her."[15] Some of those features could be harnessed within séances so that slavery became a spectacle for white audiences, something that had happened in the past and was now safely over. Its ongoing political and economic consequences were largely diminished or ignored by mediums as the century went on.

Yet what the appearance of such figures suggest, as they do in the domestic fiction of the mid-century period, is what Amy Kaplan has termed the "imperial reach of domesticity," which "extended not only to racially foreign subjects inside and outside the home, but also to the interiority of female subjectivity, the major focus of popular women's fiction in the 1850s."[16] Rita J. Smith's reading of the novel's borrowings from an evangelical Christian text set in imperial India—Martha Mary Sherwood's hugely popular *Little Henry and his Bearer Boosy* (1814)—allows for a reading of *Uncle Tom's Cabin* that locates its imperial impulse as borrowing from both U.S. and British imperial practices.[17] The shared proselytizing and its relation to a desire to tame those foreign elements that need incorporation into the home of nation and empire show the ways in which the novels are each implicated with, and produced out of, empire.

The death of Little Eva—as she is usually known—like the death of Charles Dickens' Little Nell, or Louisa May Alcott's Beth March, or of countless other young white girls in mid-nineteenth-century literary culture on both sides of the Atlantic, touched a chord for readers at the time for whom the realities of death, especially that of young children were never far distant. The subject of child death had always been a part of mainstream American literary culture, as the elegiac poetry of Anne Bradstreet shows. Though many readers particularly celebrated the three deaths of Eva, Nell, and Beth as examples of successful and moving fictions Eva's death had an iconic status that eclipsed the other two. This was in part because of its central function within a novel whose massive popularity was testimony both to its narrative power and to very careful marketing.[18] It was also to do with the significance of Eva's death within a model of death and mourning constructed on sentimental lines.

Since, in a conventional sense, spirits were not alive, the farewell performance enacted within the darkened séance room was a new event that concerned a second or further rupture, which was contained within the theatrical space of the séance. The performance that took place within the séance was certainly not a reenactment of the individual's death, though spirits occasionally alluded to the manner of their departure from this earth. The séance itself might be part of the strategy and practice of mourning for the bereaved who was either hoping to establish contact with the spirit of a loved one or wanted to maintain it after a successful initial contact.

Since the sentimental relied on a formula that aimed to provoke an empathetic reaction, it is not surprising that Eva's death was so enabling for writers and readers. Her death energized a powerful template for how to write about the processes of dying and its aftermath. Its substantial impact on literary and popular culture was, in part, due to the way in which it became a form of sentimental fetish.[19] It had a particular significance to spiritualist mediums for a number of reasons. One was Eva's youth and femininity, two features shared by many of the mediums who emerged in the 1850s and beyond. Another was the representational use of whiteness in descriptions of Eva. Whiteness in the form of illuminated or phosphorescent body parts and clothing became a common feature of many séances by the 1870s or thereabouts. Its corollary, darkness or blackness, was also the necessary condition for the production of such demonstrations of whiteness. Just as the most dramatic and effectively staged aspects of Eva's death involved a careful choreographing of whiteness and blackness, so did many (if not most) spiritualist séances.

A third feature of significance to spiritualists concerns the affective nature of what went on within séances themselves. Séance-goers often experienced a wide variety of emotional responses to what they encountered. Accounts of visits to mediums were often characterized by highly charged descriptions of meetings with spirits or messages from the other side. It was very common for séance-goers to find themselves moved by messages or spirits intended for others through empathy. Sensitivity, sympathy, and empathy were common features associated with mediums, who frequently explained that they were necessary for communicating with spirits. The same characteristics were possessed by Eva, in the kinds of quantity that overwhelmed her tentative physicality and led to her death. Yet, like the spirits who could be summoned and who could leave according to patterns confirmed by the manner of her own departure, she could be brought back into some kind of existence in the many varied recreations of her death that came into being very soon after the publication of the novel. What Eva demonstrated is that for fictional characters in novels with a long afterlife, there is no death.

SENTIMENTAL MOURNING AND THE SPIRITS

George Sand's striking comments on *Uncle Tom's Cabin* suggest that the deaths of Tom and of Eva, and the sentimental relationship that existed between them while still alive, were essentially what constituted the novel. As she puts it, "The life and death of a little child and of a negro slave!—that is the whole book! This negro and this child are two saints of heaven! The affection that unites them, the respect of these two perfect ones for each other, is the only love-story, the only passion of the drama."[20] By her deft juxtaposition of ideas of affection with those of respect, Sand microcosmically outlines key elements of the construction of the sentimental: attachments between individuals governed by emotion and by empathy, engendered through affect. The key differences between these characters in terms of age, gender, and ethnicity, though acknowledged by Sand, are not fully worked through, just as they are not by Stowe herself.

The history of the reappraisal and reclamation of the nineteenth-century sentimental novel (largely as written by women) has been associated with the pioneering writing of feminists, such as Jane Tompkins, whose seminal and acclaimed essay on *Uncle Tom's Cabin* has been a highly significant intervention in defense of sentimentalism.[21] Since her pioneering work, the sentimental tradition within American literature and its origins and influences has received renewed and serious critical attention that has demonstrated the particular qualities of sentimental writing, which gave it power over its enormous and devoted readership.

This has included some significant readings of early literature. Affective, emotional narratives in which death and grief feature prominently dominated the early novel in the United States. Julia Stern argues that what is often characterized as the "sensational and self-conscious theatricality" of the late eighteenth-century novel in the United States is a response to its location in a highly contested political period that has at one end the aftermath of the French Revolution and publication of Edmund Burke's prescient *Reflections on the Revolution in France* (1790) and at the other end the election of Thomas Jefferson and the shift from Federalist to Republican government. Her "affective" reading of the novels that appeared between 1789–1799—Susanna Rowson's *Charlotte Temple* (1791/94); Hannah Webster Foster's *The Coquette* (1797); William Hill Brown's *The Power of Sympathy* (1789); Charles Brockden Brown's *Wieland* (1789) and *Ormond* (1799)—suggests that the "republican novel fancies that, however fleetingly, Americans might imaginatively contemplate if not actually assume one another's political perspectives."[22]

This fancy is one that reappears explicitly in *Uncle Tom's Cabin*, in which the affective and the emotional are always constituted in their intricate relation to the political, albeit a politics that many commentators increasingly read as implicated in racist and imperialist ideologies. Stern's reading of these early novels allows us to see the relation of Stowe's fiction to the politics of the early Republic. This can be read chiefly through her willingness, like her predecessors, to envisage a nation in which encouraging structures of feeling—especially those that envisage empathetic relationships between sometimes very disparate individuals—is the best method of enabling Americans to avoid tyrannical institutions. Chief among them is slavery.[23] Stowe envisages the sentimental as progressive, unifying, and politically powerful. What the novel has in common with some of these fictions of the early Republic is a focus on the significance of the dead and their legacies, which are portrayed as cultural, political, and social.

The incestuous love story at the heart of William Hill Brown's epistolary novel *The Power of Sympathy* ends with the deaths of the sibling-lovers Harriot and Harrington and the discovery of a copy of *The Sorrows of Werther* by the body of Harrington, who has shot himself. The overwhelming signifying presence of Goethe's doomed lover as part of Harrington's reading experience signaled Brown's knowledge of the European tradition from which his tragic protagonists emerged and his desire to incorporate that tradition into a newly emerging national literary culture. The letter that concludes the novel nicely articulates the relation between drama and sensibility that characterizes the novel as well as the predicament of its innocent lovers. It reads,

> We have surmounted the performance of the last scene of our tragedy, with less difficulty and distress than I imagined. Great numbers crouded [sic] to see the body of poor *Harrington*; they were impressed with various emotions, for their sympathizing sorrow could not be concealed—Indeed a man without sensibility exhibits no sign of a soul.[24]

The spiritual (as distinct from the emotional) dimension of sensibility is also articulated here. For Worthy, the aptly named author of the letter, the "sympathising sorrow" of the people who come to see the body of the suicide exhibit a response that is not simply emotional and immediate but also one that emanates from a profound humanity that has its basis in a religious or spiritual sensibility.

Yet if this is taken to suggest that the "man without sensibility" is one without a soul, then is the person who exhibits the most sensibility also the one with the most highly developed soul? This would certainly seem to be the position of Stowe whose mid-nineteenth-century Christian sentimentalism explicitly articulates the relation between highly developed religious and sentimental sensibilities. The relationship between Harriot and Harrington, as unconventional (albeit in profoundly different ways) as the one that Sand identifies between Eva and Tom, is commemorated in the inscription that Harrington writes for the monument in which the siblings are buried. The last words of this—and of the novel—envisage future generations of lovers moved by pity at the moral lesson to be gleaned from the inscription,

> If ever wandering near this dark recess,
> Where guardian spirits round the ether press;

> Where, on their urn, celestial care descends,
> Two lovers come, whom fair success attends,
> " O'er the pale marble shall they join their heads,
> "And drink the falling tears each other sheds,
> "Then sadly say, with mutual pity mov'd,
> "O! may we never love as these have lov'd"[25]

The tableau envisaged by Harrington is of pitiful lovers literally con-
sumed by and drinking the outward symbol of their grief, as "the
falling tears" watched over by "guardian spirits" who seem to be trying
to break through from the spirit world to this one, as they "round
the ether press." Their private response to the publicizing of the private disasters of another couple through the device of monumental
inscription, and their mutual declaration of intent, suggests the
process by which individual responses get translated into forms of
action that are envisaged as potentially politically powerful.

This monument, envisaged by Harrington as the lovers' legacy, acts
as both memorial and warning. Others are envisaged as having their
lives changed through their tearful responses to it. In just such a way,
the highly emotional tableau that is the death of Eva was envisaged by
Stowe as acting in the manner of a trigger to encourage abolitionist
sentiments. Stowe's work is a continuation of a tradition of celebrating
the effects of iconographic death upon the living. It further extends this
into the nineteenth century and takes it into new realms of significance
that place abolition at its ethical and religious center. In *Uncle Tom's
Cabin* the appearance of spirits, or the assumed appearance of spirits, act
as warnings to those still alive, in this way operating as a prompt not just
to the characters within the novel but to its audience as well.

At a formal level, the sentimental language Stowe uses both in the
many partings, farewells, and reflective recollections of the novel,
but especially in the description of Eva's slow demise, became an
important and influential model for how to write about grief, parting, death, and mourning within nineteenth-century U.S. literary
culture. At the level of symbolism, the death of a Southern, white,
Christian child within this abolitionist novel became a reflection of
grieving that reached its height a few years later with the huge losses
involved in the Civil War. Her death allowed for an outpouring
of private, individual anguish that turned it into an iconic example of
the processes and practices of an ongoing mode of recollection that
could be known as sentimental mourning.

This took the form of articulating the processes of mourning through an affective relation both to the figure of the dead person themselves, those left behind, and a concentration on certain fetishized objects that acted as sentimental mementoes and were circulated as such. These might include hair, photographs, clothing, or other objects left by or associated with the figure of the dead—items that allowed mourners to involve themselves in what Mary Louise Kete has suggestively called "sentimental collaboration."[26] The emphasis placed upon these affect-laden objects was one that made its way from sentimental fiction into spiritualist séances.

Eva's death eclipsed and has continued to eclipse all other deaths within the novel. Many readers read the book tearfully—many no doubt in private, some in small groups—and were moved to an affective communion with the descriptions of Eva's illness and death. They certainly included the numerous writers such as Frances E. W. Harper who produced poetic or other responses to Eva's death.[27] Writings about it formed a part of the way in which the novel was marketed from the period of its first publication.

Stowe had fractious exchanges over the financial deal for the novel with her publisher, John P. Jewett. They settled on 10 percent of the sales to Stowe with a further 10 percent to be invested in advertising. Jewett paid John Greenleaf Whittier $50 to write a poem about Eva and then had the poem set to music to further its appeal. Not only did the public respond to the poem, but the Beecher family incorporated the poem and song into their domestic life. By doing so, they claimed to improve upon it. In a letter to her husband, Isabella Beecher Hooker wrote that Whittier's verses were beautiful "but you should hear Charles [Beecher] sing them, in his clear, rich voice, to know their full power."[28] Whittier's lines include the following:

> Dry the tears for holy Eva
> With the blessed angels leave her,
> Of the form so sweet and fair,
> Give to earth the tender care.
> For the golden locks of Eva
> Let the sunny south land give her
> Flowery pillow of repose,
> Orange bloom and budding rose.
> All is light and peace with Eva,

> There the darkness cometh never,
> Tears are wiped and fetters fall,
> And the Lord is all in all.[29]

Whittier's poem emphasizes a crucial part of Eva's appeal: her youth, femininity, and angelic fairness. He appeals to the reader to stop their sentimental response to Eva's death "Dry the tears for holy Eva" since she is now with "the blessed angels" and only her body has been returned to the "tender care" of the earth, which will provide sweet smelling flowers for her repose. Though the abolitionist Quaker Whittier is emphatic that Eva's death is in some way restorative and therefore does not need tears (in one place he writes, "Weep no more for happy Eva"), he also acknowledges that it is in heaven where "the darkness cometh never," that mourners are comforted and slaves freed. These were details that captivated Stowe's audience, which included her family. They also suggest the content of some séances in which such comforting scenarios dominated representation and, as has been seen, effectively effaced slavery as the century progressed.

Stowe used the register of the sentimental poem in two of her extraordinary and moving mourning poems, which suggested the terrible grief she felt after the death of her son Charley, "Only a Year" and "Below." The references to Charley's hair—"clustering curls of sunny hair," "clustering curls of golden hair," and "sunny ringlets"—closely resemble Whittier's verses.[30] Sentimental lines such as Whittier's set the tone of much of what would be written about Eva's death, and much was indeed written, on both sides of the Atlantic, some of which has seemed to some critics to take her death into the realm of travesty. The final scene of Aiken's play, for example, ends with the three most significant characters in the play coming back to life for a wordless scene, like a spirit tableau that exists nowhere else within the novel. This portrays a sentimental version of life after death: "Gorgeous clouds, tinted with sunlight. EVA, robed in white, is discovered on the back of a milk-white dove, with expanded wings, as if just soaring upward. Her hands are extended in benediction over ST. CLARE and UNCLE TOM, who are kneeling and gazing up to her. Impressive music.—Slow curtain."[31] We have already seen, though, in Emma Hardinge Britten's embodiment as Saint Cecilia, that highly dramatic—even excessive—tableaux, could be favored by mediums as well as dramatists. The novel certainly lent itself to such adaptations. Since *Uncle Tom's Cabin* never truly empowers Tom or many of the other black characters in real political terms, such an adaptation seems an extension that is all too predictable.

The visionary or prophetic character of the moment at which Stowe conceived of the scene of Tom's death has passed into mythology. Karen Halttunen describes it well. Stowe took communion one Sunday morning and found herself, soon afterward, having "a vision of a saintly slave being brutally beaten to death." Later she claimed that the novel "'can less be said to have been composed by her than imposed upon her. Scenes, incidents, conversations rushed upon her with a vividness and importunity that would not be denied.' Like a number of Gothic writers before her . . . Harriet Beecher Stowe engaged in a kind of automatic writing, producing at great speed under an inner compulsion a novel whose power drew unconsciously on her years of physical and spiritual suffering."[32]

Halttunen's description of "a kind of automatic writing" needs to be treated with some care, though it does accurately describe one part of the process of the production of the novel. The compulsion to write that Stowe described, in addition to the speed of composition, suggests a creativity that seemed to emerge without Stowe's volition. It would be dangerous to make too close an association between the idea of automatic writing and the spiritualist appropriations proposed here. Still, the idea of a creativity that was allied to a vision, links the novel to a tradition of mystical experience drawn more from religious or Romantic sensibility than from more prosaic ideas of novelistic slog, even if reality belies this to some degree. Though the novel was certainly written quickly, Stowe missed two magazine deadlines, which suggests that the process was not quite as rapid as all that and that other concerns still intruded into her writing time.

THE DEATH OF LITTLE EVA

Eva's death takes place in chapter 26 of the novel, a chapter called, simply, "Death." Two lines from Thomas Moore's 1816 poem "Weep Not for Those" preface the opening: "Weep not for those whom the veil of the tomb/ In life's early morning, hath hid from our eyes." It is a plea by Stowe to understand that her death is the start of a happier life in what Eva herself calls a "better country." The chapter starts with a lengthy description of her beautiful bedroom and moves swiftly to describe the last period of her life. Eva's death reproduced an image of an achingly told sacrifice that used a "rhetoric of transcendent vision and light" that, as Richard Dyer has noted, is part of the production of whiteness within Western culture and is particularly allied to the death of Christ.[33] This aesthetic dominated the way in which Stowe described Eva's last moments with the St. Clare household. Specifically, this takes the form of her blonde hair, pale skin (offset by blue eyes) that becomes paler during her illness (another name for tuberculosis is "white death"), and the white and rose-colored trappings of her bedroom.[34]

These carefully described luxury objects—Parisian carpeting, bamboo furniture of a highly ornamental style, a statue of Christ with children and one of an angel above her bed, vases replenished daily with flowers by Tom whose "pride and delight" it was to do this, assorted trinkets, books, and an alabaster writing stand—were purchased by her father "in a style that had a peculiar keeping with the character of her for whom it was intended." Stowe writes that Eva's "eyes never opened, in the morning light, without falling on something which suggested to the heart soothing and beautiful thoughts."[35] Such detailed description is emblematic of what Lori Merish has argued are "the practices of a sentimental domestic economy" in which items can be defined in specific ways within the home where they are "endowed with personal affectional significance and reconstituted as containers of 'sensibility.'"[36]

In this context the visual purity of the objects, combined with the shrine-like quality of the room with its daily offerings of flowers by Topsy and Tom, simultaneously suggests a material luxury that is allied to a quality of spirituality, even saintliness that might be seen as its corollary. Eva is closer to an angel than a saint, a spirit than a living human. Perversely, it is the very materiality of the luxury objects from around the globe with which her father surrounds her that suggest her immaterial qualities. Yet it is the economy of slavery that enables Eva to live in such comfort and slaves themselves who clean, decorate, and order the room. Her pale wasting form suggests an implied ghostliness that is akin both to an angelic power but also to ideas about the supernatural that are never given explicit voice within the novel, but are always just beneath its surface. Her whiteness suggests her continual proximity to the world of spirits that allows her father to feel that he is in communion with his own dead mother.

The shadows of the solemn evening closed round them deeper and deeper, as St. Clare sat silently holding the little frail form to his bosom. He saw no more in the deep eyes, but the voice came over him as a spirit voice, and, as in a sort of judgment vision, his whole past life rose in a moment before his eyes: his mother's prayers and hymns; his own early yearnings and aspirings for good; and, between them and this hour, years of worldliness and scepticism, and what man calls respectable living.[37]

Eva repeatedly reassures her father that he will join her in "our Saviour's home," and her certainty and finality elevate her prophetic words, as the passage above shows. Her slow death leaves her in close contact with the heaven she is keen to go to and to the figures who have preceded her there as if she is able to mediate between the heaven she longs for and the earth she remains part of.

Through Eva, Augustine St. Clare is given the ability to be in a form of contact with his much-mourned mother. This is not the explicit contact or communication that mourners would long for and even experience in spiritualist séances from this period onward, but is instead a psychic or spiritual closeness that comes from being in the presence of one herself believed to be close to heaven. Eva becomes a sort of substitute whose proximity to death allows her to exist in a liminal state between life and death, the material and immaterial, in some ways like a spirit. When she finally dies it is a relief to those gathered around,

The child lay panting on her pillows, as one exhausted,—the large clear eyes rolled up and fixed. Ah, what said those eyes, that spoke so much of heaven? Earth was past, and earthly pain; but so solemn, so mysterious, was the triumphant brightness of that face, that it checked even the sobs of sorrow. They pressed around her, in breathless stillness.

"Eva," said St. Clare, gently.

She did not hear.

"O, Eva, tell us what you see! What is it?" said her father.

A bright, a glorious smile passed over her face, and she said, brokenly,—"O! love,—joy,—peace!" gave one sigh, and passed from death unto life!

"Farewell beloved child! the bright, eternal doors have closed after thee; we shall see thy sweet face no more. O, woe for them who watched thy entrance into heaven, when they shall wake and find only the cold gray sky of daily life, and thou gone forever!"[38]

The prophetic quality of her death, one consistent with conventional Calvinist ideas about the significance of the utterances of the soon-to-be-dead, is striking here.[39] She becomes apparitional as she physically becomes more and more frail and white, and literally less substantial as she moves toward death. At the end of her life she is just a voice, though one imbued with remarkable power.

What is also significant, though more ambivalent, are the final words cited above that end the chapter. Yet it is never made clear in the novel who speaks them. None of the figures who witness her death—Tom, Ophelia, St. Clare, Marie, Mammy, and the slaves who watch through the windows—seem likely to make such a speech. Though St. Clare is the last to speak before Eva, Stowe writes in the next chapter that his anguish at her death had practically taken away his speech,

> from the hour that voices had said, in the dying chamber, "she is gone," it had been all a dreary mist, a heavy "dimness of anguish." He had heard voices around him; he had had questions asked, and answered them; they had asked him when he would have the funeral, and where they should lay her; and he had answered, impatiently, that he cared not.[40]

Though Aiken attributed the brief eulogy to St. Clare in his stage play it seems an unlikely sentiment from a man whose religious doubt almost overwhelms him at times. It sounds far closer to the voice of Stowe herself, who had watched the death of her son Charley in 1849 and, like St. Clare, yearned for a quick death. She wrote in a letter to her husband, "I could not help nor soothe nor do one thing, not one, to mitigate his cruel suffering, do nothing but pray in my anguish that he might die soon."[41] St. Clare, incapable of praying himself, urges Tom "Pray that this may be cut short! . . . [T]his wrings my heart."[42]

The description of Eva laid out on her deathbed in the following chapter, head to one side as if asleep, bears a strong resemblance to the postmortem daguerreotype of Charley that simultaneously asserts his youth and the fact of his death.[43] Daguerreotypes, like locks of hair and objects that belonged to the dead, all circulated within sentimental economy as exchange items.[44] The comment that follows Eva's death then, allocated speech marks but never directly attributed to any character in the novel, hangs like a direct authorial intervention of a different order even than that of the countless personal comments and asides that fill the book. Despite the affirmation of a Christian afterlife (Eva "passed from death into life"), it is the dreariness and finality for those left behind that is emphatically revealed at her final departure.

Strikingly, the chapter ends with the word "forever," a partial resurrection of Poe's celebrated "forevermore" and "nevermore" that suggests the awful despair of this moment within the novel. However the apparent finality of the moment of death within the novel is repeatedly challenged by Stowe's invocation of the idea of the significance of the dead within the lives of the living, just as the "nevermore" of Poe needs rereading in the context of the repeated instances of the apparent dead coming back to life in his work. The dead mothers of St. Clare and Simon Legree are both importantly revivified to some degree by the interventions of Eva at different moments in the novel. The significance of this will become clear later.

The death of Eva haunts the text, particularly through the invocation of her beautiful hair, which she distributes to the grieving mourners who surround her bed in one of her final public moments. Her desire to distribute locks of her hair to her father's slaves prior to her death suggests her precocious understanding of the mechanics of mourning. Once the slaves (or "servants" as Stowe calls them in one of her too frequent euphemisms) are gathered in her room, Eva becomes the center of a circle of sympathy:

> Eva lay back on her pillows; her hair hanging loosely about her face, her crimson cheeks contrasting painfully with the intense whiteness of her complexion and the thin contour of her limbs and features, and her large, soul-like eyes fixed earnestly on every one.
>
> The servants were struck with a sudden emotion. The spiritual face, the long locks of hair cut off and lying by her, her father's averted face, and Marie's sobs, struck at once upon the feelings of a sensitive and impressible race; and, as they came in, they looked one on another, sighed, and shook their heads. There was a deep silence, like that of a funeral.[45]

Eva's intense look and fragile appearance suggest her proximity to death and a new life. As she hands out her curls to her overwrought audience, the juxtaposition of her calm and their "tears and sobs" suggests both Stowe's notorious belief in essential racial differences between individuals, as well as the certainty that comes from her religious conviction.

The scene of distributing her hair has significant consequences later in the novel as hair takes on a symbolic sentimental, racial, and supernatural significance, especially as nearly every person who she gives her blonde hair to is a slave. Though the figures that surround her in this moment of domestic theater are ethnically mixed, the audience for this scene is predominantly black. This is a striking reversal of experience of reading a novel whose contemporary audience was overwhelmingly white. The manner in which Eva's hair is used in the novel draws both upon European and Africanist notions of the supernatural and of the power of artifacts.

In the mid-nineteenth century there was a revival of interest in the use of hair as a token of love or loss. The hair of the deceased might be woven into mourning rings and brooches that could also contain portraits or photographs of the deceased, or it might be kept in a special place (a breast pocket or a box, for example).[46] Women were particularly engaged in the process that went into the production of mourning objects, such as brooches. Eva's hair takes on the quality of sentimental mourning object, holy relic, and talismanic fetish. In this way it draws upon and syncretizes a series of different religious, ethnic, and cultural traditions, particularly "the surviving presence of African survivals," as Lynn Wardley has recently shown.[47] In recouping Stowe's use of an Africanist/Orientalist series of tropes within the novel, Wardley provides a persuasive reading of Stowe's interest in elements of the supernatural and of the syncretism at the heart of white bourgeois domesticity.

The power of the dead over the living, suggested by the significance given to mourning objects, such as hair, within a domestic sentimental economy, is raised suggestively later in the novel after Sambo and Quimbo have beaten Tom savagely on the orders of Legree. In a scene that deliberately invokes and rewrites Frederick Douglass's description of the mojo root given to him by another slave to ward off evil, Sambo presents Legree with an item that he has found Tom wearing around his neck—the hair of Little Eva. Sambo calls it "a witch thing. . . . Something that niggers gets from witches. Keeps 'em from feelin' when they's flogged."[48] When Legree "uneasily" unwraps the lock of hair from the paper in which it is folded, it wraps itself around his finger and he explodes in fury and fear, throwing the hair into the fire.[49] Later it is revealed that he has mistaken the hair for that of his dead mother, who had sent him a lock of her own hair on her deathbed, with her forgiveness for his past actions.

Stowe writes that he often dreamed of "that pale mother rising by his bedside, and felt the soft twining of that hair around his fingers, till the cold sweat would roll down his face, and he would spring from his bed in horror."[50] Yet, though this explains his reaction in part, it does not clarify the fearful premonition he experiences when first unwrapping the hair. This suggests knowledge (always unspoken) of the power of Africanist rituals and artifacts, and a sense of his impotence against the forms of folk belief that survived within slave populations. He is haunted by the power of his pale mother as well as by his mulatto mistress Cassy who literally haunts the house in which he lives, disrupting the domestic and familial structures he has forcibly created by his sexual and economic domination of slave women. His terror of obeah within the slave population combines with his own fear of more conventionally understood ghostliness.

Stowe effectively rescripts Douglass, making the hair of white women and the fetish objects of slaves interchangeable. By incorporating obeah and voodoo into the practices of domestic sentimentalism, she demonstrates the ways in which the domestic and sentimental operate within the frame of empire. Amy Kaplan's important formulation of the ways in which domestic ideology operates by taming the "foreign" elements that threaten the empire of the mother is instructive here. She writes that

> the discourse of domesticity was intimately intertwined with the discourse of Manifest Destiny in antebellum U.S. culture. The "empire of the mother" developed as a central tenet of middle-class culture between the 1830s and 1850s, at a time when the United States was violently and massively expanding its national domain across the continent."[51]

The hair of the white daughter and white mother recalls a Christian message, annexing the more "savage" elements of Africanist beliefs into a feminized, Christianized, white United States. In doing so, it seeks to efface those African elements that destabilize and undermine its hegemony, while remaining aware of their ongoing power. The lock of hair that simultaneously signifies Eva, Legree's mother, and Africanist beliefs literally intertwines Legree's finger in his nightmare, reminding him, and readers, of the inseparability of the violence that marks U.S. imperialism and enables middle class domesticity.

For example, key meetings between Tom and Eva are staged on the shores of Lake Pontchartrain, the site of well-known voodoo meetings led by Marie Laveau and her daughter.[52] Wardley suggests that in this scene "Tom's Christianization is arguably matched by Eva's Africanization."[53] I posit that the way in which this takes place is through a further whitening of them both. The "Africanizing" of Eva takes its strength from absorbing and redeploying the power of blackness within the frame of whiteness, which then hides and/or denies its African origins. What we will see is that within spiritualist practice, the primacy of whiteness in many instances is created precisely out of such a process of absorption and redeployment. Let us turn to one celebrated instance.

THE FAREWELL PERFORMANCES OF KATIE KING

In 1860 a book was published that made a considerable impact. This was Robert Dale Owen's *Footfalls on the Boundary of Another World*. Owen's writing on spiritualism fascinated many people, including Stowe. She avidly read both this and his subsequent work *The Debatable Land between This World and the Next* (1871) and would, like others, be intrigued by a piece he published in the *Atlantic Monthly* in which he described his personal experiences with a series of extraordinary séances.[54] Owen's short piece "Touching Visitants from a Higher Life" was subtitled "A Chapter of Autobiography." It is partly because of his fame and of the piece's status as autobiography that it was published in one of the most highly respected and widely read periodicals of the moment rather than in a specialist spiritualist journal. He anticipated a substantial and elite (though potentially skeptical) readership for his claims.[55]

The article, with its strongly articulated defense of spiritualism, became a serious personal embarrassment when he realized that he had been duped and this fact became public knowledge. The revelation of the fraud had a significant impact, for not only had the piece appeared in a prominent publication but also it occupied (physically speaking) a significant place in it.[56] "Touching Visitants from a Higher Life" was sandwiched between the first chapters of Henry James's *Roderick Hudson* and Mark Twain's *Old Times on the Mississippi*. Prior to his publicly articulated interest in spiritualism, Owen was widely known for his involvement in socialism, abolition and social justice, and in social experiments such as the New Harmony community in Indiana.[57]

By the time Owen wrote his *Atlantic Monthly* piece he was an elderly man. The spirit he encountered was that of a beautiful young woman called Katie King who claimed to be the same spirit who had materialized in London under the mediumship of Florence Cook, a young British medium, and had also appeared through other mediums, including Americans. The erotic heterosexual drama between the older man and younger woman should not be underestimated, for it was a common feature of many séances.

Katie King was the name of both the wife and the daughter of a spirit known as John King who had, it was claimed, been a buccaneer while alive. Katie did not materialize through Florence Cook when she appeared to Owen.[58] She had already claimed to have left this world altogether at a séance she gave in London with Cook as her medium. Her departure from London was a highly theatrical event. She gave three farewell séances before she left, the first and last of which were attended by Florence Marryat. At the third, on May 21, 1874, she appeared wearing a long white low-necked and short-sleeved dress with a white veil. Her hair was "of a light auburn or golden colour" and hung loose in ringlets "reaching nearly to her waist."[59]

In a gesture that was successfully reenacted in the Philadelphia sittings, she cut off portions of her white dress and veil to distribute to individuals who attended the séance. She then dramatically revealed that the clothing appeared complete and uncut so that the séance-goers were mystified as to how the fragments she distributed had been produced. She gave out these pieces of clothing in addition to flowers, hand-written notes, and locks of her hair. She promenaded around the room shaking the hands of her well-wishers. Eventually, having spoken parting words to the sitters she looked "once more earnestly at her friends" and disappeared behind the curtain of the cabinet in which Florence Cook lay. As Alex Owen writes, it "was pure theatre, complete with special effects, pathos, and timing."[60] Yet Katie King had not gone after all, and when she re-appeared in Philadelphia a few weeks later she had some explaining to do.

The Katie King who appeared over 40 times in a number of weeks to Owen in Philadelphia, differed in significant ways from the figure of the same name who materialized through Cook in London, though there were important similarities too. Both Katie King and Florence Cook were celebrated figures. Katie had been the first spirit fully to manifest herself in physical form in England, through Cook's mediumship. The popular mediums Mr. and Mrs. Nelson Holmes, who knew Cook, also claimed Katie as a spirit control.[61] Owen had received a letter only eight days after Katie had left London alluding to the curious fact that the spirit was trying to contact him. At a séance held by Mr. and Mrs. Holmes in Philadelphia, she had appeared and had requested him to travel to Philadelphia to meet her.[62] This seemed extraordinary not just because of the personal nature of the invitation but because of the very public final farewell the spirit had just made in London, of which many American spiritualists (including Owen) were already aware.

This was a matter that Katie herself addressed at the final séance Owen attended in Philadelphia, in which some of the features of her London departure (notably the distribution of hair, flowers, and clothing) were successfully reenacted. The spirit explained that there was in fact nothing extraordinary about the fact that she had departed from the world a few weeks earlier but had now reappeared. As she put it, "Some of my London friends misinterpreted my parting words. I took final leave, not of your earth, but of dear Florrie Cook, because my continuance with her would have injured her health."[63] She had not really meant to say farewell at all, it seemed—just au revoir. Katie King had left the world twice in quick succession on both sides of the Atlantic, and the way in which these farewells were enacted were strikingly similar.

Owen was fascinated by the invitation extended to him by the spirit and the possibilities for communication it offered. In a lengthy and detailed account of the many meetings he had with King and the spirits who sometimes appeared at various points, Owen makes it clear that he has no doubts about spirit communications. One important feature of their meetings was the exchange of gifts that took place: these included notes, locks of hair, and jewelry. Explicitly sentimental language is characteristic of their meetings, suggesting the extent to which a sentimental framework was the organizing principle of their encounters. There was also a clear element of sexual frisson. Such conflicting modes often combined. On one occasion he gave her a mother of pearl cross on a white silk braid with a note that said "I offer you this because, though it be simple, it is white and pure and beautiful, as you are."[64] Katie offered him a lock of her hair. He described it as "a beautiful ringlet, about four inches long, literally of a golden color, soft and fine."[65] The whiteness or paleness of King was something he noted repeatedly in his account of her.

The séances he attended included a wide range of spectacular special effects: flowers and other objects appeared and disappeared, phosphorescent hands and arms pointed or wrote on levitating sheets of paper, and King herself appeared and disappeared in dramatic ways—once she appeared literally to emerge from the floor before growing to full height in front of her select and small audience. At the final séance at which they made their farewells, their parting was represented as highly moving, though it was less overtly theatrical than her departure from London. She walked about the séance room and placed her hands upon the heads of individuals in a gesture of blessing.

Shortly before the end of the séance she disappeared inside the cabinet and appeared literally to emerge bit by bit from the floor before standing up before her audience. She kissed Owen on the forehead, spoke a few words to the others at the séance and said "I am very sorry that I shall soon have to part with you all." This was clearly the most emotional moment of the séance. Owen wrote,

> As she spoke, the tears—literal tears—stood in those large, kind eyes, and she wiped them with her veil, slowly retreating to the cabinet. Both the ladies wept; and to us all it was a sad and solemn leave-taking.[66]

The features of this séance (spectacular special effects, lachrymose moments, a full panoply of theatrical gestures) were common within many séances. The two departures of Katie King showed just the extent to which spiritualists had learned from the stage, sentimental fiction, and popular melodrama. Both used the language of sentiment; both were solemn and tearful events. Both involved the distribution of personal effects and objects that were imbued with a sentimental significance—hair, articles of clothing, jewelry, and so on. The departures of these pale white spirits, and the discipline and ritual of the farewells they performed suggest an understanding of how to enact parting scenes, one that owes a debt to the death of Little Eva.

For spiritualists, whose central claim that "there is no death" needed constant reinforcement to protect it from the ravages of grief about deaths that were all too real, Eva's death showed one way in which farewells could be conducted and could be rendered powerfully full of meaning and comfort for those left behind. Eva's distribution of her beautiful hair (a particularly affecting aspect of the representation of her death) was imitated by Cook, in a manner that showed just how powerful a symbol it could be. The distribution of King's hair on both sides of the Atlantic must partly be explained by the significance of hair as a well established token of love and mourning. But it may also be due to the extent to which Eva's death (as well as other scenes from the novel) was popularly known and widely reproduced in a variety of forms by this period. This made it available for multiple appropriations and adaptations.

Yet Eva's death, as we have seen, reconstituted elements of Africanist sensibilities and beliefs within the frame of the dominant white culture, by appropriating, refashioning, and redeploying them. Is it just a coincidence that Katie King had links to the sea via her putative father/husband the buccaneer John King? The *Oxford English Dictionary* gives the origin of the noun "buccaneer" as having connections both to the culinary habits of Indians in the Caribbean and their imitation by French hunters, as well as to the pirates of the Spanish seas in colonial America.[67] Emma Hardinge Britten argued that John King was in fact Henry Morgan, "the infamous pirate whose base was in the Bay of Panama."[68] Katie King, the pure white spirit who crossed the ocean, seems to have a powerful relation to a complex, racialized Atlantic and encounters between indigenous peoples and colonizing Europeans.

THE DEATH OF SUSIE

Stowe developed a different mode of writing about the death of a child when she wrote *My Wife and I*. The manner in which she described Susie's death suggests the extent to which her own thinking about mortality had been modified by her encounters with spiritualism. The death of Susie suggested that in *Uncle Tom's Cabin* the subject had been left as unfinished business. The subtle difference in emphasis between the deaths of Susie and Eva implies that Stowe had reached a differing understanding of its meanings when she came to write *My Wife and I*, one that emphasized that central tenet of spiritualism.

In Stowe's later writing, the representation of death is filtered through her experiences with spiritualism that made her rethink the anti-Calvinist rewritings she uses in her earlier work. She had experienced her first religious conversion at the age of 13, and then, at age 31, she had a second conversion and was seized by the desire to lead a better Christian life. Yet, around the same time, she began to investigate the possibility of leading a healthier physical and mental life by taking renewed interest in her physical well-being.

On a visit to Henry Ward Beecher and his wife Eunice in July 1844, she experimented with mesmerism and was put into a trance on three occasions by her brother Henry. She became friendly with a husband and wife team of mesmerists who were lecturing and experimenting in Cincinnati and became convinced that it could cure her headaches.[69] The emotional crisis that made Stowe investigate the possibilities of spiritualism with special vigor was the death of her son Henry in 1857. What made this particularly hard for Stowe and her family was the fear that Henry, who had expressed religious doubts, would not be saved. Had he died unregenerate? This profound anxiety fed into Stowe's novel *The Minister's Wooing* (1859), in which she symbolically reversed Henry's death by making a young sailor, James Marvyn, come back to life from a reported drowning.

Though Stowe was symbolically able to enact Henry's salvation through the novel, in her daily life she continued to try to find a way of proving that he was not lost to her forever.[70] She described the experience of seeing his dead body in a letter to the Duchess of Sutherland,

> There he lay so calm, so placid, so peaceful, that I could not believe that he would not smile upon me, and that my voice, which always had such power over him, could not recall him. There had always been such a peculiar union, such a tenderness between us. I had had such power always to call up answering feelings to my own, that it seemed impossible that he could be silent and unmoved at my grief.[71]

The crisis expressed here about the failure of the power of the voice is in part about the failure of empathy. She could not call back the dead beloved, or make him respond to her voice and, above all, could not "call up answering feelings to my own," which is the epitome of successful sentimental empathetic responses. Her anguish, to the Duchess of Sutherland, that the "power" of her voice failed to produce a reaction in her dead son is related to her experiences with mesmerism, sharing its language.

Later, in the same decade, Stowe and her husband both started to try health cures. She spent 11 months at a water cure in Brattleboro,

Vermont, in 1846 and became an enthusiastic convert to its methods, persuading her husband to try it himself.[72] Such cures often incorporated techniques that included mesmerism and other of the quasi-medical practices that were introduced to the United States in the late eighteenth century. The water cure advocated healthy eating, exercise, avoidance of drugs and alcohol, as well as douching, showering, washing, and sweating—all of which involved a great deal of water. Stowe's adoption of the water cure restored her health and suggested a secular counterpart or conversion experience that mirrored her earlier religious experience. She continued with her interest in such alternatives to allopathic medicine. In the autumn of 1869 Stowe, her husband, and her sister Catharine all attended Dr. Taylor's Swedish Movement Cure in New York, in which vigorous exercise was the chief cause of the cure offered. Taylor was a spiritualist and while attending the cure she took part in a number of séances held by Kate Fox Jencken.[73]

Stowe and her brothers and sisters were receptive to many of the mid-nineteenth-century beliefs that are associated with the radical political belief systems that emerged within the new republic. Each moved away from the Calvinism into which they had been born and several experimented with ideas familiar within the culture of the period: dietary reform, sexual abstinence within marriage, a belief in the pre-existence of souls. Isabella Beecher Hooker became especially interested in spiritualism.[74] Stowe's participation in such attempts to strengthen, cure, and purify the body are consistent with a pattern of middle-class interest in popular culture and fashionable cures that could often lead to spiritualism, or at least are consistent with a propensity to consider its claims in a serious and engaged manner.

She was frequently skeptical about the motives and honesty of professional mediums, however. She acknowledged later, in a letter to her children, that individuals often turned to spiritualism following the death of a loved one. She wrote that "When we hear sometimes of persons of the strongest and clearest minds becoming credulous votaries of certain spiritualist circles, let us not wonder: if we inquire, we shall almost always find that the belief has followed some stroke of death; it is only an indication of the desperation of that heart-hunger which in part it appeases."[75] Her supposition certainly seems to be correct.

In *My Wife and I*, Susie's death, of scarlet fever, is not given the prominent place of Eva's death: it registers as the symbolic striking of a bell six times that the novel's protagonist, Harry, hears through his own fevered state. Instead, Stowe concentrate's upon an important scene in which Harry has a dream vision of his dead playmate (who he, somewhat confusingly, calls Daisy) who comforts him from the other world. His dream resembles the two dreams that Tom has of Eva after her death that appear to have been partial templates. On the first occasion, which takes place just before St. Clare's death, Tom "saw her coming bounding towards him, just as she used to come . . . but, as he looked, she seemed to rise from the ground; her cheeks wore a paler hue,—her eyes had a deep, divine radiance, a golden halo seemed around her head,—and she vanished from his sight."[76] Just as she disappears, Tom is woken abruptly by a knocking at the gate, which turns out to signify that St. Clare has been fatally stabbed. The experience seems, therefore, to have been a sort of premonition that precedes a moment of crisis in the novel—the death of a man who has lapsed from his faith. As St. Clare lies dying, he rejects the offer of a visit from a clergyman and instead is ministered to by Tom, whose sentimental praying—"literally prayer offered with strong crying and tears"—leads to the domestic image, which St. Clare himself suggests, of his soul coming home "at last" as he returns to his faith and sees the image of his mother as he dies.[77] Tom's own faith has without doubt been boosted by his dream of Eva, and though it is his mother that St. Clare calls out to on his deathbed, the reader is comforted in the thought that he will soon be reunited with his beloved daughter.

The second occasion takes place just after Tom has been sold to Legree, and it acts as a consolatory reminder of the existence of God. It is prompted by the doubts of two slave women whom Tom helps. He dreams that Eva is reading the Bible to him by Lake Pontchartrain. She reads from Isaiah 43:2–3, which tells of God's constancy and protection. As Tom listens, the dream starts to fade.

> Gradually the words seemed to melt and fade, as in a divine music; the child raised her deep eyes, and fixed them lovingly on him, and rays of warmth and comfort seemed to go from them to his heart; and, as if wafted on the music, she seemed to rise on shining wings, from which flakes and spangles of gold fell off like stars, and she was gone.[78]

George Aiken may have been interpreting this somewhat literally when he incorporated the scene of Eva rising to heaven on a white dove into his stage play, but Stowe leaves it to the reader to decide how to read the scene. She intervenes to ask, "Was it a dream? Let it pass for one" before ending indecisively with four lines of verse that suggest that the dead may not have left their loved ones forever: "It is a beautiful belief,/ That ever round our head/ Are hovering, on angel wings,/ The spirits of the dead."[79] This "belief" is further developed in the dream Harry has of Susie as well as in Stowe's visits to séances and in the poetry she published in the few years that followed. All this suggests that these spirits were reachable and could be communicated with. This culminated in moments in which the distinction between her more conventional religious beliefs and the new possibilities offered by spiritualism became mixed.

Harry's dream borrows from both visions that Tom has of Eva. His mother explaining to him that Susie was "a fair white angel" in heaven, and the anguish this causes him when he realizes he will never see her again prompts it. He cries himself to sleep, and has a dream of her.

> It seemed to me that I was again in our meadow, and that it was fairer than ever before; the sun shone gaily, the sky was blue, and out great, golden lily stocks seemed mysteriously bright and fair, but I was wandering lonesome and solitary. Then suddenly my little Daisy came running to meet me in her pink dress and white apron, with her golden curls hanging down her neck. "Oh Daisy, Daisy!" said I running up to her. "Are you alive?—they told me you were dead."
>
> "No, Hazzy, dear, I am not dead,—never you believe that," she said, and I felt the clasp of her soft little arms round my neck. "Didn't I tell you we'd see each other again?"
>
> "But they told me you were dead," I said in wonder—and I thought I held her off and looked at her,—she laughed gently at me as she used to, but her lovely eyes had a mysterious power that seemed to thrill all through me.
>
> "I am not dead, dear Hazzy," she said. "We never die where I am—I shall love you always," and with that my dream wavered and grew misty as when clear water breaks an image into a thousand glassy rings and fragments.
>
> I thought I heard lovely music, and felt soft, clasping arms, and I awoke with a sense of being loved and pitied and comforted.[80]

The key difference between the dreams of Tom and Harry is the importance of speech in Harry's dreams. Though Tom hears Eva's voice in his second dream, she only reads from the Bible. Susie, on the other hand, speaks directly to Harry and tells him first that death is a myth and second, that she loves him forever. The experience of comfort he receives from Susie takes place both through the consolatory message she gives him of the impotence of death and through the reassurance of the continuation of her love after her departure.

Crucially, too, he experiences the comfort of two occasions of physical contact with her, a contact that has been an ordinary part of their affectionate relationship prior to her death. Whereas Stowe uses an analogy of the process of the fading away of Tom's vision of Eva as being like that of music—"as in a divine music"—Harry believes he actually hears "a lovely music" before he feels Susie's last embrace. When he awakes it is "with a sense of being loved and pitied, and comforted," whereas Stowe writes simply of Tom's waking up: "Tom woke." Though at one level Stowe is representing the differing ages and ethnic and socioeconomic positioning of Tom and Eva, Harry and Susie, the disparity between these dream sequences cannot be dismissed so easily. What is also being reflected is a new understanding of what death meant to Stowe, and how she might reconsider the processes of parting and mourning in the light of this. Harry's dream of Susie most closely resembles the experience of a séance-goer for whom music and the embrace of a materialized spirit, as well as the feeling of comfort this brought was a regular part of the séance. The language of the meeting, with the mutual recognition, the reassurance of the impotence and unreality of death, and the physicality and materiality of the occasion with its accompanying music all read like one of the many accounts of séances reported throughout this period.

Though it is not clear that Stowe encountered the materialized spirits of either of her sons at the séances she attended, she did write to Calvin Stowe that when she sat with an American medium in Florence she felt "sustained and comforted, as if I had been near to my Henry and other departed friends. This has been at times so strong as greatly to soothe and support me." She went on to claim that

One thing I am convinced of,—that spiritualism is a reaction from the intense materialism of the present age. Luther, when he recognized a personal devil, was much nearer right. We ought to enter fully, at least, into the spiritualism of the Bible. Circles and spiritual jugglery I regard as the lying signs and wonders, with all deceivableness of unrighteousness; but there is a real scriptural spiritualism which has fallen into disuse, and must be revived, and there are, doubtless, people who, from some constitutional formation, can more readily receive the impressions of the surrounding spiritual world. Such were apostles, prophets, and workers of miracles.[81]

Through this personal definition of spiritualism, which saw the phenomena as part of a tradition within Christianity that had been neglected at some cost, Stowe was able to feel the reassurance that spiritualism could bring. At the same time, she was able to distance herself from the practices of professional mediums that she thought likely to be fraudulent, and the political radicalism of some spiritualists that did not sit happily with her own political beliefs. Stowe was able to rationalize the experiences she had with spiritualists and incorporate them within a framework both of Christianity and of natural laws. In this manner she domesticated spiritualism and made it accessible to the processes of mourning, which she so brilliantly delineated in *Uncle Tom's Cabin*.

CHAPTER 5

"THERE IS NO DEATH": SPIRITUALISM AND THE CIVIL WAR

"GIVE ME BACK MY DEAD"

The title of this chapter comes from the famous spiritualist denial of the existence of death. The kind of dispelling of belief implied by this claim is particularly striking when it is considered that spiritualism gained new adherents at key moments of trauma associated with widespread levels of death—notably, the period of the Civil War in the United States, and the 1914–1918 war. At each of these moments there was a revival of interest in the spirit world.[1] What are the difficulties, or even the opportunities, faced by a system of beliefs that denies the existence of death when confronted with the devastation it causes?

The violent internal struggle of the Civil War and the assassination of Abraham Lincoln were two events that particularly tested the degree to which such a denial might appeal to, or repel, Americans. The kinds of comforts and euphemisms that spiritualism might offer at periods of massive internal turmoil and unprecedented crisis had found their moment. Violence on the scale experienced during this period produced problems of language as well as comprehension. Such catastrophes test the limits of language and understanding and require new explanations and ways of dealing with crisis, mourning, and loss.[2]

Spiritualists responded to this in a number of ways. One was through consolatory writings that emphasized the reconstitution of broken and disfigured bodies within a realm that was rendered accessible and comprehensible through spiritualist ideology. Another was through a preoccupation with Lincoln as an iconic figure that, especially for Northerners, could act as a surrogate or substitute for the dead soldiers they mourned.

The war was often seen as a fratricidal conflict. With the president (in conventional terms) seen as both leader and father of the nation, metaphors of the familial abounded. The status of dead soldiers as fathers, brothers, or sons was frequently invoked and reminded Americans of the networks of the bereaved that were left behind while soldiers headed into battle. Visceral images of bloodied bodies brutally vivisected by the war were also common. Emma Hardinge Britten utilized such a rhetorical trope in an oration she made after Lincoln's death. She described him as "uniting again in one fraternal clasp the severed hands of North and South."[3] The reunion of the traumatized and amputated hands provides an image that suggests both the massive death caused by the war and its brutalizing human consequences.

The two events—the war and the assassination—were often played out as strikingly domestic dramas within a familial/local set of parameters. Yet at the same time the limits of what constituted the domestic were also being tested by the implications of the events overtaking the nation and this, in turn, suggested the limitations of the kinds of language being used to describe disaster on such a gigantic scale. Spiritualism was well positioned to take its place within such constructions. Its role as a provider of comfort to bereaved families who healed grief by allowing for hands to be joined, literally, once more, was well established by the time of the war. Séances frequently took place within domestic environments in which the families were significant both as living participants and as returning spirits.

The war brought substantial challenges to the ways with which the dead were dealt, building on changes that had already been taking place within antebellum culture. In addition to this, meanings of death and the imaginative responses to it were undergoing significant shifts during the period. The ways in which death and mourning were conceived of changed considerably throughout the nineteenth century. The developments of new ways of dealing with the bodies of the dead—the emergence of the funeral parlor, the improvement in techniques of embalming and preserving the body—took corpses out of the domestic space they had once occupied and into a new commercial realm governed by professionals, often male, who made it their business to manage the processes that took place after death. The growth of the rural cemetery movement and the philosophy associated with it also assisted in changing understandings of death and providing new ways of talking about death and its ramifications.

A number of novels written by women addressed the impact of the war on the families who were left behind. The most celebrated of these is the best-selling *Little Women* (1868). Set during the war, Louisa May Alcott's novel shows the way in which the war divided the March family. Mr. March is away at the front, and Mrs. March (Marmee) remains at home taking care of their four daughters, Amy, Beth, Jo and Meg. For Alcott, families include the dead as well as the living. The novel shows that the dead can return to comfort and to teach those left behind. The presence of Teddy Laurence (Laurie) in the house of his grandfather Mr. Laurence is a constant physical reminder of the son Mr. Laurence has lost, as well as the dead daughter-in-law whose marriage to his son he opposed so strongly. Through his resemblance to his parents, Laurie extends and main-tains their impact on the living, particularly his grandfather. Beth's resemblance to Mr. Laurence's dead granddaughter allows the elderly man to articulate his feelings of loss and grief and to come to terms with the actions of his son and reconcile himself with his grandson. Toward the end of the novel, when Mr. Laurence accom-panies Laurie to Europe, Alcott represents his journey as a form of atonement to his dead son prompted by the lessons he has learned from his re-engagement with the familial, here represented by the March family. The novel shows the ways in which tensions and rebel-lions within the nation can be represented and resolved through and within the family.

Yet one particular challenge that the Civil War posed to bereaved Americans on both sides of the conflict was the absence of the dead from families, both figuratively and literally. The dead often did not return to their places of origin, marking, in huge numbers, a new prob-lem for Americans. About 42 percent of the dead were not identified.[4] While many American immigrants, by definition, did not have access to the graves of their ancestors, which could be located in other countries, the events of the war made the dislocation between the living and the dead in these tangible ways even more evident.

How could the dead—the unidentified, absent figures whose bodies had not been returned—be mourned fully? The difficulties faced by the families of the dead were partly overcome, at least for Unionists, by public mourning that followed the assassination of Lincoln. His visibility and familiarity was envisaged as both unifying and comforting to bereaved families, especially those of unionists. Other strategies were invoked that dealt with the pressing emotional needs of the huge numbers of women whose lovers, brothers, fathers, sons, and cousins had been killed.

The anguish that the bereaved felt is vividly expressed in the comments of a Northern man describing his wife's frantic expressions of longing for the return of her son's body: "Day and night she cried: 'Give me back my dead,' a desire that many desperate Northerners echoed, with no expectation that it could ever be realized."[5] It was not only Northerners who experienced such emotions, of course, but one of the most celebrated and successful examples of consolatory writing that dealt explicitly with the mourning practices of women in just such a situation was aimed at them. This was Elizabeth Stuart Phelps's *The Gates Ajar*, published in the same year as *Little Women*. Phelps's success with this novel, which sold upward of eighty thousand copies in the United States before the end of the century (and more than that in Britain in addition to the translations that were sold in other countries), suggested to her that fiction on related topics might be commercially successful. She published two related novels, *Beyond the Gates* (1883) and *The Gates Between* (1887).[6]

These three novels do not exactly represent a trilogy, in the strictest sense. Given their related thematic preoccupations and the associations suggested by their titles, it is interesting to read them in tangent. The most celebrated, *The Gates Ajar*, is explicitly linked to the experience of being a bereaved woman in the period of the war. At the start of the novel, Mary Cabot is in mourning for her soldier brother Royal (Roy) who has been shot. The novel articulates a vision of life after death in which continuation of the familial and domestic in a perfected way predominates. Mary's despair is gradually lifted by the arrival of her youthful widowed Aunt Winifred whose theology resembles that of spiritualists.

While there is some doubt about Phelps's involvement with spiritualism, her family-centered, optimistic vision of what happens after death accords with spiritualist ideas. Without doubt, the novel was aimed at the many women whose lives had been permanently changed by Civil War deaths. Phelps's related novels, however, aimed more at considering ideas of death and future lives more within their own terms rather than in the context of the war.

The final novel is narrated by the spirit of a well-intentioned doctor who has neglected his wife and child in life, but finds that he is able to make up for this after he dies in a carriage accident. His son dies shortly after him, of a disease he might have recognized and even cured had he not been so preoccupied. Given the opportunity to prove that he can be a good postmortem parent to his spirit son he obliges and is rewarded by being reunited with his beloved wife who dies soon after this. Even so brief account as is given here will show the ways in which ideas of reunion and idealized domesticity are at the heart of Phelps's own ideological vision of what happens after death. Crucially, too, her novels give voice not just to the anguish of those left behind, but to the experiences of spirits themselves.

Phelps's invocation of a world beyond that of the living is largely stripped of any association with the grotesque, the gothic, or the horrific—unlike, for example, the work of Poe. Instead she aims to provide reassurance, stability, and comfort—a bourgeois heaven with all the material comforts of the domestic, notoriously including pianos.[7] She saw herself as engaging with a matter of supreme importance in the lives of women who, even more than men in the same period, were likely to take more responsibility for the management of grief and mourning within the family. She figured this political project within the larger politics of the nation. Her view of heaven was premised on ideas of bourgeois domesticity; the United States that her characters retreated from was shaped by capitalism and imperialism.[8] She had no doubt about the degree of shift that had affected the spiritual beliefs of individuals, particularly within the dominant New England culture. As the daughter of a prominent Calvinist theologian, she was well positioned to see how the kinds of reconfigurations of belief and practice that her books contributed to and represented had already transformed U.S. life.

This was an aspect of her world-view she certainly shared with spiritualist culture. Many spiritualists understood themselves to be involved in a set of beliefs with profound political implications, explicitly in relation to women's rights and abolition but also in terms of reshaping attitudes to the domestic. The deaths of the president, on the one hand, and of thousands of ordinary soldiers, on the other, as well as the different ways in which their corpses were treated, represented a moment of significant change in attitudes toward death. Attempts by spiritualists to claim Lincoln as a believer (which they did before and after his assassination) may tellingly be read as a strategic recognition of his symbolic value on either side of that event, and an understanding of the ways in which his death marked a shift in cultural and social practice that might have been very useful to them.

ABRAHAM LINCOLN AND THE SPIRITUALISTS

The death of the fictional Little Eva was a highly significant moment within nineteenth-century literary culture in which concepts of death and the practices of mourning could be dramatized in a sentimental manner before a reading public envisaged and constructed as sympathetic by Harriet Beecher Stowe. This, as we have seen, went on to have an important influence on the ways in which spiritualists managed the production of spirits within séances. The death of Abraham Lincoln and its immediate aftermath, in contrast, showed the way in which the real consequences of death could be played out to the full before a public comprised of individuals from a range of political perspectives and sympathies in an international context. His death—and the extensive period of formalized performances of public mourning that followed it—is a fascinating phenomenon that reveals a great deal about the ritualized staging of national mourning, the politics of citizenship, and the way that collective grief can be acted out on a huge scale.

In Lincoln's case, the struggle between his wife and politicians who appropriated his corpse for legitimating and symbolic purposes suggests the ways in which both wanted to contain and maintain the meaning of his body and the legacy it represented. Both sides recognized the iconic status of his body within a nation in which bloody internecine conflict had dominated the previous few years. Lincoln, both dead and alive, was available to be appropriated as a symbol of the nation, a democratic union that was represented as being unique in the world's history. Poets and others did just that, and no more so than Walt Whitman who repeatedly returned to the figure of Lincoln, after his assassination, as a source and subject of some of his best-known poetry. His four poems on Lincoln—"When Lilacs Last in the Dooryard Bloom'd," "O Captain! My Captain," "Hush'd Be the Camps Tonight," and "The Dust Was Once the Man"—appeared at various dates but were collected in the second issue of the 1871 edition of *Leaves of Grass*, under the title "President

Lincoln's Burial Hymn." The better-known title, "Memories of President Lincoln," was given in the 1881 edition.[9]

A number of American presidents—especially Jefferson and Washington—were frequently invoked within national discourse as examples of great, dead leaders whose lives had didactic value. As such, they appeared with some regularity within popular expressions of loss, remembrance, and aspiration. These included nineteenth-century séances where from an early period the two might appear and dispense advice and good counsel. Lincoln, however, is an example of an American president who famously took this a stage further. He both attended séances while he was alive (even at the White House itself) and appeared in them (including in a celebrated spirit photograph) after his death—a fact much commented on both at the time and afterward.[10]

This suggested the extent to which he was a figure of special interest to spiritualists, many of whom claimed him as a fellow believer. Indeed there has always been a great deal of debate about whether Lincoln, who was raised as a Baptist, could be described as having conventional Christian beliefs at all. Jon Butler has argued, persuasively, that he represented a spiritual heterodoxy that was shared by many Americans. He claims that Lincoln was a religious man, whose belief system is of profound importance to anyone seeking to understand his presidency, even arguing that it is "impossible to discuss him apart from religion."[11] His beliefs drew from his encounters with a variety of sources. Lincoln attributed "divine significance" to his dreams, which corresponds to "the spiritual world of his youth, where Methodists or other itinerants, such as Lorenzo Dow, regularly described dreams as they enunciated, justified, and explained the ways of God. . . . Yet Lincoln also expressed a bitter fatalism that resonated both with traditional American lay skepticism and with some aspects of American occultism." He did not join a church, and he expressed no interest in the historical or religious figure of Jesus.[12]

This complex debate about what his religious beliefs actually were and how this might be interpreted in the light of his actions as a President has led some critics to, for instance, investigate his rhetorical practices (the language of the Gettysburg Address for example, as Garry Wills has done) and his recorded comments, as ways of probing his beliefs.[13] Butler writes, "Lincoln's religious rhetoric was abstract, grand, fatalistic—almost Judaic in its emphasis on providence and, certainly, deliverance, but only loosely Christian at best and perhaps not substantially Christian at all."[14] Out of such debates, spiritualists and others have constructed a popular mythology about his purported mysticism, belief in premonitions, gifts of prophecy, and involvement with mediums.

The many interpretations of his religious beliefs suggest a number of different agendas, but most imbue Lincoln with some kind of supernatural mystique, as critics regularly note. The titles of a number of books suggest this. Nettie Colburn Maynard's *Was Abraham Lincoln a Spiritualist?* (1891) cashes in on Maynard's fame as one medium that gave Lincoln advice, purportedly from the spirit world, during his lifetime. Francis Grierson's *Abraham Lincoln: The Practical Mystic* (1919) concentrates upon Lincoln's apparent mysticism and prophetic nature (a detail of some debate in the aftermath of his death). Harriet M. Shelton's *Abraham Lincoln Returns* (1957) is the first person account by Shelton (an American medium) of Lincoln's communications with her through an English medium. It contains detailed accounts of Colburn Maynard's encounters with Lincoln in the White House and reflections on how it might be possible to understand his involvement with mediums.[15]

His encounters with them were far fewer than that of Mary Todd Lincoln whose grief at the deaths of their sons Eddie in 1850 and Willie in 1862 certainly prompted her to look to the spirit world for solace. She believed that she had received messages from Willie through raps on walls and furniture and scratched writing on wainscoting. In addition to this, she thought that after Willie's death his smiling form appeared to her at the end of her bed, which greatly reassured her.[16] This was a pattern established by many celebrated figures who visited mediums. Lincoln's engagement with spiritualism was no doubt partly due to his own sorrow, but also the fact that spiritualism's profile was increasing and mediums were already visiting the White House.

Spiritualists claimed that spirits played an important role in the government of the country during the Civil War. Rumors abounded during Lincoln's lifetime and after his death about this involvement. The memoirs of Maynard, as well as works such as *Abraham Lincoln Returns* were designed to suggest that Lincoln was indeed a firm believer in spiritualism, therefore adding his name to the list of celebrated figures who experimented with spiritualism at some point in their lives. Lincoln's premature death meant that spiritualists could claim him as a figure who was still actively involved in séances at the end of his life: he had not become disillusioned as others had.

Despite their claims, a more skeptical reading of Lincoln's numerous cryptic, often ambivalent, even hostile, responses is certainly possible, indeed sensible. It is without doubt that his wife Mary Todd Lincoln was a firm believer in spiritualism, for at least a part of her life, and she encouraged her husband to attend séances with her.[17] Yet it is highly unlikely that Lincoln's widely documented informal investigations into spiritualism actually became formalized into belief in any significant way. The investigations he undertook are of consequence, in part, because of their reflection on the relationship between spiritualism, the politics of abolition, and the Civil War.[18] In the period of the war, death and politics were intermingled in public life in vivid and inescapable ways.

Spirit mediums certainly visited the White House, then, and gave Lincoln advice on military and political tactics during the war period, which they represented as coming from the spirit world and as being welcomed by Lincoln. It was even rumored that the Emancipation Proclamation had been prompted by a spirit message transmitted to the President by Colburn Maynard.[19] Other accounts gave details of a variety of spiritualist activities within the White House. A widely reprinted newspaper article in the *Boston Gazette* described a séance conducted at the White House at which Lincoln, his wife, and a number of others were present.

The medium Charles E. Shockle produced a message from General Henry Knox, the first Secretary of War, in response to a question by the President about the future of the country. When he asked when the war would be over, Knox revealed that the spirits had an interest in such issues.

> Washington, Lafayette, Franklin, Wilberforce, Napoleon, and myself have held frequent consultations on this point. There is something which our spiritual eyes cannot detect which appears well formed. Evil has come at times by removal of men from high positions, and there are those in retirement whose abilities should be made useful to hasten the end. Napoleon says, concentrate your forces upon one point; Lafayette thinks that the rebellion will die of exhaustion; Franklin sees the end approaching, as the South must give up for want of mechanical ability to compete against Northern mechanics. Wilberforce sees hope only in a negro army.[20]

This is an unlikely transatlantic political alliance to claim a wartime advisory role. The séance was marked by many droll asides from

Lincoln, and the dramatic finale was the appearance of the spirit of Napoleon, speaking through the person of Shockle (whose physical gestures "resting his left arm on the back [of a chair], his right thrust into his bosom" rendered him unmistakable), who advised Lincoln "to listen to the wishes of the people" and to restore the Union. Lincoln's cryptic response was as follows: "I believe that . . . whether it comes from spirit or human."[21] A similar response was given to Robert Dale Owen, who at another point read to him at some length about related matters. Having listened patiently to him, Lincoln responded, "for those who like that sort of thing, I should think it is just about the sort of thing they would like."[22] One of the notable spirits who appeared to Owen, in the series of séances he attended in Philadelphia, was that of Lincoln, though his conversation (if indeed he spoke on that occasion) is not recorded.

Much of this has been well documented by critics who see it as an example of eccentricity, genuine faith, the expression of a bereaved man trying to come to terms with the loss of his son, Willie, in one of the modes of the period, or a man being pressured by a wife that some went on to believe was not sane on the subject. Though spiritualist beliefs could be interpreted as symptoms of insanity, particularly in the cases of women, it could prove hazardous to make such a charge, even in this period. When, in 1875, Robert Lincoln accused his mother of insanity and had her committed to a sanitarium, her belief in spiritualism was not mentioned as part of the case against her, though her passion for shopping was.[23] This was represented as a form of mania, of manic obsession with purchasing, and such representation can be read as a displacement or deflection from her spiritualist beliefs into a commercial realm.

One reason for avoiding the mention of spiritualism in the trial that led to her commitment may well have been that it would have raised the well-known campaign of Elizabeth Packard, tried seven years earlier for insanity. Packard's husband, a Congregationalist minister, had regarded his wife's interest in spiritualism, Swedenborgianism, Universalism, and phrenology with a great deal of suspicion, and eventually had her certified as insane. When she eventually regained her freedom she began to work highly effectively for the reform of the law under which she had been imprisoned and to gain the right, in Illinois, to jury trial for individuals accused of insanity.[24] Privately, Robert Lincoln was greatly concerned by her involvement with spiritualism. Among the symptoms noted by a physician, who had treated her since 1873, were her claims that wires were being pulled out of her eyes and bones from her cheeks by an Indian spirit who also some-times lifted and then replaced her scalp.[25] Her physician initially interpreted her illness as one emanating from a diseased psychology, though he eventually diagnosed a physiological cause for some of her symptoms.

While figures like Emma Hardinge Britten and Walt Whitman were finding public modes to address their sorrow at the death of the president, his bereaved widow continued her private search to allay her grief at the deaths of her sons and husband. In 1871 she visited Moravia, New York, and saw the faces of 22 spirits, including that of her son Tad, who had died that year, leaving her with only one surviving child, Robert. Later she visited a spiritualist in Boston and attended séances for a fortnight, at which point the spirit of her hus-band appeared, much comforting her.[26]

She also visited the first spirit photographer, William H. Mumler, to try to obtain a spirit photograph of Lincoln. Spirit photography emerged in the early days of the new technology and became another proof by which spiritualists could prove their beliefs to skeptics. Mumler was working as an engraver in Boston when he discovered his gift and soon moved to New York where he set up a successful business. As the phenomena of spirit photography became increas-ingly common, spiritualist supporters often repeated details from his book *The Personal Experiences of William H. Mumler in Spirit-Photography* (1875). He also found that spiritualists could be antagonists as well as allies. He wrote,

> Before commencing to take spirit-pictures I had a reputation as an honest and trustworthy person, enjoying for many years the confi-dence of the leading jewellers of Boston, in whose emply I was, and often being entrusted with their valuables to a large amount. But this reputation, that I had been years in establishing, vanished like a soap-bubble when I commenced to take spirit-photographs. I was condemned as a trickster, branded as a fraud, and deserted by those who were happy to acknowledge my acquaintance when in—to them—a more honorable business. And, strange as it may seem, many of my strongest opponents have been professed Spiritualists—men who have seen and are familiar with the difficulties that attend the demonstration of spiritual truths; who, while endeavoring to enlighten a skeptical and bigoted world with new truths will, at the same time, with the same skepticism and bigotry, denounce other truths of which they have not been convinced.[27]

In 1869 Mumler was tried in a celebrated case in which he was accused of obtaining money under false pretences by fraudulently claiming to take spirit photographs. He was cleared in a trial covered by newspapers including the New York *Herald,* whose investigations had prompted the charge, helped by the testimony of a judge who was also a spiritualist.[28]

Mumler gives a full, if biased, account of Mary Todd Lincoln's visit. He gave details of a heavily veiled woman appearing at his studio and giving her name as Mrs. Lindall. She removed her veil ("so thick that it was impossible to distinguish a single feature of her face") and sat for a photograph. Once it was taken, she left, agreeing to return in three days to collect the photographs. The negatives were sent to the printers and were returned "only a few moments" before she returned at the appointed time. Mumler had been away, and claimed that he had not seen the developed photographs and still did not know her real identity. Mrs. Mumler, who was talking to a friend when Lindall/Lincoln returned, handed the envelope containing the photograph to Lindall/Lincoln and carried on talking to the friend who then asked Lindall/Lincoln if she recognized the likeness in the photo. This is a repetition of the question Mary Todd Lincoln had herself asked of the sitter whose photograph was taken just before hers was done. Yet this obvious symmetry was not matched by what then followed:

> Mrs L. replied, hesitatingly, "Yes." My wife was almost instantly entranced, and, turning to Mrs. L., said: "Mother, if you cannot recognize father, show the picture to Robert; he will recognize it." "Yes-yes, dear," Mrs Lincoln said; "I do recognize it; but who is now speaking?" she asked. The control replied: "Thaddeus!" A long conversation ensued. Mr. Lincoln afterwards controlled and talked with her—so the lady-friend informed me who had thus unexpectedly been a witness of this excellent test.

> When my wife resumed her normal condition, she found Mrs. L. weeping tears of joy that she had again found her loved ones, and apparently anxious to learn, if possible, how long before she could join them in their spirit home. But this information of course could not be given.

Mumler concludes that "The picture of Mr. Lincoln is an excellent one. He is seen standing behind her, with his hands resting on her shoulders, and looking down, with a pleasant smile."[29] Mary

Todd Lincoln's response to and belief in the commercially obtained image of her husband's spirit may be difficult to comprehend. Yet, read against the popularity of postmortem photographs in the same period, the kinds of evidence marshaled by William Lloyd Garrison as proof of spirits, or (in contrast) the celebrated and macabre account of Ralph Waldo Emerson examining the remains of his son Waldo some fifteen years after his death as a way of denying sentimentalism's claims and repudiating mourning, it needs further examination.

Garrison's experiences with Mumler divided those who heard about it. He had been interested in photography and photographs (or "counterfeit presentments." as he called them) for some time before they met.[31] His family had given him a much-treasured photograph album in 1861, which happens to have been the year in which Mumler took his first spirit photograph. By the time Garrison visited him in Boston in 1874, he was an experienced spirit photographer. His subjects were often prompted to approach him by spirits whom they encountered in séances. Departed friends or relatives suggested that they would appear photographically if they would go to Mumler. They did, of course, in numbers.

According to Garrison, the photographer had no idea of his identity, at the time of his sitting. Since he was a highly visible public figure and had been for years, this seems implausible, to say the least. The negative was shown to him "immediately after it was taken from the camera" and it turned out to reveal the spirit of Charles Sumner suspended above him holding a broken chain.[32] Garrison was profoundly moved by what he saw and was robust in his championing of what he interpreted as an indisputable piece of evidence. Yet many critics questioned this interpretation, not least because the chain held by the spirit was hanging at an impossible angle.

In an August 1874 letter to his wife, he continued defending it against the doubts of others. In a striking argument in favor of the validity of the photograph he claimed that since Sumner's spirit did not actually materialize but was only visible once the photograph was developed it was not therefore "amenable to the rules of art" and should not have the same criteria attached to it as a "materialized form." It seemed to Garrison that the rules of gravity need not apply in this instance and it was too literalistic to interpret what was clearly a symbolic image in this manner. He wrote in an exasperated manner of one critic, complaining that

He says that the broken chain on my breast would hang vertically *by its own weight*, and not diagonally as it is seen in the picture; but this is absurdly assuming that the spirit (if a spirit) was holding in his hand, at the time, literally an iron chain! Enough that the chain appears at all as a symbol of emancipation. Mr. S's conclusion, that "the picture is a transparent fraud," is so sweeping and self-sufficient as to indicate a foregone conclusion on his part not to indicate the possibility of any such phenomenon. It must be remembered that he has no belief in a future state of existence.[33]

It is easy to use Garrison's argument against himself to suggest that since he had a belief in future existence, his evidence might also be suspect. Marshaling the spirits of Coffin and Webb as witnesses, a subsequent critical move, was not the most persuasive mode of argument.

In addition to that, belief that a professional medium and professional spirit photographer might not have good reason to stand together seems extraordinarily naive. The photograph utilized highly familiar iconography associated with abolition. Garrison confusingly wanted to apply two different and competing standards to the image of Sumner and the chain. The first was that of verisimilitude—did the image look like its subject? In other words, could the spirit be recognized as Sumner? The second was that of symbolism, envisaged as being separate from and not subject to the laws governing realistic representation. What is curious is his belief that a materialized spirit, visibly present at the sitting, would be subject to the laws governing the material world. Part of what the example of the image of Sumner and the chain suggests is that issues of photographic representation were themselves still the subjects of debate. The conjunction of the new technology and spiritualism produced images that were subject to wildly different interpretations.

THE AFTERLIFE OF LINCOLN

One week after Lincoln's death the poet Edmund Clarence Stedman wrote to Bayard Taylor describing the mood of Washington, DC. He wrote,

I would that you were here to see this town, converted into a vast mausoleum by the national calamity. You know that a *vulgar* woman appears a lady *in mourning*; and that a lady is never so elegant as when in black. Something of the same effect has been produced on our superb, but bizarre and inharmonious, city. It looks like an immense black and white flower, with leaves and petals spreading grandly and in perfect keeping, to every point of the compass. Such an effect I never saw, or dreamed of. It is overwhelming, sombre, sublime. Just the same feeling, of the spirit of which all of this is the outward symbol, flows like a mighty river through the hearts of the million. It can never be changed or lessened.[34]

To see the transformation of the city in terms of the sublime, and to see the sublime being produced by and through grief, is to suggest the massiveness and the significance of the occasion, as well as the self-consciousness of figures, such as Stedman who had no doubt about the gravity and possibility of the event that had overcome them. The language of the feminized, widowed city made transcendent by the apparatus of mourning further eclipsed the proper role of Mary Todd Lincoln who became insignificant within the context of such monumental sorrow. The language of the sublime, used by Stedman as a way of best articulating the effect of Lincoln's death on the mourning city, was one currently used for thinking about cemeteries in a connected context.

The sublime was frequently invoked in influential ways in relation to death and the treatment of the body, specifically in relation to the rural cemetery movement. Here it was often a Burkean definition of the sublime that was invoked. On occasion, this was strikingly like the language used for the "vast mausoleum" of Washington, DC. William Saunders, the planner of the Gettysburg Cemetery, described the qualities of the planned cemetery in the following terms:

The prevailing expression of the Cemetery should be that of *simple grandeur*. Simplicity is that element of beauty in a scene that leads gradually from one object to another, in easy harmony, avoiding abrupt contrasts and unexpected features. Grandeur, in this application, is closely allied to solemnity. Solemnity is an attribute of the sublime. The sublime in scenery may be defined as a continuity of extent, the repetition of objects in themselves simple and commonplace. We do not apply this epithet to the scanty tricklings of the brook, but to the collected waters of the ocean. To produce an expression of grandeur, we must avoid intricacy and great variety of parts; more particularly must we refrain from introducing any intermixture of meretricious display or ornament.[35]

The connection between the appropriate absence of "meretricious display or ornament" of Saunders's description echoes Stedman's description of the mourning Washington, DC, transcending vulgarity. The "solemnity" of Saunders's cemetery likewise has its counterpart in the description of Washington, DC, as "somber." The key quality of "harmony," invoked by Saunders to describe the effect cemetery planners must strive for is achieved naturally by the plunging of the "inharmonious" Washington, DC, into mourning. It is as if the city itself has been transformed by the ideals of the rural cemetery; even down to the water metaphors that Stedman uses to describe the mourning city and its people. The massive display of public mourning that followed Lincoln's death was unprecedented in the United States and is still remarkable when reflecting on its full scope.

Lincoln's funeral was a highly choreographed national event. It brought the fact of his assassination into the lives of the public much in the way that television did in the case of John F. Kennedy's assassination in the twentieth century. It showed the ways in which the language of death and mourning was being molded within the period. Such a massive public event was only possible within the context of new technologies of travel, information flow, and developments in the treatment of corpses. Increasingly, new ways of dealing with the dead, and new technologies that emerged in the period, made them increasingly distant from the lives of the living. The funeral of the sixteenth president tells a decisively modern story, one of how the dead could become symbolically significant in highly resonant ways.[36]

His body was embalmed immediately after his death. It was then displayed in the East Room of the White House, which was decorated in somber crepe. A queue more than a mile long and six or seven deep rapidly formed to view the body. The following day a private religious service was held in the same room for some 500 invited guests. The body was then moved to the Capitol where the public again gathered to view it. All the paintings and statues within the rotunda, except for that of George Washington, were covered—implying a direct line of descent between the first and the sixteenth presidents. The relation between the two was further developed after Lincoln's death and effective canonization within American history, a fact celebrated in, among other items, a *carte-de-visite* of 1865 that shows the two men in an embrace as Washington welcomes Lincoln into heaven where he crowns him with a laurel wreath.[37]

A funeral train took Lincoln's body, along with the remains of his son, Willie, north to its final resting-place in Springfield, Illinois, amid scenes of collective grief. Along the way the train was viewed by tens of thousands of people as it passed through urban centers including Philadelphia, New York, and Chicago. The body of the dead president was the focus of a series of ceremonies.[38] The places that the funeral train passed through on Lincoln's long final journey were transformed as people came out to pay their respects to the assassinated president. His body, always striking even in life, became the focus for intense public attention and scrutiny. It was as if, in some macabre way, in glimpsing the dead man, the public would share in the events that had taken over the nation in a more personal and profound way than might otherwise be possible.

After a war in which the bodies of fathers, brothers, sons, and friends had been spectacularly and brutally effaced, the embalmed and publicly displayed body of the dead president offered the chance for Northerners to mourn a concrete substitute for those who had died. Here was a body that could be shown to the people in a whole form: it could be brought to them so that they could come out of their homes and pay their respects.

The problem of how the dead president could become a truly national symbol was not fully overcome. Taking his body to Southern states was out of the question given the sentiments of some Southerners and the suspicion of Northerners. Yet a compromise was arrived at by the federal government, which aimed for a "symbolic rehabilitation of the entire nation through a westward tour in the North."[39] The return of the body to its place of origin was a fantasy that many families of soldiers were denied but desperately sought. The hideous state of many of the key battlefields can be suggested by Garry Wills's vivid description of the aftermath of Gettysburg, where

> thousands of fermenting bodies, with gas-distended bellies, [were] deliquescing in the July heat. . . . Eight thousand human bodies were scattered over, or (barely) under, the ground. Suffocating teams of soldiers, Confederate prisoners, and dragooned civilians slid the bodies beneath a minimal covering, as fast as possible. . . . It was work to be done hugger-mugger or not at all, fighting clustered bluebottle flies black on the earth, shoveling and retching by turns.[40]

Within a very short period, desperate relatives began to uncover these hastily disposed of bodies looking for their own beloved dead, and the battlefield began sprouting a hideous harvest of decomposing heads and limbs as they emerged from the earth.[41]

Walt Whitman repeatedly described the bloody scenes of battle-fields and the sheer numbers of the dead in *Specimen Days* (1882) in passages that emphasized the vivid visual and olfactory oppressiveness of the war. In a frequently quoted passage, he writes,

> The dead in this war—there they lie, strewing the fields and woods and valleys and battle-fields of the south—Virginia, the Peninsula—Malvern hill and Fair Oaks—the banks of the Chickahominy—the terraces of Fredericksburgh—Antietam bridge—the grisly ravines of the Manassas—the bloody promenade of the Wilderness—the varieties of the *strayed* dead, (the estimate of the War department is 25,000 national soldiers kill'd in battle and never buried at all, 5,000 drown'd—15,000 inhumed by strangers, or on the march in haste, in hitherto unfound localities—2,000 graves cover'd by sand and mud by Mississippi freshets, 3,000 carried away by caving-in of banks, &c.,)—Gettysburgh, the West, Southwest—Vicksburg—Chattanooga—the trenches of Petersburgh—the numberless battles, camps, hospitals everywhere—the crop reap'd by the mighty reapers, typhoid, dystentery, inflammations—and blackest and loathsomest of all, the dead and living burial-pits, the prison-pens of Andersonville, Salisbury, Belle-Isle, &c., (not Dante's pictured hell and all its woes, its degradations, filthy torments , excell'd those prisons)—the dead, the dead, the dead, our dead—or South or North, ours all, (all, all, all, finally, dear to me)—or East or West—Atlantic coast or Mississippi valley—somewhere they crawl'd to die, alone, in bushes, low gullies, or on the sides of hills—(there, in secluded spots, their skeletons, bleache'd bones, tufts of hair, buttons, fragments of clothing, are occasionally found yet)—our young men once so handsome and so joyous, taken from us—the son from the mother, the husband from the wife, the dear friend from the dear friend—the clusters of camp graves.[42]

Whitman's extraordinary, loaded and cumulative prose, with its repetition of the word "dead," finishes in a reflection of the anonymous character of many of the dead men, "And everywhere among these countless graves—everywhere in the many soldier Cemeteries of the Nation . . . we see, and ages yet may see, on monuments and gravestones, singly or in masses, to thousands or tens of thousands, the significant word Unknown."[43]

The fact of anonymous death, the lack of recognition of the body, the fragmentation of the body that becomes merely bits of bones "tufts of hair" and remnants of clothing, is always a central fact of warfare. But, as Benedict Anderson has argued, the commemorative possibilities associated with the unknown dead are a peculiarly modern phenomenon. The development of public memorials to celebrate Unknown Soldiers was, he argued, without precedent.[44] Since the tombs of Unknown Soldiers are deliberately constructed around the fact of anonymity, they therefore gesture to ideological inclusiveness. As he puts it, "void as these tombs are of identifiable mortal remains or immortal souls, they are nonetheless saturated with ghostly *national* imaginings."[45]

Further, though, he suggests that the developments of national and religious imaginaries are closely proximate not least because of their shared engagement with ideas of death.[46] Certainly, the function of Lincoln's elaborate funeral procession was closely tied in with the ideological processes of constructing a unified nation out of one recently torn by civil war. Here was a figure whose potential for creating a revitalized national consciousness was due not to his anonymity but to his very familiarity, even to the idiosyncratic body shape that made him a powerful physical icon. Many of the extant photographs of Lincoln show him towering above a group of men— soldiers or political allies—his physical height, augmented by his hat, suggesting that he literally occupied a different realm to those around him. At the same time, his biography suggested that he was simultaneously just like them.

This possibility of belonging to two positions simultaneously was something that spiritualist séances also capitalized on. Spirits, including that of Lincoln, were recognizably like those to whom they appeared, and this gave solace and hope to those who came to see or hear them. At the same time they had access to knowledge and places outside the experience of the bereaved and this maintained a degree of distance that the séance repeatedly seemed to undo. This powerfully conflicting message of affinity and difference often drew believers in and kept them engaged with the possibilities of spiritualism.

The realities of dealing with wartime dead had provided a massive challenge to antebellum religious beliefs about the sanctity of the body and symbolic representation of the soul. Whereas sentimental writers had consistently emphasized the importance of empathy and a personal affective relationship to the scene of death and the dead body in their literary representations of death, those working at the front often argued that distance, impersonality, and rationality rather than emotion were the necessary features of good nursing.

Katherine Prescott Wormeley, who worked with the Sanitary Commission in 1862, suggested that "We are here with health, strength, and *head*. To think or speak of the things we see here would be fatal. No one must come here who cannot put away all feelings. Do all you can and be a machine—that's the way to act; the only way."[47] This appeal to the mechanical coincided with the growth of the funeral industry and the increasing distance between death and the domestic. Whitman's prose is some long way from the mechanical and the rational with its weighty repetitions and its insistence on the impossibility of representing a catastrophic event that nonetheless it gets very close to bringing alive to readers. The death of Lincoln, and the symbolic function of his dead body, allowed for a process of mourning that the grisly and anonymous fates of the unknown rendered highly problematic. It also shows a return to emotion, albeit in a contained, rationalized manner, away from the appeals to the mechanical outlined above.

The image of the assassinated president, whose body decayed visibly during its last journey despite the best attentions of embalmers and undertakers, was very unlike that of the damaged, unrecognized, and unrecognizable corpses of many of the war dead. It was a far cry too from the sentimentalized, idealized, sanitized figure of the saintly female child, Little Eva whose courtly slow demise had the kind of impact in an antebellum era that would not be possible after the war. Beyond a pallor and thinness constructed as a symptom of her sanctity (or incorporeality), she never exhibited any symptoms of bodily decay (or corporeality) before or after her death. While postmortem photographs of children continued to enjoy tremendous popularity, and the deaths of children continued, of course, to be important and moving subjects within literary texts, the certainty with which Stowe writes of Eva's future would not be possible again. Like the postmortem daguerreotypes of children, Eva was frozen in time. The war changed all that, though.

The relative bathos of the death of Beth March in *Little Women*, which takes place after her father's return from the war, provides an interesting contrast to the death of Eva. Alcott writes,

> Seldom, except in books, do the dying utter memorable words, see visions, or depart with beatified countenances; and those who have sped many parting souls know, that to most the end comes as naturally

and simply as sleep. As Beth had hoped, the "tide went out easily";
and in the dark hour before the dawn, on the bosom where she had
drawn her first breath, she quietly drew her last, with no farewell but
one loving look and a little sigh.[48]

The simplicity and quiet of Beth's death differs substantially to the
lengthy stylized death of Eva. The register used by Alcott is some
distance from the sentimental language used by Stowe. The diminution
of the sentimental mode and emphasis on a more practical and
action-based definition of human relations was a key difference between
the two celebrated novels.

Gary Laderman has argued that one aspect of Lincoln's funeral
that is particularly striking is the fact that the symbolism of his dead
body was dependent on its dislocation from the domestic and the
sentimental, in this case represented by his family and particularly his
wife.[49] While she tried to reclaim his body for a private, familial act
of mourning, contemporary politicians and advisors saw it as a
national symbol with crucial meanings at a time of crisis. Yet the
death of Lincoln, like that of Eva, was redolent with a symbolism
that was only too evident to his contemporaries.

The question of appropriate language was central to responses to
Lincoln's death and funeral. The death of Lincoln could not be
envisaged, allayed, or recouped for long by using the language of
sentiment, though it was certainly possible to read aspects of his
death through a sentimental focus. Attempts at this were paralleled
in the efforts made by some Northern Protestant leaders to work
against the prevalent mode of subsuming the individual soldier into
a collective national and world historical focus and instead "a coun-
tervailing tendency to remember, personalize, and glorify the deaths
of single individuals as well." The manner in which this took place
was through "personal accounts of redemptive deaths described in
newspapers, letters and diaries, and songs and poems."[50] Instead, a
different sort of discourse needed to be invoked, one that simultaneously suggested the grandiose as well as the calamitous.

Though the personally catastrophic was well within the realm of
the sentimental (the death of a beloved child, or indeed a soldier,
form obvious examples), a collective catastrophe on such a vast scale
exceeded the discourses available within the sentimental and threatened to overwhelm them. The president had always been associated
with (and often mocked for) his use of a popular vernacular that
blurred the distinctions between his public role as father of the

nation and his status as self-made man.[51] The question of appropriate language had long been associated with him precisely because of the idiosyncrasies of his speech. Yet it was Lincoln himself who had brilliantly demonstrated the ways in which apparently simple language could have a dramatic power and an elegiac and memorializing function in his Gettysburg Address of 1863.

The task of having to invent a language to describe his assassination and legacy was one willingly undertaken by poets, who produced unprecedented numbers of elegies and other forms of commemorative verse in honor of the dead president.[52] Though many of these were indeed sentimental in tone, the most successful—notably Whitman's "When Lilacs Last in the Dooryard Bloom'd" (1865)—worked with a register and language that, though profoundly personal and touched with pathos, set up Lincoln's death within the frame of history and a symbolic apparatus. This took it to new levels of intellectual and emotional understanding as well as historical significance. Newspapers, too, had to find ways of reporting his assassination, having spent the previous four years reporting the deaths of many nameless soldiers throughout the war period.

"THROUGH ME MANY LONG DUMB VOICES"

Walt Whitman, a self-styled national poet, produced numerous poetic responses to Lincoln's death and in addition gave a commemorative public lecture on nine occasions, between 1879 and 1890 in New York, Philadelphia, Boston, and Camden. Such public commemorations also exist within spiritualist culture—for example, Emma Hardinge Britten's extemporized funeral oration, given as a public performance two days after he was shot. Britten had campaigned for his election during 1864 and lectured on "The Coming Man; or The Next President of America" to audiences who may have been more familiar with her as a spiritualist and reformer than as a proselytizer for Lincoln. After the success of her initial lecture, she gave 32 more, in 38 days (many lectures lasting about two hours or more) in a period in which women speakers were regarded with suspicion and hostility.[53]

The first lecture probably provided the basis for the extemporized funeral oration she gave in New York two days after his death. She was keen to explain to those around her, though they were not always willing to believe her, that her public speaking was inspired by spirits, and that she spoke "only as the spirit gave me utterance."[54] Little about the funeral oration gives any evidence of its spiritual origin. Were it not for the fact of Britten's known beliefs, and her comments about her earlier lectures, it would be difficult to identify any aspects of the speech that revealed any spiritualist beliefs at all. The only clue to the idea that it may have had an origin outside of the speaker is the insistence, in the short preface, that the speech was "*entirely extemporaneous.*"[55] The fact of it existing in writing, therefore, is explained in the preface to the published version, in which it is explained that it was "phonographically reported" and has been reproduced due to demand.[56]

Britten's lengthy oration emphasizes the facts of Lincoln's early life and the difficulties of the tasks facing him while in office. Her chief strategy, in considering the political and ideological significance of his death, is to envisage it as a catastrophe confronting the entire nation, rather than just the North. Her method of constructing his assassination in this manner is by first emphasizing her belief in Lincoln's role as a peacemaker and a man of judgment and forgiveness, and second repudiating any notion of his death as being part of a wider political conspiracy. She launches into a series of rhetorical questions in order to assert her sense of a national catastrophe, demanding,

> where is the plea which we can hand down to a candid posterity in exculpation, wholly or partially, of the parricidal act which has robbed the American nation of a father, every American citizen of a friend, factious parties of their most generous judge, a relentless enemy of their best protector, and the whole world of an HONEST MAN? Where is the precedent in history for the insanity which destroys in a nation's preserver a nation's institutions; in a nation's noblest man her brightest jewel; and in the hoar of his noblest recorded acts inflicts on him the blow that recoils in an immortal stain upon a nation's honor?[57]

The repetition of the idea of a nation at this moment of national crisis (albeit in a somewhat incoherent fashion) represents a strategic recognition of the significance of rapidly recuperating an idea of collective grief (even where it did not exist) for the purposes of nation building.

While history tells us that the South's response to Lincoln's death was deeply divided, "men now who sit beneath the southern orange and magnolia and weep for him as we weep" and "southern Rachels" who weep, too, people Britten's account.[58] She may have thought that this fantasy of Southern life with images straight out of popular fiction would appeal to the New Yorkers who came to her oration. She may even have been right. Britten casts the dead president (in words that oddly anticipate the language used for the dead Princess Diana by the British Prime Minister Tony Blair) as "the PEOPLE'S ABRAHAM LINCOLN."[59] Her movement into such nonspecific and democratizing language allows Lincoln, the man she has represented as being emphatically of the people in the details she gives of his life, to be symbolically returned to the people in death.

Given the rumors already emerging at this period, her emphasis on the anti-American character of the perpetrator(s) of the assassination is significant. She states,

> In view of the special infamy which time, circumstance, and person all so fearfully aggravate, permit me here to speak my deep conviction that this act, however fatally we know it is the work of plot and rebellion, still cannot be, for the honor of humanity, the organized act of any great section of the land we call *American*. I cannot believe it the work of South, North, West, the common enemy, or even a foreign foe. The act of a demon scarcely suffices to brand a whole humanity; and we should pause ere long we accept, as conclusive, evidence to show that a knot of inhuman serpents wearing the shape of men, or a coil of conspirators doing the deeds of demons, should represent the country of our birth and manhood. Of this I shall speak more hereafter, but having entered my protest against the belief that an enemy we once called brother, still Americans, and always men, could have wrought the deed that none but Earth's Cains are capable of doing. [sic][60]

It might sound simple-minded to ask why, given the spirit origins of her speech, she did not have special access to some of the facts that puzzled her. Might the spirits be able to tell her who the conspirators (if there were any) were? Britten's desire is to read the assassination as the act of evil that is not available to readings other than ones that cast it as evil. In doing so, she separates such ideas of evil from ideals of American national identity while invoking a notion of national identity predicated on masculinity and the rights of birth. Though this might seem a curious strategy for a woman of British birth to take, it is one that recognizes the affinity in this period between debates about the nation and masculinity.

Certainly it resonates with the account cited in her autobiography of her next encounter with Lincoln, the viewing of his corpse as it lay in the State House in Philadelphia. This casts Lincoln as a tragic and heroic actor in a drama of nation building and preservation based on the history of dead men. It says,

> In that place, where the sires of the American nation had signed the famous instrument which made America a nation; and there with the painted faces of all that nation's heroes, veiled in the drapery of death, face to face with the only uncovered canvas on the walls, which bore the effigy of Washington, "the Father of his country," lay Abraham Lincoln—*its preserver*—dead![61]

Like Britten, Whitman used images of the nation's history to reflect upon Lincoln's life and death in his speech on the dead President. He described first seeing Lincoln in New York in February 1861. Lincoln was on his way to his inauguration in Washington. When he appeared amongst the vast crowd Whitman recollected the "sulky, unbroken silence," that met his appearance.[62] He recounted seeing Lafayette in the same area in 1825 and seeing or hearing of the visits of a range of other eminent men—Andrew Jackson and Kossuth, for instance—who had been met with great cheers and celebrations, very unlike the way in which Lincoln's presence created silence was met. He repeatedly invokes theatrical metaphors to describe Lincoln, at one point noting,

> Lincoln was fond of the theatre. I have myself seen him there several times. I remember thinking how funny it was that He, in some respects, the leading actor in the stormiest drama known to real history's stage, through centuries, should sit there and be so completely interested and absorb'd in those imaginary doings.[63]

The theatrical trope extends into reading Lincoln's assassination as a form of dramatic tragedy whose meanings are intricately woven into the mode in which it took place. Whitman argues that Lincoln's legacy, in terms of the future of the nation, is in the poetic, literary, and dramatic qualities of his death, rather than his presidency or the fact of his death, which allows him to embody nationhood precisely through his death.

For Whitman, death and citizenship, death and nationhood, are mutually constitutive. Lincoln's violent death can be read as being exemplary and even necessary. He writes,

> The final use of the greatest men of a Nation is not with reference to their deeds in themselves, or their direct bearing on their times or

lands. The final use of a heroic-eminent life—especially of a heroic-eminent death—is its indirect filtering into the nation and the race, and to give, often at many removes, but unerringly, color and fibre to the Personalism of the youth and maturity of that age, and all ages, of mankind. Then there is a cement to the whole People, subtler, more underlying, than any thing in written Constitution, or courts or armies—namely, the cement of a first-class tragic incident thoroughly identified with that People, at its head, and for its sake. Strange, (is it not?) that battles, martyrs, blood, even assassination, should so condense—perhaps only really, lastingly condense—a Nationality.[64]

Whitman posits the death of a leader or "the grand deaths of the race—the dramatic deaths of every Nationality" as being central to the construction and maintenance of national identity.[65] This argument might itself be an exemple of Benedict Anderson's claim that diminishing power of systems of religious belief in the eighteenth century brought with it questions of how to find new ways of explaining suffering. He argues that "What then was required was a secular transformation of fatality into continuity, contingency into meaning. As we shall see, few things were (are) better suited to this end than an idea of nation."[66] The readings that both Whitman and Britten produced of Lincoln's death were each posited on its trans-formatory capacity in national terms. Despite the overwhelming problem of his role as the opponent of the South, his birth and child-hood in Kentucky, and his upbringing in Illinois allowed him to some extent to overcome more narrow definitions of his regional allegiances and to be fashioned into a national emblem in death.

Whitman's chosen position as national poet articulating the voices of the disenfranchised allowed him to assume a role close to that of a medium and to use language that suggests the process of possession. When he celebrates the possibility of articulating the words of the disenfranchised in "Song of Myself," his words suggest a powerful fantasy of a kind of possession. He writes,

> Through me the afflatus surging and surging, through me the cur-rent and index. . . .
> Through me many long dumb voices,
> Voices of the interminable generations of prisoners and slaves,
> Voices of the diseas'd and despairing and of thieves and dwarfs,
> Voices of cycles of preparation and accretion,
> And of the threads that connect the stars, and of wombs and of the

father-stuff,
And of the rights of them the others are down upon,
Of the deform'd, trivial, flat, foolish, despised,
Fog in the air, beetles rolling balls of dung.
Through me forbidden voices,
Voices of sexes and lusts, voiced veil'd and I remove the veil,
Voices indecent by me clarified and transfigur'd.[67]

His fantasy of possession and transformation, for all its overtly democratizing language, is also a one of control. Whitman as inspired poet, has a totalizing ability to shape and articulate the experiences of others whose voices are otherwise marginal or ignored. Like a medium, he is a channel for such voices, embodying them and giving them a platform and an audience.

LINCOLN AND THE NATION

Lincoln's death, and the treatment of his body after death, is far from the only example of a death that has had significant impact on public rituals of negotiating with the consequences of mortality. Other prominent examples include British royalty, such as Prince Albert and Princess Diana, as well as political icons, such as Eva Perón, Martin Luther King, Jr., and John F. Kennedy.[68] Perón's corpse was embalmed in a process that took six months. Its macabre afterlife, in which it was kidnapped by anti-Perónists for 15 years, shows the significance of her remains, which, according to one scholar, were an example (like Lenin's body and presumably Lincoln's) of "Sacred political immanence."[69] The televised funerals of Kennedy and Martin Luther King, Jr., took the impact of their deaths into those American homes that had access to televisual technology.

Karla Holloway has noted that though these funerals were represented as occasions of national mourning, that of King (like that of political figures such as Supreme Court Justice Thurgood Marshall and Commerce Secretary Ron Brown) "did not lose their black specificity, which was apparent in the music (including the 'Negro National Anthem' and 'Lift Every Voice and Sing') and the lengthy orations."[70] While their bodies were available for readings that allowed them to represent the nation state, they subtly resisted being read only within the contexts of legitimation and continuation. The aural signifiers of songs that signified blackness and a mode of funeral address that refused to be constrained by artificial time constraints and instead considered length and detail a form of approbation and respect, in a manner that Holloway argues is associated with black funerary tradition, these occasions spoke to at least two intended audiences.[71] The issue of the extent to which the meanings of death or funerals could be harnessed by one group is interestingly laid open in the cases outlined by Holloway. Likewise, Lincoln's death spoke to and had meanings for, a variety of audiences, as we have seen.

Michael Kearl has argued that it was precisely because of the new dominance of the national ideal and its effect of diminishing other kinds of allegiances and "social groups" that the dead came to have a new significance within the nation state. Bodies can be symbols of their political legitimacy and are available to be harnessed into national discourses, which help resolve the problem of the nation state's increasing control over meanings in the modern era. However the "expanding influence over the final rite of passage" by the nation state created a "'much more problematic relation between political authority and ultimate meaning than had ever been thought before."[72] He writes that

> The resolution of this problem can be found in the symbolic treatment of the dead by political systems. . . . By extending immortality to their citizenry, polities create a sense of continuity with past and future generations while simultaneously addressing the transcendence anxieties of individuals who must have both a sense of uniqueness and a sense of place in the cosmic scheme of things. However . . . tensions between these two functions can emerge, leading either to the extinction or recasting of one's memory, of the dead becoming an antiregime symbol.[73]

Seen in this light, the ways in which spiritualism extended "immortality to its citizenry" by keeping them available to be contacted and engaged with in perpetuity might be read as one response (albeit not one emanating from the political mainstream) to political marginality. Certainly this makes sense in relation to the youth and gender of many of the most celebrated mediums for whom their apparent gifts allowed them access to power normally way outside their sphere of expectation.

We have seen, too, that early on the Shakers involved in the manifestations that characterized a key moment in the history of that movement were largely the young, especially young women. Likewise the Fox sisters and others all found that spiritualism gave them access not just to the spirit world but to other worlds as well, in which politicians, newspaper editors, writers, and others all wanted to hear what they had to say. They recognized that the marginality that would usually have been their lot was radically transformed by having access to spirit messages. While they could have little final control over the ways in which they were read by such figures, the fact that they wanted (and felt they needed) to hear and witness their performances, suggested their power. While Kearl's comments help us to think through the question of what it was that allowed spiritualism to emerge and flourish from the mid-nineteenth century onward, he also shows the ways in which the dead function within political discourse, writing that, "[i]n the United States, political eulogies and the themes of sacrifice and rebirth are central components of civil religion."[74]

Lincoln's dead body was available to be appropriated by figures, including spiritualists, with a range of interests. It was certainly used as a symbol that legitimated the regime at the time. This is one of the ways in which, both before and after his assassination, he is used within Whitman's poetry and also in séances in which he appeared after his death. But what of other, more unruly dead figures who also appear in séances—figures who are not citizens and who tend instead toward disrupting and critiquing the authority of the regime by their presence and sometimes their actions and words? Those ostracized or ignored (or persecuted) by the dominant regime can literally come back to haunt it, reminding Americans that the past is never really over.[75]

CONCLUSION

THE AFTERLIFE OF SPIRITUALISM

The occult, spiritualism, séances, mesmerism, Theosophy, mind cure, Christian Science and New Thought, trance speaking, and a wide range of associated practices were all subjects that received significant attention within the literary culture of the United States from its earliest inception onward. From the uses of Gothic in the late eighteenth century to Modernist explorations of automatic writing in the early twentieth by Gertrude Stein and others, the engagement with forces that seemed to resist rationalist explanations and produce new modes of aesthetic productivity remain a crucial aspect of artistic exploration. Many examples might be given of varied literary practices in the twentieth-century United States that engage with such ideas from T. S. Eliot's Madame Sosostris and the "crowd" of the dead pouring over the River Thames in *The Waste Land* (1922) to the clairvoyant practices of the performance artist and poet Hannah Weiner.[1] Spiritualism, frequently thought of as an esoteric nineteenth-century phenomenon, has a gestation period that precedes its emergence in the mid-century and an afterlife that continues to the present.

Of course, spiritualism was also the subject of many overtly satirical attacks by writers who found a rich source of material in some of the obvious instances of fraud that took place.[2] Such things happened on both sides of the Atlantic. While Harriet Beecher Stowe found a sympathetic interlocutor in Elizabeth Barrett Browning, who shared her interest in spiritualism, Robert Browning's "Mr. Sludge, The Medium" (1864) was a recognizable satire on the infamous and theatrical antics of Daniel Douglas Home, whom Browning despised. The huge number of texts satirizing or otherwise critiquing spiritualism suggests how significant it was as a subject to all kinds of writers.

Some writers produced critiques of spiritualists that placed them at the center of reforming political movements. These could focus on the dangers spiritualism posed to vulnerable young women. George Ellington's book *The Women of New York: Or the Underworld of the Great City* (1869) warns of clairvoyants, astrologers and spiritualists in the lengthy section of his book titled "Wicked Women." (Other chapters under this heading include "Infanticide in the Great Metropolis," "Female Pickpockets and Shoplifters," and "Baby-Farmers.") He traces a common history among the class of "female necromancers" whom he attacks.

> Some have been dressmakers, milliners and even shop-girls, in the early stages of their career in life. Many of them have been Spiritualists, but have been of the scientific class of that very peculiar class of individuals; and their investigations carrying them into scientific studies, and among them the study of astronomy, they have given up their search as to the various "spheres" supposed to exist, and ideas of "spent life," for the more solid, tangible and (supposed to be) practical state of their relation to the events of human life.[3]

His claim that there is a general class of women involved in a range of activities that draw on the occult as well as the supernatural is one that seems to be consistent with other evidence that connects between otherwise unconnected practices. Other critics, particularly men, claimed that there was a direct relation between madness and spiritualism. In a number of celebrated instances on both sides of the Atlantic some men tried to divorce their spiritualist wives on the grounds of insanity.[4] Defenders of spiritualism gave feisty ripostes, such as Eugene Crowell's *Spiritualism and Insanity* (1877).[5]

By attacking spiritualism, some critics extended justifying the limitation of women's freedom to more general conservative critiques of the working class. John Hay's *The Bread-Winners* (1883) uses spiritualism as a way of considering social organization. It contains a range of unflattering references. One description of a public séance describes the crowd who gathered to see the mediums perform as merely out to watch the latest form of popular performance.[6] Hay's suggestion that spiritualism could be merely a form of public entertainment for some, and a form of escapism and opportunity for others, is linked by the consistent voice of patrician scorn with which he treats the subject and those who believe in its possibilities.

Despite Hay's (and his narrator's) disdain, it was not true that spiritualists were only to be found among the working classes who, he suggested, needed to be distracted from mundane and difficult lives. Spiritualists emerged from every part of society, even from those who were perfectly accustomed to what Hay alludes to as the center of cosmopolitan intellectual life: "the opera, the ballet, and the annual Zola."[7] It may not have suited Hay to acknowledge or accept that, however, it remains an undisputable fact. Part of what he found so discomforting about what spiritualism offered was that, beyond the merely false elements of what clearly amounted to charlatan acts, there could often also simultaneously be expressions of popular belief in the possibility of subverting existing structures of power and the desire to do so. Spiritualism often united believers across class and gender lines, like many other forms of belief. While elements of what took place in séances could take the form of the conservative and consolatory, the structures of the séances in which, often young, women were in charge of the way in which events took place challenged conventional expectations. The absence of clear power structures or strict organization within spiritualism was part of what made it very appealing to many practitioners, notably women.

But what Hay's work also reveals is the extent to which spiritualist practice had altered in the decades since it first appeared. His male medium performing before the credulous for financial reward was a very different figure to the young women mediums offering private séances to like-minded people more characteristic of earlier periods. What Hay describes is a form of cheap popular theatrical entertainment, which people paid to go and see. This was a development from the kinds of private séance circles that individuals formed within their own homes at which they sought some kind of contact with dead friends and relatives. Spiritualism encompassed both these (and other) divergent forms.

Hay's use of a motif centered around spiritualism to allow for a critique of contemporary culture is echoed in the work of other writers of fiction. The preoccupation of a number of late nineteenth-century writers with spiritualism and related phenomena is remarkable. It is notable that not only Hamlin Garland, a firm proponent of "veritism," and W.D. Howells, a feisty defender of realism, both wrote fiction on the subject of spiritualism. Garland's longstanding interest and involvement in psychical research is well known. His novel *The Shadow Land* (1908), unpublished last novel *The Mystery of the Buried Crosses* (1939), and memoir *Forty Years of Psychical Research* (1936) might all be read as evidence of a merely personal interest were it not for the fact that so many other writers were also investigating other worlds.[8] The plot of Howells's 1880 novel *The Undiscovered Country* centers on a spiritualist and the daughter he believes to be a medium. Howells sets his novel in the past, "at a time when the rapid growth of the city was changing the character of many localities," a moment in which spiritualism was in the ascendance.[9] Like much of Howells's work, the novel is set in and around Boston.

Six years after *The Undiscovered Country* came out, one of the most celebrated fictional critiques of spiritualism was published. Henry James's *The Bostonians* takes a satirical and coolly critical look at the power struggle dominating the United States following the Civil War. The novel is dominated by metaphorical and actual invocations of death—of soldiers of the North and South, of a culture dominated by New England and New York culture—and their haunting legacy. Though many parts of the novel draw explicitly on spiritualist culture and its relation to radical reform, one part of the novel that brilliantly suggests more subtle preoccupations comes when Basil Ransom and Verena Tarrant visit the Harvard Memorial Hall. James writes of Ransom's expectations before he enters the building that "Basil Ransom had heard of the great Memorial Hall; he knew what memories it enshrined, and the worst that he should have to suffer there."[10] Nonetheless at the end of a chapter spent surrounded by memories of the Civil War dead, he seems ill prepared for the unhappiness he experiences at the uncertainties in his future with Verena. James reveals, through the ill-matched relationship of Basil and Verena, the uneasy future of a nation that has not come to terms with its radical, yet profoundly flawed and problematic past.

At a less explicit level, recent critics have argued that accounts of psychical investigation, encounters with spirits, and spirit photography may have influenced James's aesthetic and political transformation of the ghost story in a tale such as "The Turn of the Screw" (1898). Both James and Howells had fathers who were careful readers of the Swedish mystic Emmanuel Swedenborg (James's elder brother William was of course one of the foremost American investigators of psychic phenomena) and their mutual interest in writing about spiritualism emerged out of a recognition of the complexities of religious belief and social practice in the new nation.[11]

By the late nineteenth century and early twentieth century it was not just spiritualism that interested writers, but new systems of thought—notably New Thought, Christian Science, and Theosophy. Spiritualism no longer had the novelty value or power it had once possessed. It remained (and remains) a significant set of practices as the sales figures for popular books by mediums continue to demonstrate. Yet writers began to be absorbed by new kinds of systems of belief and by new ways of writing about spiritualism once the many satirical attacks had their inevitable effect. In a passage that emulates Henry James' famous list of what was absent from American life, William Leach writes,

> Mind cure produced new religious ideas and groups—for example New Thought, Unity, Christian Science, and theosophy. As a general spiritual mentality, it was wish-oriented, optimistic, sunny, the epitome of cheer and self-confidence, and completely lacking in anything resembling a tragic view of life. In mind cure there was no darkness, no Melville or Hawthorne, no secrets, no sin or evil, nothing grim or untidy, only the safe shore and "the sunlight of health," in one mind-curer's words.[12]

This was indeed a far cry from the doubt and despair of earlier U.S. writers. Figures such as Eleanor Porter, through her celebrated protagonist Pollyanna, invited readers to play the "glad game" and use the power of positive thinking to change the conditions of their lives. Louisa May Alcott wrote detailed accounts of her attempts to rid herself of headaches by a form of what she alternately and inconsistently referred to as "mind cure" and "mesmerism." She even appropriated the language of spiritualists to describe one encounter with the woman who attempted the cures as a "séance."[13] Alcott's father had also been drawn to Christian Science, corresponded with Mary Baker Eddy, and began a study of the new movement.[14] Theodore Dreiser, Willa Cather, L. Frank Baum, Eleanor Porter, and others were all interested in the promises offered by Christian Scientists and similar groups.[15]

Mark Twain found spiritualism a ready source for satire, though his relationship to it was complicated. He went on to write about

Christian Science, a subject with which his relationship was equally complex, in "The Secret History of Eddypus, the World-Empire" (1901–1902) and *Christian Science* (1907).[16] Christian Science had become, briefly, the subject of international notoriety after the death of the novelist and journalist Harold Frederic in 1898. His lover and a Christian Science healer were accused of manslaughter, in a case covered salaciously by the international press.[17] The founder of Christian Science, Mary Baker Eddy, had been involved in spiritualism, mesmerism, and faith-healing early in her career. She came under the influence of Phineas Quimby, who had himself become interested in mesmerism after attending a lecture by Robert Collyer in 1838. Eddy went on to repudiate much of her engagement with both spiritualism and mesmerism, yet the connections between such beliefs and Christian Science are apparent.

Willa Cather and Georgine Milmine jointly wrote *The Life of Mary Baker Eddy and the History of Christian Science* (1909). The book partly focused on the extraordinarily forceful persona who had forged a system of beliefs that captured the contemporary imagination in an era of change. It was serialized the same year as Mark Twain's book on Eddy.[18] Ella Wheeler Wilcox, whose poetry sold in enormous numbers in her lifetime, was engaged by a set of beliefs propounded by another vivid and dominant woman, Helena Blavatsky. Wilcox became an avid theosophist. She wrote extensively about her early interest in psychic phenomena, experience of automatic writing, experiments in spiritualism, and encounters with spirit photography in her autobiography *The Worlds and I* (1918). Though she explicitly moved from her early interest in spiritualism to a more developed relationship to theosophical beliefs, her autobiography consistently articulated the idea (central to both) of unmediated relationships between the living and other worlds.[19] Though the high point of spiritualism was well over by the turn into the twentieth century, its legacy in the consciousness of twentieth century writers still lived on. Writers such as Jack London and Djuna Barnes acknowledged its influence on them.[20]

But quite apart from the individuals listed above whose works were not usually read in terms of an engagement with spiritualism, a number of nineteenth-century writers can only be considered in that light. These were figures who saw themselves as producing literature that came directly from the world of spirits. They claimed to reproduce material revealed to them from higher sources. The work of such writers varies enormously in quality (and quantity), but it is a part of the literature and the legacy of spiritualism and suggests the more quirky and esoteric aspect of spiritualist belief. Many writers, including Twain and Poe, were credited with continuing their writing careers after their deaths. Poe was particularly active in the spirit world, producing, through the medium Lizzie Doten, poems that appeared as *Poems from the Inner Life* (1862).[21]

Figures who were not themselves writers but believed themselves to have special access to them also tried to publicize posthumous work from the spirits of the celebrated dead. Grace Crane, mother of the poet Hart Crane, tried to publish the "Posthumous Works," which his spirit dictated to her after his suicide in 1932.[22] Sarah Helen Whitman, Poe's former fiancée claimed that he dictated poetry to her from the spirit world.[23] Achsha Sprague wrote a number of poems following her conversion to spiritualism, one of which—her long account of an illness and its cure (by angels), "The Angel's Visit"—is an interesting work of spiritual conversion and literature.[24] As these and other examples will demonstrate, spiritualists were keen to show that spirits still engaged with the world of the living and could maintain important roles.[25]

Spiritualists brilliantly adapted themselves to contemporary culture and to what they perceived as a justified longing to continue communicating beyond the grave. Spiritualism became a trope within U.S. culture that frequently found ample expression within literary texts, as the brief survey over the last few pages demonstrates. It gained more followers at times of crisis, such as war, and maintained itself by mutating into new forms. It appropriated available technologies, finding, in the existing spectral metaphors used to explain them, ways of exploiting and explaining its own presence and processes. Its numbers expanded and declined with regularity, but it has proved itself remarkably tenacious and adaptable. It might be true to say then, that for spiritualism itself, there is no death.

NOTES

INTRODUCTION

1. Mark Twain, "Among the Spirits" (1866) in *The Complete Humorous Sketches and Tales of Mark Twain*, ed. Charles Neider (New York: Doubleday, 1961), 66–67.
2. Ann Douglas, *Terrible Honesty: Mongrel Manhattan in the 1920s* (London: Papermac, 1995), 154.
3. Shelley Streeby, *American Sensations: Class, Empire, and the Production of Popular Culture* (Berkeley: University of California Press, 2002), 290.
4. Joseph Roach, *Cities of the Dead: Circum-Atlantic Performance* (New York: Columbia University Press, 1996), 4. See also Helen Taylor, "Looking Transatlantically," in *Circling Dixie: Contemporary Southern Culture through a Transatlantic Lens*, (New Brunswick, NJ: Rutgers University Press, 2001), 6–27.
5. Roach, *Cities of the Dead*, 4.
6. She writes that "the adjective 'American' in *American Sensations* indicates both the hemispheric dimensions of . . . imperial activity and the process whereby U.S. Americans appropriated the term 'America' for themselves, a process that was both bolstered and complicated by what I call the 'culture of sensation.'" Streeby, *American Sensations*, 7.
7. Wai Chee Dimock, *Through Other Continents: American Literature Across Deep Time* (Princeton, NJ: Princeton University Press, 2006), 3.
8. Logie Barrow, *Independent Spirits: Spiritualism and English Plebeians, 1850–1910* (London: Routledge, 1986); Alex Owen, *The Darkened Room: Women, Power and Spiritualism in Late Victorian England* (London: Virago, 1989); Ruth Brandon, *The Spritualists: The Passion for the Occult in the Nineteenth and Twentieth Centuries* (London: Weidenfeld and Nicolson, 1983); Philip Hoare, *England's Lost Eden: Adventures in a Victorian Utopia* (London: Fourth Estate, 2005); Roger Luckhurst, *The Invention of Telepathy, 1870–1901* (Oxford: Oxford University Press, 2002); Janet Oppenheim, *The Other World: Spiritualism and Psychical Research in England, 1850–1914* (Cambridge: Cambridge University Press, 1985); Pamela Thurschwell,

Literature, Technology and Magical Thinking, 1880–1920 (Cambridge: Cambridge University Press, 2001); Ann Braude, *Radical Spirits: Spiritualism and Women's Rights in Nineteenth-Century America* (Boston: Beacon, 1989); Bret E. Carroll, *Spiritualism in Antebellum America* (Bloomington: Indiana University Press, 1997); Howard Kerr, *Mediums, Spirit-Rappers and Roaring Radicals: Spiritualism in American Literature, 1850–1900* (Urbana: University of Illinois Press, 1972); R. Laurence Moore, *In Search of White Crows: Spiritualism, Parapsychology, and American Culture* (New York: Oxford University Press, 1977); John J. Kucich, *Ghostly Communication: Cross-Cultural Spiritualism in Nineteenth-Century American Literature* (Hanover, NH: Dartmouth College Press, 2004). Key works on mesmerism include, Robert Darnton, *Mesmerism and the End of the Enlightenment in France* (Cambridge, MA: Harvard University Press, 1968); Robert C. Fuller, *Mesmerism and the Cure of American Souls* (Philadelphia: University of Pennsylvania Press, 1982); Alan Gauld, *A History of Hypnotism* (Cambridge: Cambridge University Press, 1992); Alison Winter, *Mesmerised: Powers of Mind in Victorian Britain* (Chicago: University of Chicago Press, 1998). As this book was going to press, another two significant works were published. The first is Marina Warner's magisterial *Phantasmagoria: Spirit Visions, Metaphors, and Media into the Twenty-first Century* (Oxford: Oxford University Press, 2006). The other is Sarah A. Willburn, *Possessed Victorians: Extra Spheres in Nineteenth-Century Mystical Writings* (Aldershot, England: Ashgate, 2006).

9. Other readings of the Rochester rappings include those by Russ Castronovo, *Necro Citizenship: Death, Eroticism, and the Public Sphere in the Nineteenth-Century United States* (Durham, NC: Duke University Press, 2001), 131–32; and Braude, *Radical Spirits*, especially 10–12 and 19–20.

10. Owen, *Darkened Room*, 42, 48.

11. Braude, *Radical Spirits*, 27.

12. See Lisa A. Long, "'The Corporeality of Heaven': Rehabilitating the Civil War Body in *The Gates Ajar*," *American Literature* 69, no. 4 (December 1997), 781–811.

13. Braude, *Radical Spirits*, 25. For more details of the spread of spiritualism see Geoffrey K. Nelson, *Spiritualism and Society* (London: Routledge, 1969), 3–18.

14. On the cultures of performance and rhetoric in revolutionary America see Jay Fliegelman, *Declaring Independence: Jefferson, Natural Language, and the Culture of Performance* (Stanford, CA: Stanford University Press, 1993).

15. For more on social and cultural practices and their relation to death see Douglas J. Davies, *Death, Ritual and Belief: The Rhetoric of Funerary Rites* (London: Cassell, 1997), especially 1–22; Michael Kearl, *Endings: A Sociology of Death and Dying* (New York: Oxford University Press,

1989); Phillipe Ariès, *The Hour of Our Death*, trans. Helen Weaver (London: Allen Lane, 1981). For a more historical account of death in America see Gary Laderman, *The Sacred Remains: American Attitudes to death, 1799–1883* (New Haven, CT: Yale University Press, 1996). For a theorized account of representing the dead and dying body in contemporary culture, see Laura E. Tanner, *Lost Bodies: Inhabiting the Borders of Life and Death* (Ithaca, NY: Cornell University Press, 2006).

16. Mary Louise Pratt, *Imperial Eyes: Travel Writing and Transculturation* (London: Routledge, 1992), 6.

17. They can certainly be traced within contemporary U.S. culture, which has recently experienced what Jeffrey Weinstock has called a "spectral turn." Jeffrey Andrew Weinstock, ed., *Spectral America: Phantoms and the National Imagination* (Madison: University of Wisconsin Press, 2004), 5. He writes that "Millennial specters ask us to what extent we can move forward into a new millennium when we are still shackled to a past that haunts us and that we have to face and mourn fully." Ibid., 6.

18. Benedict Anderson, *Imagined Communities: Reflections on the Origin and Spread of Nationalism*, rev. ed. (London: Verso, 1991), 198.

19. Ibid., 199. Emphasis original.

20. For more on the relationship between African Americans, spiritualism, and literary culture see Akasha (Gloria) Hull, "Channeling the Ancestral Muse: Lucille Clifton and Dolores Kendrick," in *Female Subjects in Black and White: Race, Psychoanalysis, Feminism*, ed. Elizabeth Abel, Barbara Christian, and Helene Moglen (Berkeley: University of California Press, 1997), 330–48; and Carolyn Martin Shaw, "The Poetics of Identity: Questioning Spiritualism in African American Contexts," in Abel, Christian, and Moglen, eds., *Female Subjects*, 349–62.

21. See Lynn Wardley, "Relic, Fetish, Femmage: The Aesthetics of Sentiment in the Work of Stowe," in *The Culture of Sentiment: Race, Gender, and Sentimentality in Nineteenth-Century America*, ed. Shirley Samuels, 203–20 (New York: Oxford University Press, 1992), 204. Wardley notes that "Mecha Sobel's examination of black and white values in eighteenth-century Virginia demonstrates that it is a surviving West African perception of death as a homecoming and heaven as a home, that by the end of the century becomes 'an American expectation.'" See also Timothy E. Fulop and Albert J. Raboteau, eds., *African-American Religion: Interpretive Essays in History and Culture* (London: Routledge, 1997); George Eaton Simpson, *Black Religions in the New World* (New York: Columbia University Press, 1978.) On black mediumship in the New World (especially the British Caribbean), see Sylvia R. Frey and Betty Wood, *Come Shouting to Zion: African American Protestantism in the American South and British Caribbean to 1830* (Chapel Hill: University of North Carolina Press, 1998), 58–60.

22. For more on this see Renée Bergland, *The National Uncanny: Indian Ghosts and American Subjects* (Hanover, NH: Dartmouth College, 2000), 159–69.

23. There are too many examples of the appearance of Indian spirits in séances to be mentioned in detail. Two examples from that of famous American spiritualist mediums will suffice here. One is the series of séances given by Mrs. J. H. Conant at the meeting rooms of the spiritualist journal *The Banner of Light* over the course of 18 years. Many spirits, including Indians, spoke through her, and a process of signing their names through her by automatic writing confirmed their identities. The issue of literacy seems not to have been considered here. See Allen Putnam, ed., *Spirit Invocations: or, Prayers and Praises* (Boston: Colby and Rich, 1876.) The second is that of the spirit of Ouina who communicated through the celebrated medium Cora L. V. Richmond. Her life story was published as: Cora L. V. Richmond, *Ouina's Canoe and Christmas Offering, Filled with Flowers for the Darlings of the Earth* (Ottumwa, IA: D. M. and N. P. Fox, 1882.) The title page says that it is "Given through her Medium, "Water-Lily.""

24. See, for instance, Florence Marryat, *There Is No Death* (London: Psychic Book Club, 1938), 217–18.

25. Bergland, *National Uncanny*, 3.

26. Ibid., 87, 106.

27. Ibid., 7. Bergland writes that "America was haunted by the ghosts of African American slaves and Indians as well as disenfranchised women and struggling workers. The people who were described and imagined as ghosts were those whose existence challenged developing structures of political and economic power." See also Kucich, Ghostly Communion, 55.

28. Ibid., 187.

29. Eric Lott, *Love and Theft: Blackface Minstrelsy and the American Working Class* (New York: Oxford University Press, 1993), 19. An example of the impact of minstrelsy on a séance can be found in Emma Hardinge Britten, *Autobiography of Emma Hardinge Britten*, ed. Margaret Wilkinson (Manchester: John Heywood, 1900), 120–21.

30. Paul Gilmore, *The Genuine Article: Race, Mass Culture, and American Literary Manhood* (Durham, NC: Duke University Press, 2001), 7.

31. Ibid.

32. Orlando Patterson, *Slavery and Social Death: A Comparative Study* (Cambridge, MA: Harvard University Press, 1982), 5.

33. Sharon Patricia Holland, *Raising the Dead: Readings of Death and (Black) Subjectivity* (Durham, NC: Duke University Press, 2000), 15. Emphasis original.

34. Russ Castronovo, *Necro Citizenship*, 3. In the brilliant reading of the complex relationship between disembodiment, ethnicity, citizenship,

and the supernatural that he gives in chapter 4 of his work, he argues that "Whites, not blacks, have an interest in misrecognizing African Americans as ghosts, as barely historical presences" (152).

35. Amy Kaplan, *The Anarchy of Empire in the Making of U.S. Culture* (Cambridge, MA: Harvard University Press, 2002), 13.

36. Clarke Garrett, *Spirit Possession and Popular Religion: From the Camisards to the Shakers* (Baltimore: Johns Hopkins University Press, 1987), 10. For more on the relation between haunting and performativity see Joshua Gunn, "Mourning Speech: Haunting and the Spectral Voices of Nine Eleven," *Text and Performance Quarterly* 24, no. 2 (April 2004): 91–114.

37. Sheri Weinstein, "Technologies of Vision: Spiritualism and Science in Nineteenth-Century America," in Weinstock, ed., *Spectral America*, 124.

38. Richard Schechner, "From Ritual to Theater and Back," in *Performance Theory*, ed. Schechner (London: Routledge, 2003), 130.

39. Schechner, *Performance Theory*, 130.

40. Roach, *Cities of the Dead*, 2.

41. Ibid., 3. Emphasis original.

42. Susan Castillo, *Performing America: Colonial Encounters in New World Writing, 1500–1786* (London: Routledge, 2006), 10.

43. Terry Castle, *The Female Thermometer: Eighteenth-Century Culture and the Invention of the Uncanny* (Oxford: Oxford University Press, 1995), 17. Emphasis original.

44. I appropriate this from Christine Buci-Glucksman's term "baroque reason." See Christine Buci-Glucksman, *Baroque Reason: The Aesthetics of Modernity*, trans. Patrick Camiller (London: Sage, 1994).

45. Susan Gillman, *Blood Talk: American Race Melodrama and the Culture of the Occult* (Chicago: University of Chicago Press, 2003), 9.

46. Ibid. Emphasis original. On the relationship between secret rituals, the occult and masculinity in the nineteenth-century United States, see Mark C. Carnes, *Secret Ritual and Manhood in Victorian America* (New Haven, CT: Yale University Press, 1989).

47. Castle, *The Apparitional Lesbian: Female Homosexuality and Modern Culture* (New York: Columbia University Press, 1993), 6.

48. The British novelist and spiritualist Florence Marryat gave an example of the spirit of a woman who had died leaving two young children behind appearing to her mother in Boston to give advice on clothing patterns and the hiring of a children's nurse. She cited this as an example of "how much more the American spiritualists regard their departed friends as still forming part of the home circle, and [are] interested in their domestic affairs. . . . She [the spirit] perused the servants' characters as practically as her mother might have done, but said she would

have none of them, and Mrs. Seymour was to wait till she received some more. The right one had not come yet." Marryat, *There Is No Death*, 205.

49. Jon Butler, *Awash in a Sea of Faith: Christianizing the American People* (Cambridge, MA: Harvard University Press, 1990), 241–44.

50. Carroll, *Spiritualism in Antebellum America*, 20.

51. R. Laurence Moore, "Insiders and Outsiders in American Historical Narrative and American History," in *Religion in American History*, ed. Jon Butler and Harry S. Stout, 199–221 (Oxford: Oxford University Press, 1998), 199.

52. X. Theodore Barber, "Phantasmagorical Wonders: The Magic Lantern Ghost Show in Nineteenth-Century America," *Film History* 3 (1989): 82.

53. See Castle, "Phantasmagoria and the Metaphorics of Modern Reverie," in Castle, *Female Thermometer*, 140–67; G. A. Household, ed., *To Catch a Sunbeam: Victorian Reality through the Magic Lantern* (London: Michael Joseph, 1979); Steve Humphries, *Victorian Britain through the Magic Lantern* (London: Sidgwick and Jackson, 1979). One of the most celebrated American spiritualist photographers of the mid-century period was William Mumler. See Fred Gettings, *Ghosts in Photographs: The Extraordinary Story of Spirit Photography* (Montreal: Optimum, 1978); Tom Patterson, *A Hundred Years of Spirit Photography* (London: Regency, 1965); James Coates, *Photographing the Invisible: Practical Studies in Supernormal Photography, Script, and Other Allied Phenomena* (London: L. N. Fowler, 1921); William Mumler, *The Personal Experiences of William H. Mumler in Spirit Photography* (Boston: Colby and Rich, 1875).

54. See, for example, Alison Chapman "'A Poet Never Sees a Ghost': Photography and Trance in Tennyson's *Enoch Arden* and Julia Margaret Cameron's Photography," *Victorian Poetry* 41, no. 1 (Spring 2003): 47–71. See especially, 49–51.

55. Marina Warner, "In the Mind's Eye: Thought-Pictures and Ethereal Presences in the Photography of Julia Margaret Cameron (1815–79)," *archive* (February 2004): 32.

56. Roland Barthes, *Camera Lucida*, trans. Richard Howard (London: Vintage, 2000), 92.

57. Brady's work, cited above, is a good example of this.

58. Peggy Phelan, "Francesca Woodman's Photography: Death and the Image One More Time," *Signs: Journal of Women in Culture and Society* 27, no. 4 (2002): 981–82.

59. Julie Rugg, "From Reason to Regulation: 1760–1850," in *Death in England: An Illustrated History*, ed. Peter C. Jupp and Clare Gittings, 202–29 (Manchester: Manchester University Press, 1999), 209.

60. Pat Jallard, "Victorian Death and Its Decline: 1850–1918," in Jupp and Gittings, eds., *Death in England*, 235.

61. They helped to establish "the photograph as an unimpeachable witness and cornerstone of journalistic claims to objectivity." Jay Ruby, *Secure the Shadow: Death and Photography in America* (Cambridge: Massachusetts Institute of Technology Press, 1995), 13.

62. Cited in Ruby, *Secure the Shadow*, 13–15.

63. Cited in ibid., 58.

64. Many such instances are recorded in Coates, *Photographing the Invisible*.

CHAPTER 1

1. For details of the urban and technological transformation of the late 1840s–1850s see Shelley Streeby, *American Sensations: Class, Empire, and the Production of Popular Culture* (Berkeley: University of California Press, 2002), 10–13.

2. Logie Barrow, *Independent Spirits: Spiritualism and English Plebeians, 1850–1910* (London: Routledge, 1986); Janet Oppenheim, *The Other World: Spiritualism and Psychical Research in England, 1850–1914* (Cambridge: Cambridge University Press, 1985).

3. Oppenheim, *Other World*, 11.

4. Amy Kaplan, *The Anarchy of Empire in the Making of U.S. Culture* (Cambridge, MA: Harvard University Press, 2002), 17. Kaplan writes that "I challenge the way the history of U.S. imperialism has often revolved around a central geographic bifurcation between continental expansion and overseas empire, and the related, yet not identical, division between territorial annexation and deterritorialized forms of global domination."

5. Donald Pease, "The Global Homeland State: Bush's Biopolitical Settlement" *boundary* 2, no. 3 (2003): 4.

6. The term comes from Michael Paul Rogin, *Subversive Genealogy: The Politics and Art of Herman Melville* (Berkeley: University of California Press, 1979), 19.

7. The work of Shelley Streeby and Amy Kaplan is particularly significant. In a key critical move Shelley Streeby argues that she "seeks to trouble the distinction between the 'continental frontier' of 1848 and the 'imperial frontier' of 1898." Andy Doolen's work has taken on the challenges posed by the works of Kaplan, Streeby, and others. See Andy Doolen, *Fugitive Empires: Locating Early American Imperialism* (Minneapolis: University of Minnesota Press, 2005). Bruce Burgett has argued for "the interdependence of the categories 'foreign' and 'domestic' in early debates concerning nationality." Bruce Burgett, *Sentimental Bodies: Sex, Gender, and Citizenship in the Early Republic* (Princeton, NJ: Princeton University Press, 1998), 62.

8. Rogin, *Subversive Genealogy*, 20.
9. Sheri Weinstein, "Technologies of Vision: Spiritualism and Science in Nineteenth-Century America," in *Spectral America: Phantoms and the National Imagination*, ed. Jeffrey Andrew Weinstock (Madison: University of Wisconsin Press, 2004), 127. Weinstein writes, "In arguing that the boundaries between heaven and earth and between life and death are permeable, spiritualism dramatized a general and pervasive American spirit of boundless expansion, a 'manifest destiny' ideology motivating the nation, and especially its technological innovations and sociopolitical agendas, in both the antebellum and postbellum years." Ibid.
10. Alex Owen, *The Darkened Room: Women, Power and Spiritualism in Late Victorian England* (London: Virago, 1989), 19.
11. Ibid. Her profound interest in spiritualism has been amply documented.
12. Owen, *Darkened Room*, 19, letter from Mary Howitt to her husband.
13. *Le Charivari*, June 21, 1853, p. 3. Sarah Meer kindly alerted me to this extraordinary cartoon.
14. Kaplan, *Anarchy of Empire*, 26–27. She cites the work of Thomas Hietala to augment her argument.
15. It is well known that a circle of British and American expatriates in Florence experimented with spiritualism, for example. Harriet Beecher Stowe wrote to her husband of having had meetings with a Mrs. E of Boston while in Florence in 1860 that were of great comfort to her. Though Mrs. E was anxious about calling herself a spiritualist, Beecher Stowe was sure that she was a "very powerful medium" and encouraged her to "try the spirits whether they were of God—to keep close to the Bible and prayer, and then accept whatever came." Annie Fields, ed., *The Life and Letters of Harriet Beecher Stowe* (Cambridge, MA: Houghton Mifflin, 1898), 253. Letter to Calvin Stowe, January 16, 1860. A fair amount of work has been done on groups of spiritualists (especially expatriate groups of spiritualists) outside Britain and the United States.
16. See, for example, Howard Kerr, *Mediums, Spirit-Rappers, and Roaring Radicals: Spiritualism in American Literature, 1850–1900* (Urbana: University of Illinois Press, 1972); R. Laurence Moore, *In Search of White Crows: Spiritualism, Parapsychology, and American Culture* (New York: Oxford University Press, 1977); Bret E. Carroll, *Spiritualism in Antebellum America* (Bloomington: Indiana University Press, 1997). I am indebted to each of these works.
17. James Dunkerley, *Americana: The Americas in the World, around 1850* (London: Verso, 2000), 27.
18. William Verhoeven, ed., *Revolutionary Histories: Transatlantic Cultural Nationalism, 1775–1815* (Basingstoke, England: Palgrave, 2002), 3. Emphasis original.
19. Paul Giles, forward to *Transatlantic Studies*, ed. Will Kaufman and Heidi Slettedahl MacPherson (Oxford: University Press of America,

2000), x. See also Paul Giles, *Transatlantic Insurrections: British Culture and the Formation of American Literature, 1730–1860* (Philadelphia: University of Pennsylvania Press, 2001).

20. Two recent biographies of Woodhull (though several others have also appeared) have details of her interest in spiritualism. See Lois Beechy Underhill, *The Woman Who Ran for President: The Many Lives of Victoria Woodhull* (London: Penguin, 1995); and Barbara Goldsmith, *Other Powers: The Age of Suffrage, Spiritualism, and the Scandalous Victoria Woodhull* (New York: Knopf, 1998).

21. On the transatlantic dimensions of revivalism see Richard Cawardine, *Transatlantic Revivalism: Popular Evangelicalism in Britain and America, 1790–1865* (Westport, CT: Greenwood, 1978); and Ruth H. Bloch, *Visionary Republic: Millennial Themes in American Thought, 1756–1800* (Cambridge: Cambridge University Press, 1985).

22. Ronald E. Shaw, *Erie Water West: A History of the Erie Canal, 1792–1854* (Lexington: University of Kentucky Press, 1966), 11–12.

23. Cited in ibid., 12.

24. Cited in ibid., 13.

25. Ibid., 13.

26. Cited in ibid., 22. Emphasis original.

27. Cited in David Kazanjian, *The Colonizing Trick: National Culture and Imperial Citizenship in Early America* (Minneapolis: University of Minnesota Press, 2003), 42.

28. Among the vessels that followed her on her voyage was the *Noah's Ark*, which "carried an assortment of birds, fishes, insects, two young bears, and two Seneca boys." Shaw, *Erie Water West*, 185. For the relationship between landscape art and imperial ambitions see Tim Barringer, "The Course of Empires: Landscape and Identity in America and Britain, 1820–1880," in *American Sublime: Landscape Painting in the United States 1820–1880*, ed. Andrew Wilton and Tim Barringer, 39–65 (London: Tate Publishing, 2002), 59; Ibid., 58–59.

29. Ibid., 181, 189.

30. Jackson Lears, *Fables of Abundance: A Cultural History of Advertising in America* (New York: Harper Collins, 1994), 64.

31. Ibid., 63–74.

32. See Paul Gilroy, *The Black Atlantic: Modernity and Double Consciousness*, 2nd ed. (London: Verso, 1995), 14.

33. A useful account of the current state of transatlanticist scholarship is Laura M. Stevens, "Transatlanticism Now," *American Literary History* 16, no. 1 (Spring 2004): 93–102.

34. Dickens's *American Notes for General Circulation* was published in 1842, Fanny Trollope's *Domestic Manners of the Americans* in 1832, and Frederick Marryat's *A Diary in America* in 1842.

35. Charles Dickens, *American Notes for General Circulation*, eds. Arnold Goldman and John Whitley (London: Penguin, 1985), 290.

36. Owen, *Darkened Room*, 19.

37. For details see Bret E. Carroll, "The Structure of the Spirit World," *Spiritualism in Antebellum America*, 60–84.

38. Ibid., 35. Also, see chapter 3 "Spiritualist Republicanism," 35–59.

39. On transatlantic spiritualism as progressive and novel, see Edward S. Cutler, *Recovering the New: Transtlantic Roots of Modernism* (Hanover, NH: University Press of New England, 2003), 46–48.

40. Barrow, *Independent Spirits*, 10.

41. These include Ann Braude, Bret E. Carroll, and Russ Castronovo. There is much exciting work to be done to add to the scholarship that already exists, most particularly, in the area of the Black Atlantic, and in the representations and interventions of race within spiritualism.

42. He argues, "I am not so concerned with the origins of spiritualism, then— the Fox sisters in upstate New York, Mrs. W. R. Hayden's first visit to England, Daniel Dunglas Home's incursions into France and Russia—as I am in the cultural appeal and power, the evident meaning, that this movement proved to have." Daniel Cottom, *Abyss of Reason: Cultural Movements, Revelations, and Betrayals* (New York: Oxford University Press, 1991), 13.

43. Ibid., 13.

44. The British actor Fanny Kemble wrote in her memoirs of an occasion in 1850 when the black mesmerist H. E. Lewis put the spiritualist Cathleen Crowe into a trance in which she walked naked into the streets of Edinburgh. See W. D. King, "'Shadow of a Mesmerist': The Female Body on the 'Dark' Stage," *Theatre Journal* 49 (1997): 191.

45. Geoffrey K. Nelson, *Spiritualism and Society* (London: Routledge, 1969), 16–17.

46. Ann Braude, *Radical Spirits: Spiritualism and Women's Rights in Nineteenth-Century America* (Boston: Beacon, 1989), 29–30. She argues that Southern spiritualists were more likely to see themselves as Christians than Northern spiritualists. She writes that they "tended to focus on communication with the dead while ignoring both the reform agenda and the heterodox theology that many believed such communication implied," 30.

47. Braude, *Radical Spirits*, 29–30. The periodicals were *Spiritualiste de la Nouvelle-Orleans* and *Echo-Mensuel* and *La Salut*.

48. Henri Louis Rey, "Communications Spiritualistses, " in *Paroles d'Honneur: Écrits de Créoles de coleur néo-orléanais 1837–1872*, ed. Chris Michaelides,189–210 (Shreveport, LA: Éditions Tintamarre, 2004). Toussaint L'Ouverture is reported as saying:

> Un Roi! C'est un maître tôt ou tard!
> Un pape! C'est le Despote politique et religieux à la fois.

Meure la Tyrannie!
Vive la Liberté!

49. Emma Hardinge Britten, *Autobiography of Emma Hardinge Britten*, ed. Margaret Wilkinson (Manchester: John Heywood, 1900), 145–47.

50. See Angela Jorge, "*Mesa Blanca*: A Puerto Rican Healing Tradition," in *Spirit Versus Scalpel: Traditional Healing and Modern Psychotherapy*, ed. Leonore Loeb Adler and B. Runi Mukherji, 109–20 (Westport, CT: Bergin and Garvey, 1995); and Regina Spires-Robin and Peggy McGarrahan, "The Healing Practices of Mexican Spiritualism," in Adler and Mukherji, eds., *Spirit Versus Scalpel*, 121–35.

51. Margaret McFadden, *Golden Cables of Sympathy: The Transatlantic Sources of Nineteenth-Century Feminism* (Lexington: University Press of Kentucky, 1999), 4.

52. Ibid.

53. Ann Braude has done the most sustained critical work tracing such relationships.

54. Cited in Carroll, *Spiritualism in Antebellum America*, 69. Emphasis original. For further arguments about the significance of the telegraph see, for example, Emma Hardinge [Britten], *Modern American Spiritualism* (New York : n.p., 1869).

55. Carroll, *Spiritualism in Antebellum America*, 69.

56. Ibid., 65–71. Some spiritualists claimed that science in fact borrowed from spiritualism. Writing in 1872, a spiritualist claimed that, in private, scientists "adopt the idioms of Spiritualists, and unwittingly give expression to the fact that they entertain the same convictions as to the existence of spirits, their agency as mediums, and their communion with those in the flesh." Cited in Cottom, *Abyss of Reason*, 35.

57. Cottom, *Abyss of Reason*, 195.

58. Ibid.

59. Ibid., 193–4.

60. Ibid., 195.

61. Ibid., 10–11.

62. Jon Butler, *Awash in a Sea of Faith: Christianizing the American People* (Cambridge, MA: Harvard University Press, 1990), 88.

63. Britten, *Autobiography*, 22–23. For accounts of predictions of Atlantic shipping disasters, see 31–34.

64. Ibid., 22–3. Emphasis original.

65. Gilroy, *Black Atlantic*, 4 and see indexed references. He writes, "Ships immediately focus attention on the middle passage, on the various projects for redemptive return to an African homeland, on the circulation of ideas and activists as well as the movement of key cultural and political artifacts: tracts, books, gramophone records, and choirs."

66. Frederick Marryat, *A Reply to Captain Marryat's Illiberal and Incorrect Statements Relative to the Coloured West Indies, as Published in his Work, Entitled, "A Diary in America"* (London: E. Justins and Son, 1840).

67. See ibid., 3. The claim is made by a figure signed "A Coloured West Indian." For details of Frederick Marryat's life, see David Hannay, *Life of Frederick Marryat* (London: Walter Scott, 1889); and Florence Marryat, *Life and Letters of Captain Marryat* (London: Richard Bentley and Son, 1872). The question of his ancestry is raised in highly coded ways, chiefly through the notion that biographers of Marryat would do well to avoid making unproven assumptions. See, for example, *The Athenaeum*, no. 3212, May 18, 1889, p. 633. Four notes in *Notes and Queries* deal with the issue of which street in Westminster Marryat was born. The attention to this detail and deference to family authority on the subject is not particularly unusual. Yet given the claims made in Grenada it does suggest that there was still a question hanging over Marryat's ancestry. See *Notes and Queries* 7, no. 7 (1889): 9, 74, 177, 294.

68. Gilroy, *Black Atlantic*, 13.

69. See Robert S. Tilton, *Pocahontas: The Evolution of an American Narrative* (Cambridge: Cambridge University Press, 1994); Alden T. Vaughan, "Trinculo's Indian: American Natives in Shakespeare's England" in *"The Tempest" and Its Travels*, ed. Peter Hulme and William H. Sherman, 49–59 (London: Reaktion, 2000); Karen Robertson, "Pocahontas at the Masque," *Signs* (Spring 1996): 551–83.

70. Owen, *Darkened Room*, 57.

71. In 1877 she had been discovered impersonating Pocha in Blackburn and the story was published in the *Blackburn Times*. She defended herself by blaming evil spirits, "Miss Wood, speaking in the voice of the child spirit, 'Pocha,' said that she had been controlled by an evil spirit who 'had all but stripped her naked' and sent her out into the circle." Ibid., 64, 70.

72. Britten, *Autobiography*, 211.

73. Barrow, *Independent Spirits*, 36.

74. Britten, *Autobiography*, 210–12.

CHAPTER 2

1. T. S. Eliot, *Collected Poems, 1909–1962* (London: Faber and Faber, 1963), 55.

2. Nathaniel Hawthorne, *The Scarlet Letter: A Romance* (New York: Penguin, 2003), 28. A cognate argument is made by Jessica Catherine Lieberman in her discussion of nineteenth-century *fugeurs*, notably

Ansel Bourne, the subject of one of William James' investigations that he discussed in *The Principles of Psychology* (1890). She asks, "Does the past disappear? Does it persist? And, if so, in what form? . . . in Bourne's America, answers came framed in an atmosphere of vagabondage and military desertion and of the American interpretation of fugue in a time of popular Spiritualism." Jessica Catherine Lieberman, "Flight from Haunting: Psychogenic Fugue and Nineteenth-Century American Imagination," in *Spectral America: Phantoms and the National Imagination*, ed. Jeffrey Andrew Weinstock, 141–56 (Madison: University of Wisconsin Press, 2004), 143.

3. Leslie A. Fiedler, *Love and Death in the American Novel* (New York: Criterion, 1960), xxi.

4. Julia A. Stern, *The Plight of Feeling: Sympathy and Dissent in the Early American Novel* (Chicago: University of Chicago Press, 1997), 2.

5. Ibid.

6. Russ Castronovo, *Necro Citizenship: Death, Eroticism, and the Public Sphere in the Nineteenth-Century United States* (Durham, NC: Duke University Press, 2001), 10. Emphasis original.

7. Toni Morrison, *Playing in the Dark: Whiteness and the Literary Imagination* (London: Picador, 1993), 35.

8. Andy Doolen, *Fugitive Empire: Locating Early American Imperialism* (Minneapolis: University of Minnesota Press, 2005)., xv, xxi.

9. Ibid, xxi.

10. David Kazanjian, *The Colonizing Trick: National Culture and Imperial Citizenship in Early America* (Minneapolis: University of Minnesota Press, 2003), 156. Maddox has shown that this is a tactic employed by Hawthorne too. See Lucy Maddox, *Removals: Nineteenth-Century American Literature and the Politics of Indian Affairs* (New York: Oxford University Press, 1991), 130.

11. Nathaniel Hawthorne, from his journal for 1837–1840, cited in Maddox, *Removals*, 113.

12. "Literary magazines of the period were filled with programmatic calls for the founding of an authentic American culture derived from Europe, but from 'indigenous'—that is, white settler colonial—sources, thereby turning white colonists into the proper subjects of America and invoking Native Americans only as obstacles or backdrops." Kazanjian, *Colonizing Trick*, 143.

13. Tim Barringer, "The Course of Empires: Landscape and Identity in America and Britain, 1820–1880," in *American Sublime: Landscape Painting in the United States 1820–1880*, ed. Andrew Wilton and Tim Barringer, 39–65 (London: Tate Publishing, 2002), 59.

14. A number of highly significant Americans belonged to Masonic orders, for instance. George Washington and Benjamin Franklin were just two of the best-known and most powerful men to be involved with freemasonry.

For a detailed account of the significance of Masonry within the United States in the nineteenth century see Mark C. Carnes, *Secret Ritual and Manhood in Victorian America* (New Haven, CT: Yale University Press, 1989.) When Washington dedicated the U.S. Capital on September 18, 1793, he wore a Masonic apron and used Masonic symbols to represent the connection between masonry and the Republic. Steven C. Bullock, *Revolutionary Brotherhood: Freemasonry and the Transformation of the American Social Order, 1730–1840* (Chapel Hill: University of North Carolina Press, 1996), 137.

15. Larry Kutchen, "The 'Vulgar Thread of the Canvas': Revolution and the Picturesque in Ann Eliza Bleeker, Crèvecoeur, and Charles Brockden Brown," *Early American Literature* 36, no. 3 (2001): 395–425. Kutchen argues that the American picturesque is "an English Atlantic aesthetic. . . . [W]e see authors and narrators drawing on the aesthetic resources of a truly imperial extension of the idealized English countryside into North America, in search of repose from the disintegrating influences of revolution" (396–97). Another celebrated story, "The Legend of Sleepy Hollow" shows Irving's interest in magical beliefs, fortune telling, witchcraft, and Puritanism.

16. Ralph Waldo Emerson, *Nature and Selected Essays*, ed. Larzer Ziff (New York: Penguin, 2003), 35–36. Karen Sánchez-Eppler provides an illuminating reading of this passage in relation to Emerson's attitudes to mourning and, in particular, a focus on the death of his son, Waldo, in 1842 and Emerson's act of looking into his grave when the child's remains were being moved to the cemetery in Sleepy Hollow. Karen Sánchez-Eppler, "Then When We Clutch Hardest: On the Death of a Child and the Replication of an Image," in *Sentimental Men: Masculinity and the Politics of Affect in American Culture*, ed. Mary Chapman and Glenn Hendler (Berkeley: University of California Press, 1999), 64–85.

17. Ibid., 77.

18. Emerson, *Nature*, 36.

19. Karl Marx, *The Revolutions of 1848: Political Writings: Volume 1*, ed. David Fernbach (London: Penguin, 1993), 67.

20. Jacques Derrida, *Specters of Marx: The State of the Debt, the Work of Mourning, and the New International*, trans. Peggy Kamuf (New York: Routledge, 1994).

21. For Hawthorne's use of the ghostly in *The Scarlet Letter*, see Renée Bergland, *The National Uncanny: Indian Ghosts and American Subjects* (Hanover, NH: Dartmouth College, 2000), 156–58.

22. Hawthorne, *The Scarlet Letter*, 9–10.

23. Edward S. Cutler has written of this, "That Marx would draw upon the stock image of the spiritualist era is . . . doubly relevant—the figure of the dancing table is not merely a helpful analogy for depicting the

phantasmic character of the commodity form of value, it is also a conditional analogy, one that intuitively locates in nineteenth-century spiritualism a peculiar reflection of commodification itself." Edward S. Cutler, *Recovering the New: Transtlantic Roots of Modernism* (Hanover, NH: University Press of New England, 2003), 49.

24. Jon Butler, *Awash in a Sea of Faith: Christianizing the American People* (Cambridge, MA: Harvard University Press, 1990), 228–56. George M. Beard argues that while belief in witchcraft had largely vanished by 1879, many individuals believed in clairvoyance. He writes, "Outside of negroes and spiritualists, there are probably not a thousand persons in this country who have even a lingering fiath in witchcraft; on the other hand, there are probably not a thousand intelligent persons in the country . . . who wuld be willing to state, with absolute positiveness, that clairvoyance and animal magnetism were utter delusions." George M. Beard, "The Delusions of Clairvoyance," *Scribner's Monthly* 18 (May–October 1879): 433.

25. For an account of the relation between late nineteenth-century economic theory and theories of the supernatural see David A. Zimmerman, "Frank Norris, Market Panic, and the Mesmeric Sublime," *American Literature* 75, no. 1 (March 2003): 61–90.

26. Jackson Lears, *Fables of Abundance: A Cultural History of Advertsing in America* (New York: Harper Collins, 1994), 44.

27. Ibid., 44–46.

28. Ann Douglas, *Terrible Honesty: Mongrel Manhattan in the 1920s* (London: Papermac, 1995), 153.

29. For a reading of Hawthorne's story in relation to contemporary daguerreotyping practice see John Stauffer, "Daguerreotyping the National Soul: The Portraits of Southworth and Hawes, 1843–1860," *Prospects: An Annual of American Cultural Studies* 22 (1997): 69–107. Hawthorne's use of visual tropes includes references to the panoramas and the phantasmagoria in *The House of the Seven Gables*.

30. Nathaniel Hawthorne, *The House of the Seven Gables*, ed. Milton R. Stern (New York: Penguin, 1986), 182–83.

31. See, for example, Maddox, *Removals*, 110–30.

32. Margaret Fuller, *Summer on the Lakes, in 1843*, introd. Susan Belasco Smith (Urbana: University of Illinois Press, 1991), 12.

33. Ibid.

34. Ibid.

35. Ibid., 4. Fuller wrote a review of the Norwegian composer and violinist Ole Bornmann Bull in December 1844 who was touring the United States performing pieces, which included his compositions "In Memory of Washington," "The Solitude of the Prairies," and "Niagara." Susan Belasco, "'The Animating Influences of Discord': Margaret Fuller in 1844," *Legacy* 20, no. 1 (2003): 76–93, especially 76, 90. Her

"enthusiastic review" appeared in the *New-York Tribune* on December 20, 1844.

36. W. J. T. Mitchell, cited in Tim Barringer, "Course of Empires," 59. On the relationship between American landscape and national and imperial ambitions see Thomas Patlin, "Exhibitions and Empire: National Parks and the Performance of Manifest Destiny," *Journal of American Culture* 22, no. 1 (Spring 1999): 41–60; and Albert Boime, *The Magisterial Gaze: Manifest Destiny and American Landscape Painting c. 1830–1865* (Washington, DC: Smithsonian Institution Press, 1991).

37. Ibid., 4.

38. Ibid., 3.

39. Such a fear, learned from reading "sensationalist accounts of white homes under savage siege" was shared by Helen Hunt Jackson, author of the Indian reform novel *Ramona* (1884). See John M. Gonzalez, "The Warp of Whiteness: Domesticity and Empire in Helen Hunt Jackson's *Ramona*," *American Literary History* 16, no. 3 (2004): 445.

40. Ibid., 4, 5, 8.

41. Kerner, "The Seeress of Prevorst," *Spiritual Telegraph* 4:122–23. The article concludes that "It may not be improper to say, in this connection, that Kerner's biography of the Seeress of Prevorst is for sale at this office, and may be read with interest and profit by all who are engaged in the investigation of spiritual subjects. The Seeress died upward of twenty years ago, and consequently long before the recent and more general unfolding of Spiritualism had its origin."

42. Ibid., 78.

43. Ibid., 77–78.

44. Ibid., 120, 121.

45. Ibid., 102.

46. For more on this see Annette Kolodny, "Margaret Fuller's First Depiction of Indians and the Limits on Social Protest: An Exercise in Women's Studies Pedagogy," *Legacy* 18, no. 1 (2001): 1–20.

47. Robert C. Fuller, *Mesmerism and the Cure of American Souls* (Philadelphia: University of Pennsylvania Press, 1982), 10–11. See also Robert Darnton, *Mesmerism and the End of the Enlightenment in France* (Cambridge, MA: Harvard University Press, 1968), 58.

48. See Darnton, *Mesmerism*, 68–71.

49. Fuller, *Mesmerism*, 12.

50. Ibid.

51. For more on *Trilby* and the use of mesmerism as a literary device see Daniel Pick, *Svengali's Web: the Alien Enchanter in Modern Culture* (New Haven, CT: Yale University Press, 2000).

52. Derek Forrest, *Hypnotism: A History* (London: Penguin), 37.

53. Darnton, *Mesmerism*, 75–77.

54. Forrest, *Hypnotism*, 35.

55. Cited in Alan Gauld, *History of Hypnotism* (Cambridge: Cambridge University Press, 1992), 4.
56. Cited in Darnton, *Mesmerism*, 88–89.
57. Forrest, *Hypnotism*, 37–38.
58. Darnton, *Mesmerism*, 23.
59. Ibid., 44.
60. Fuller, *Mesmerism*, 15. He argues that this characterizes the United States in the first five decades of the nineteenth century.
61. See Darnton, *Mesmerism*, 62–66.
62. Fuller, *Mesmerism*, 16–17.
63. Cited in Darnton, *Mesmerism*, 65–66.
64. See Darnton, *Mesmerism*, 67, 68. On page 71 he writes that "By 1789 this eclectic, spiritualist form of mesmerism, the form that was to be revived in the nineteenth century, had spread throughout Europe."
65. Louis Gottschalk, *Lafayette between the American and French Revolution (1783–1789)* (Chicago: University of Chicago Press, 1950), 101. Undoubtedly this was a reference to Franklin's "Remarks on the Savages of North America" published the same year.
66. X. Theodore Barber, "Phantasmagorical Wonders: The Magic Lantern Ghost Show in Nineteenth-Century America," *Film History* 3 (1989): 78.
67. Ibid., 78.
68. Richard D. Altick, *The Shows of London* (Cambridge, MA: Harvard University Press, 1978), 217.
69. Ibid., 117. See also 46.
70. Cited in Terry Castle, *The Female Thermometer: Eighteenth-Century Culture and the Invention of the Uncanny* (New York: Oxford University Press, 1995), 149.
71. It continues, "A young fop asked to see the apparition of a woman he had tenderly loved, and showed her portrait in miniature to the phantasmagorian, who threw on the brazier some sparrow feathers, a few grains of phosphorus and a dozen butterflies. Soon a woman became visible, with breast uncovered and floating hair, gazing upon her young friend with a sad and melancholy smile. A grave man, seated next to me, cried out, raising his hand to his brow: 'Heavens! I think that's my wife'; and ran off, not believing it to be a phantom any more." Armand Poutier, *L'Ami des lois,* 8 Germinal Year VI (March 28, 1798), cited in Castle, *Female Thermometer,* 147–48. The Jacobin Jean-Paul Marat was murdered in his bathtub by Charlotte Corday in 1793.
72. John Barnes, "The History of the Magic Lantern," in *Servants of Light: The Book of the Lantern,* ed. Dennis Crompton, Richard Franklin, and Stephen Herbert, 8–33 (Ripon: Magic Lantern Society, 1997), 30.
73. Cited in ibid., 30.
74. *European Magazine* 43 (1803): 186–88. Cited in Altick, *Shows of London,* 218.

75. Barber, "Phantasmagorical Wonders," 80–81.

76. Ibid., 81.

77. Ibid., 82.

78. Ibid.

79. See *Reynolds Newspaper* (London), December 19, 1895, p. 8; and Jann Pasler, cited in Davinia Caddy, "Variations on the Dance of the Seven Veils," *Cambridge Opera Journal* 17 (2005): 37–58, 140. Catherine Pedley-Hindson kindly pointed this out to me.

80. Castle, *Female Thermometer*, 155. For detail of the writers referred to here see 155–59. Many writers had first-hand experience of such performances. Harriet Martineau visited a phantasmagoria show and found it very alarming. See Steve Humphries, *Victorian Britain through the Magic Lantern* (London: Sidgwick and Jackson, 1979), 16.

81. She writes, "The entire Rowena/Ligeia transformation is very much like the phantasmagorical effect known as the transmutation, achieved by shifting two magic-lantern slides together." Castle, *Female Thermometer*, 161.

82. A powerful account of Poe's engagement with the bodies of dead women can be found in chapter 4, "The most 'poetic' topic" in Elisabeth Bronfen, *Over Her Dead Body: Death, Femininity and the Aesthetic* (Manchester: Manchester University Press, 1992), 59–75.

83. Edgar Allan Poe, *The Science Fiction of Edgar Allan Poe*, ed. Harold Beaver (London: Penguin, 1976), xv.

84. See, for example, Eliza Richards, "Lyric Telegraphy: Women Spirits, Spiritualist Poetics and the 'Phantom Voice' of Poe," *The Yale Journal of Criticism* 12, no. 2 (1999): 269–94; and Shawn James Rosenheim, *The Cryptographic Imagination: Secret Writing from Edgar Poe to the Internet* (Baltimore: Johns Hopkins University Press, 1997).

85. Fuller, *Mesmerism*, 15.

86. Ibid., 20. Details of the tour are taken from 18–21.

87. Fuller, *Mesmerism*, 26–28. Collyer writes of this in his autobiography *Lights and Shadows of American Life* (Boston: Brainard, 1843).

88. Ibid. Again it is Harold Beaver who makes this point with particular acuteness when he notes that, "The doctrines of Swedenborg, Lavater and Saint-Martin now grew intellectually fashionable. Had not natural forces been harnessed? So too would supernatural. Progress, Democracy, Manifest Destiny, were the cry of the day. All things physical and metaphysical, would be annexed—like Texas, Cuba, Mexico—to the American Dream. Father Miller and Prophet Joseph Smith, Mormons and Second Adventists, vied with each other for disciples. Mysticism, spiritualism, hypnotism, mesmeric trances, galvanic resuscitation, phrenology, flourished. In 1849, with a greedy rush, Eldorado itself was besieged." Beaver, *Science Fiction*, ix.

89. A detailed account of Hawthorne's use of mesmerism can be found in Samuel Chase Coale, *Mesmerism and Hawthorne: Mediums of an American Romance* (Tuscaloosa: University of Alabama Press, 1998).

90. Nathaniel Hawthorne, *The Blithedale Romance*, ed. Tony Tanner (Oxford: Oxford University Press, 1998), 5.

CHAPTER 3

1. Emma Hardinge Britten, *Autobiography of Emma Hardinge Britten*, ed. Margaret Wilkinson (Manchester: John Heywood, 1900), 59. Emphasis original .
2. Ibid., 60.
3. Ibid., 61.
4. Garrett appropriates a term used originally to describe spirit possession in the south of France in the seventeenth century. Clarke Garrett, *Spirit Possession and Popular Religion: From the Camisards to the Shakers* (Baltimore: Johns Hopkins University Press, 1987), 5.
5. Philip J. Deloria, *Playing Indian* (New Haven, CT: Yale University Press, 1998); Laura Browder, *Slippery Characters: Ethnic Impersonators and American Identities* (Chapel Hill: University of North Carolina Press, 2000).
6. Garrett, *Spirit Possession*, 4.
7. Ibid., 4–5.
8. Ibid., 5.
9. See Alex Owen, *The Darkened Room: Women, Power and Spiritualism in Late Victorian England* (London: Virago, 1989), 227.
10. At the London trial of the American medium Susan Willis Fletcher, for example, a house decorator explained how he had helped to fake certain spectral effects within séances. When he accidentally trod on some matches during a séance, he was revealed to the séance-goers and thought that he had been caught out. Instead he was claimed as a relative by one of the women present, and so escaped detection. "Charges against a Spiritualist," *Times* (London), January 29, 1881, p. 10.
11. See, for example, the arrangements as outlined in the diagram of a séance in Mrs. Mould, *Miss Wood in Derbyshire: A Series of Experimental Seances* (London: J. Burns, 1879), 36.
12. Owen, *Darkened Room*, 54–5. Victoria Woodhull pursued an acting career before her involvement with spiritualism, and Britten was already involved in acting long before she thought of becoming a medium.
13. Caroline Levander's (otherwise wide-ranging) book on the female public voice in nineteenth-century America fails to mention this important aspect of female oratory. See Caroline Field Levander, *Voices of the Nation: Women and Public Speech in Nineteenth-Century American Literature and Culture* (Cambridge: Cambridge University Press, 1998).

14. The best account of the relation between political activism and spiritualism is Ann Braude's *Radical Spirits: Spiritualism and Women's Rights in Nineteenth-Century America* (Boston: Beacon, 1989).

15. Henry James, *The Bostonians*, ed. Charles R. Anderson (London: Penguin, 1986), 83–84.

16. On Henry Irving's burlesque of the Davenport Brothers see Helen Nicholson "Henry Irving and the Staging of Spiritualism," *New Theatre Quarterly* 16, no. 3 (August 2000): 278–87. For more detail on Houdini's interest in spiritualism see Ruth Brandon, *The Life and Many Deaths of Harry Houdini* (London: Secker and Warburg, 1993.)

17. See Owen, *Darkened Room*, 64–65, 73.

18. Charles Nordhoff, *American Utopias* (Stockbridge, MA: Berkshire House, 1993), 118. Originally published in 1875 as *The Communistic Societies of the United States.*

19. Ibid., 250–51. See also 134.

20. Julia A. Stern, *Plight of Feeling: Sympathy and Dissent in the Early American Novel* (Chicago: University of Chicago Press, 1997), 5. Emphasis original.

21. See Stephen J. Stein, *The Shaker Experience in America: A History of the United Society of Believers* (New Haven, CT: Yale University Press, 1992), 184–89. Stein notes that "the ultimate step in the effort to control the gifts came when members of the central ministry and other society leaders began to receive spirit communications themselves" (186). For extensive detailing of the experiences of spiritual gifts by other religious groups see Garrett, *Spirit Possession.*

22. Stein, *Shaker Experience*, 174

23. See ibid ., 165–200; and Edward Deming Andrews, *The People Called Shakers: A Search for the Perfect Society* (New York: Dover, 1963), 152–76.

24. Jon Butler, *Awash in a Sea of Faith: Christianizing the American People* (Cambridge, MA: Harvard University Press, 1990), 226.

25. Ruth Brandon, *The Spiritualists: The Passion for the Occult in the Nineteenth and Twentieth Centuries* (London: Weidenfeld and Nicholson, 1983), 37–38.

26. Stein warns that "many writers in recent years have adopted an overly sympathetic, if not romantic, perspective on this sect. Some seem uninterested in distinguishing the historical record from interpretations offered of it." Stein, *Shaker Experience*, 2–3.

27. Ibid., 5–6.

28. Ibid., 5.

29. Ibid., 167. Unless otherwise noted, much of the information on Shakers is from Stein.

30. Unless otherwise noted, all quotations are from Nordhoff, *American Utopias*, 232–35.

31. See Deloria, *Playing Indian*; and Browder, *Slippery Characters*.

32. Nordhoff reports a conversation he had with Elder Frederick W. Evans of Mount Lebanon who informed him that spiritual manifestations were experienced by Shakers "many years before Kate Fox was born," implying a clear understanding of the potential relation between spiritualism and Shakerism. Nordhoff, *American Utopias*, 157. Andrews also discusses the relation between the two. See Andrews, *People Called Shakers*, 175–76.

33. Cotton Mather, *The Wonders of the Invisible World* to which is added Increase Mather *A Farther Account of the Tryals of the New-England Witches* (London: John Russell Smith, 1862), 201–2. Emphasis original.

34. Sprague's posthumously published collection *The Poet and Other Poems* (Boston: William White, 1864) includes a number of poems that are explicit about their relation to spiritualism. Related developments within spiritualism were the speeches of trance mediums (again often young women) who spoke when inspired, often on subjects such as women's rights or abolition. Such poets were often (like these Shakers) young women who believed that they were conduits between this world and the next. Sprague's work contains "Songs from Spirit Land" that have a relation to the Shaker songs. See Sprague, *Poet*, 286–87.

35. See Susan McCully, "Oh I Love Mother, I Love Her Power: Shaker Spirit Possession and the Performance of Desire," *Theatre Survey* 35, no. 1 (May 1994): 90. In a discussion of a lithograph of a Shaker line dance from the late eighteenth century, McCully notes that "It is as if the church service is also a performance for the non-Shaker visitor in the corner of the lithograph. . . . The picture also suggests that the non-Shaker guests were viewing a kind of theatricalized public performance."

36. Nordhoff, *American Utopias*, 225.

37. Andrews, *People Called Shakers*, 169.

38. See Nicholas Griffiths and Fernando Cervantes, eds., *Spiritual Encounters: Interactions between Christianity and Native Religions in Colonial America* (Birmingham: University of Birmingham Press, 1999), especially David Murray, "Spreading the Word: Missionaries, Conversion and Circulation in the Northeast," 43–64; Tracy Neal Leavelle, "Geographies of Encounter: Religion and Contested Spaces in Colonial North America," *American Quarterly* 56, no. 4 (2004): 913–43; Peter Benes, "Fortune-Tellers, Wise-Men, and Magical Healers in New England, 1644–1850," in *Wonders of the Invisible World: 1600–1900*, ed. Peter Benes, 127–56 (Dublin Seminar for New England Folklife Annual Proceedings, 1992). Later published (Boston: Boston University, 1995).

39. Nelson, *Spiritualism and Society*, 55–58. For detail of the "shaking tents," which closely resemble the cabinets adopted by some spiritualists, see Peter Nabokov, ed., *Native American Testimony: A Chronicle of*

Indian-White Relations from Prophecy to the Present, 1492–1992 (Harmondsworth, England: Viking Penguin, 1991), especially 10–12; Selwyn Dewedney, ed., *Legends of my People: The Great Ojibway,* illus. and told by Norval Morrison (Toronto: McGraw-Hill Ryerson, 1977), 70–81.

40. Britten, *Autobiography,* 138–41. She also writes about seeing Indian spirits in a number of other contexts in her autobiography, for example, 131–33, 138–41. See also, for example, Nelson, *Spiritualism and Society,* 55–58, 75–76; an account of an encounter with a so-called shaking tent in 1764 in "Spiritual Manifestations Among the Indians," in *The Spiritual Telegraph,* vol. 4, ed. S. B. Brittan (New York: Partridge and Brittan, 1854), 116; Nabokov, ed., *Native American Testimony,* 10–12. There are also other complex relationships between black spiritualism and Indian heritage. Over twenty black spiritualist churches in New Orleans "venerate the Native American Indian Chief Black Hawk as a martyr, in keeping with the teachings of Leith Anderson, a half Mohawk woman who preached the doctrine of 'spirit returning." George Lipsitz, *Time Passages: Collective Memory and American Popular Culture* (Minneapolis: University of Minnesota Press, 2001), 237.

41. Annette Leevier, *Psychic Experiences of an Indian Princess* (Los Angeles: Austin Publishing, 1920).

42. See Jean McMahon Humez, ed., *Gifts of Power: The Writings of Rebecca Jackson, Black Visionary, Shaker Eldress* (Boston: University of Massachusetts Press, 1981), 229–70. For more on Jackson see Etta Madden, "Reading, Writing, and the Race of Mother Figures: Shakers Rebecca Cox Jackson and Alonzo Giles Hollister," in *A Mighty Baptism: Race, Gender and the Creation of American Protestantism,* ed. Susan Justner and Lisa McFarlane, 210–34 (Ithaca, NY: Cornell University Press, 1996); Sylvia Bryant, "Speaking into Being: The Gifts of Rebecca Cox Jackson, 'Black Visionary, Shaker Eldress,'" in *Women's Life-Writing: Finding Voice/ Building Community,* ed. Linda S. Coleman, 63–80 (Bowling Green, OH: Bowling Green State Popular Press, 1997).

43. Charles Dudley Warner's somewhat negative response to his experience of visiting the Shakers typifies one strand of contemporary writings. See "Out of the World" *Scribner's Monthly,* vol. 18 (New York: Scribner, 1879), 549–58.

44. Though his gender is never made explicit it seems, from some of his comments, that he is a man.

45. Anonymous [A Guest of the "Community" Near Watervliet, NY], *A Revelation of the Extraordinary Visitation of Departed Spirits of Distinguished Men and Women of all Nations, and Their Manifestation Through the Living Bodies of the 'Shakers'* (Philadelphia: L. G. Thomas, 1869), 6–7. Emphasis original.

46. Ibid., 7. Emphasis original.

47. Stein, *Shaker Experience*, 225. Britten notes that when she visited New Zealand Peebles had already been lecturing there. See Britten, *Autobiography*, 246.

48. Stein, *Shaker Experience*, 320–37.

49. Charles Dickens, *American Notes for General Circulation*, ed. John S. Whitley and Arnold Goldman (London: Penguin, 1985), 256.

50. Ibid., 257–58.

51. Ibid., 258.

52. Stein, *Shaker Experience*, 176.

53. Anonymous, *Revelation*, 8.

54. Anonymous, *Revelation*, 9.

55. Ibid. Emphasis original.

56. Ibid.

57. Ibid. Emphasis original.

58. Ibid, 10.

59. Dana D. Nelson, *The Word in Black and White: Reading "Race" in American Literature, 1638–1867* (New York: Oxford University Press, 1993), 51.

60. Cited in ibid., 45.

61. Isaac Post, *Voices from the Spirit World: Being Communications from Many Spirits* (Rochester, NY: Charles H. McDonnell, 1852). Messages are from, among others, John Quincy Adams, James Fenimore Cooper, George Fox, Benjamin Franklin, Elias Hicks, Andrew Jackson, Thomas Jefferson, Margaret Fuller, Napoleon, William Penn, Swedenborg, Voltaire, George Washington, and George Whitfield.

62. Anonymous, *Revelation*, 33.

63. Karen Robertson also makes this claim, see "Pocahontas at the Masque," *Signs: Journal of Women in Culture and Society* 21, no. 3 (1996): 556. See also Susan Scheckel, *The Insistence of the Indian: Race and Nationalism in Nineteenth-Century American Culture* (Princeton, NJ: Princeton University Press, 1998), 41–69; Philip Gould, "The Pocahontas Story in Early America," *Prospects: An Annual of American Cultural Studies* 24 (1999): 99–116.

64. Robert S. Tilton, *Pocahontas: The Evolution of an American Narrative* (Cambridge: Cambridge University Press, 1994), 38.

65. Alden T. Vaughan, "Trinculo's Indian: American Natives in Shakespeare's England," in *"The Tempest" and Its Travels*, ed. Peter Hulme and William H. Sherman (London: Reaktion Books, 2000), 51. See also Vaughan, "Learning to Curse: Aspects of Linguistic Colonialism in the Sixteenth Century," in *Learning to Curse: Essays in Modern Culture*, ed. Stephen Jay Greenblatt, 16–39 (London: Routledge, 1990).

66. Vaughan, "Trinculo's Indian," 50–51.

67. Ibid., 56.

68. Robertson, "Pocahontas at the Masque," 570–71.
69. Ibid., 573.
70. For more on visual representations of Pocahontas, see Tilton, *Pocahontas*, 93–144.
71. They are too numerous to mention here, however.
72. Tilton, *Pocahontas*, 54.
73. Rosemarie K. Bank, "Staging the 'Native': Making History in American Theatre Culture, 1828–1838," *Theatre Journal* 45 (1993): 462.
74. Nordhoff, *American Utopias*, 197. He cites details of other communities too. My point though, is to establish a probability rather than to try to pursue the precise nature of knowledge of the Pocahontas story.
75. Altick, *Shows of London*, 275–79.
76. Baringer, "The Course of Empires," 50.
77. Some Indian showmen, for example Frank Loring, took advantage of these possibilities. See Harald E. L. Prins, "Chief Big Thunder (1827–1906): The Life History of a Penobscot Trickster," *Maine History* 37, no. 2 (1998): 140–58.
78. For instance, Baringer writes that Catlin "was both a critic and an agent of . . . fundamentally imperialist processes; his ethnographic work, despite its protective sentiments towards Indian culture, allowed for greater control to be exerted over the Indians by the US government." Baringer, "The Course of Empires," 50.
79. Robert Dale Owen who became an enthusiastic convert to spiritualism published a Pocahontas drama in 1837, one example of the many varying texts that took her as their subject.
80. Reviewers noted the accuracy of the dress. Bank, "Staging the 'Native,'" 483.
81. Ibid. Emphasis original.
82. Ibid., 484.
83. Ibid.
84. As Robertson puts it "the presence of the colonized other does not interrupt or even provoke hesitation in the court mechanisms, one element of the apparatus of European ideological, economic, and military force engaged in the erasure of her people, language, and culture." Robertson, "Pocahontas at the Masque," 553.
85. Ibid. Emphasis original.
86. See Bank, "Staging the 'Native,'" 476. See also Scheckel, *Insistence of the Indian*, 99–126. Within a very few years spiritualists claimed that the spirits of Black Hawk and George Fox collaborated in a humanitarian message warning that a child was very ill therefore beating the regular telegraph system. See Scheckel, "Black Hawk against Morse and Blaine," *Spiritual Telegraph* 4:447–48.
87. See Jeffrey D. Mason, "The Politics of *Metamora*," in *The Performance of Power: Theatrical Discourse and Politics*, ed. Sue-Ellen Case and

Janelle Reinelt (Iowa City: University of Iowa Press, 1991), 92–110. Mason writes that Forrest "commissioned *Metamora* as part of a nationalist agenda which supported his personal ambitions as the first major American touring star" (99).

88. Cited in Mason, "The Politics of *Metamora*," 104–5. Emphasis original.
89. Cited in ibid., 100. See also 100–102.
90. Paul Gilmore, *The Genuine Article: Race, Mass Culture, and American Literary Manhood* (Durham, NC: Duke University Press, 2001), 30.
91. Ibid., 32.
92. Eric Lott, *Love and Theft: Blackface Minstrelsy and the American Working Class* (New York: Oxford University Press, 1993), 28.
93. Gilmore argues that audiences could respond enthusiastically to the disruptive possibility of *Metamora*. Gilmore, *Genuine Article*, 32.
94. Nordhoff, *American Utopias*, 235.
95. Lott, *Love and Theft*, 29.
96. "Logan's Speech," *The Spiritual Telegraph* 4:235. The speech is given "through Mr. L" on January 15, 1854.
97. "Spirits in Keokuk," ibid., 409. One of the mediums also spoke in Latin and sang "in the Swiss language" though the piece does not mention which of the languages spoken there it might be.
98. He writes that "Internal evidence of the genuineness of literary productions are usually very different for one mind to present to another—indeed, the very nature of the most potent ones fit them for perception by intuition, rather than reason—by the heart rather than the head." Allen Putnam, *Spirit Invocations: or, Prayers and Praises* (Boston: Colby and Rich, 1876), 6.
99. Stein, *Shaker Experience*, 176.
100. Deloria, *Playing Indian*, 14. But see also 10–37.
101. Ibid.
102. For instance see Anonymous, *Revelation*, 11–12.
103. Catharine Maria Sedgwick, *Redwood: A Tale* (New York: E. Bliss and E. White, 1824), i, 137.
104. Emphasis original.
105. Butler, *Awash in a Sea of Faith*, 232–33.

CHAPTER 4

1. Recent revisionist work on the sentimental includes, crucially, Jane P. Tompkins, "Sentimental Power: *Uncle Tom's Cabin* and the Politics of Literary History," in *The New Feminist Criticism: Essays on Women, Literature and Theory*, ed. Elaine Showalter, 81–104 (London: Virago, 1986); Shirley Samuels, ed., *The Culture of Sentiment: Race, Gender,*

and Sentimentality in Nineteenth-Century America (New York: Oxford University Press), 1992; Joanne Dobson, "Reclaiming Sentimental Literature," *American Literature* 69, no. 2 (June 1997): 263–88; Mary Chapman and Glenn Hendler, eds., *Sentimental Men: Masculinity and the Politics of Affect in American Culture* (Berkeley: University of California Press, 1999); Mary Louise Kete, *Sentimental Collaboration: Mourning and Middle-Class Identity in Nineteenth-Century America* (Durham, NC: Duke University Press, 2000); Jocelyn Moody, *Sentimental Confessions: Spiritual Narratives of Nineteenth-Century African American Women* (Athens: University of Georgia Press, 2001); Elizabeth Maddock Dillon, "Sentimental Aesthetics," *American Literature* 76, no. 3 (2004): 495–523).

2. A key account of the development of divides between high and low culture in nineteenth-century America is Lawrence W. Levine, *Highbrow/Lowbrow: The Emergence of Cultural Hierarchy in America* (Cambridge, MA: Harvard University Press, 1988.)

3. The Cassell edition of *Uncle Tom's Cabin*, reprinted repeatedly for more than forty years, used illustrations by George Cruikshank, which were themselves copied by other editions of the novel. See Marcus Wood, *Blind Memory: Visual Representations of Slavery in England and America, 1780–1865* (Manchester: Manchester University Press, 2000), 151–52. Cruikshank would later write and illustrate a series of so-called discoveries about ghosts to which he appended an attack on spiritualism. See George Cruikshank, *A Discovery Concerning Ghosts: With a Rap at the "Spirit-Rappers"* (London: Routledge, Warne, and Routledge, 1864).

4. Rita J. Smith has argued that the novel bears a close resemblance to the very popular genre of the "memoir of the dying child." See Rita J. Smith, "Those Who Go before: Ancestors of Eva St. Clare," *The New England Quarterly* 70, no. 2 (June 1997): 314–18.

5. For details of this as well as references to other work on adaptations see Wood, *Blind Memory*, 143–214.

6. Annie Fields, the wife of James Fields, cited this letter in her 1898 work on Stowe. Stowe wrote, "There is a lady of my acquaintance who has developed more remarkable facts in this way than I have ever seen; I have kept a record of these communications for some time past, and everybody is very much struck by them. I have material to produce a very curious article. Shall you want it? And when?" Fields, ed., *Life and Letters*, 316–17. See also Joan D. Hedrick, *Harriet Beecher Stowe: A Life* (New York: Oxford University Press, 1994), 338–39. Frank Luther Mott notes that though James Fields was de facto editor from 1861 to July 1871, W. D. Howells "became virtual editor in 1866 and titular editor in 1871." See Frank Luther Mott, ed., *A History of American Magazines*, 5 vols. (Cambridge, MA: Harvard University Press, 1957),

3:32. Howells's 1896 novel *The Landlord at Lion's Head* includes an odd subplot featuring the use of a planchette by a man stricken with tuberculosis.

7. On the ways in which such mementoes are implicated in commodity culture see "Then When We Clutch the Hardest: On the Death of a Child and the Replication of an Image," in Chapman and Hendler, eds., *Sentimental Men*, 80.

8. For Calvin Stowe's account of his experiences see Charles Edward Stowe, *Life of Harriet Beecher Stowe Compiled from Her Letters and Journals* (London: Sampson Low, Marston, Searle, and Rivington, 1989), 419–39. See also Lyman Beecher Stowe, *Saints, Sinners and Beechers* (London: Ivor Nicholson and Watson, 1935), 220–22. For details of Horace's vision see chapter 17, "The Visit to the Haunted House" of *Oldtown Folks*. Stowe wrote to George Eliot that her husband was the basis for Horace Holyoke. The pair exchanged a number of letters that included reflections on the subject. See, for example, George Eliot to Harriet Beecher Stowe, July 11, 1869, in *The George Eliot Letters*, 12 vols., ed. Gordon Haight (New Haven, CT: Yale University Press, 1954), 5:47–49. See also George Eliot to Harriet Beecher Stowe, March 4, 1872, 5:252–53; June 24, 1872, 5:279–82; October [?], 1872, 5:321–22. Eliot also corresponded with a number of others about spiritualism. For more on Calvin Stowe's visions, see Forrest Wilson, *Crusader in Crinoline* (London: Hutchinson, 1942), 333–35; Edward Wagenknecht, *Harriet Beecher Stowe: The Known and the Unknown* (New York: Oxford University Press, 1965), 45–48.

9. See Ann Braude, *Radical Spirits: Spiritualism and Women's Rights in Nineteenth-Century America* (Boston: Beacon, 1989), 154–57.

10. Karen Halttunen, "Gothic Imagination and Social Reform: The Haunted Houses of Lyman Beecher, Henry Ward Beecher, and Harriet Beecher Stowe," in *New Essays on "Uncle Tom's Cabin,"* ed. Eric J. Sundquist (Cambridge: Cambridge University Press, 1993), 107–34.

11. Cited in Lyman Beecher Stowe, *Saints, Sinners and Beechers*, 221. For details of Barrett Browning's interest in mesmerism see Alison Winter, *Mesmerized: Powers of Mind in Victorian Britain* (Chicago: University of Chicago Press, 1998), 233–45. Winter makes useful reference to earlier work on the subject.

12. See Norman Swaine, *Autobiography of Two Worlds* (London: Rider, 1937).

13. On Samoa's relationship to imperialism in the Pacific, see Damon Salesa "Samoa's Half-Castes and Some Frontiers of Comparison," in *Haunted by Empire: Geographies of Intimacy in North American History*, ed. Ann Laura Stoler, 71–93 (Durham, NC: Duke University Press, 2006).

14. W. T. Lhamon, Jr., *Raising Cain: Blackface Performance from Jim Crow to Hip Hop* (Cambridge, MA: Harvard University Press, 1998), 143.

15. Ibid., 63.
16. Kaplan, *Anarchy of Empire*, 43. She notes that, "Susan Warner's *The Wide Wide World* sends its heroine to Scotland, while the world of Maria Cummins's *The Lamplighter* encompasses India, Cuba, the American West, and Brazil. The geographic coordinates of *Uncle Tom's Cabin* extend to Haiti, Canada, and, most notably, Africa; in E.D.E.N. Southworth's *The Hidden Hand*, the resolution of multiple domestic plots in Virginia relies on the participation of the male characters in the Mexican-American War." Ibid.
17. She argues that the significance of this model for Stowe is both in terms of its genre but also in terms of textual specificities. Rita J. Smith, "Those Who Go Before," 314. I am grateful to an anonymous reader for the *Journal of American Studies* who drew my attention to this article.
18. See "Beyond the Cover: *Uncle Tom's Cabin* as Global Entertainment," in Wood, *Blind Memory*, 143–214.
19. Ellen J. Goldner, "Arguing with Pictures: Race, Class, and the Formation of Popular Abolitionism through *Uncle Tom's Cabin*," *Journal of American Culture* 24, no. 1–2 (Spring/Summer 2001): 77.
20. Cited in Harriet Beecher Stowe, *Uncle Tom's Cabin, or, Life among the Lowly*, ed. Elizabeth Ammons (New York: W. W. Norton, 1994), 462.
21. Tompkins, "Sentimental Power," 81–104. The essay was first published in 1978. Critics who have carried out such reclamation work on behalf of the sentimental tradition have shown the extent to which canonical male writers such as Hawthorne and Melville have also used it.
22. Stern, *Plight of Feeling*, 2, 4–5.
23. This is a relationship that Elizabeth Barnes articulates explicitly in recent work in which she interprets sympathy as an American form. Elizabeth Barnes, *States of Sympathy: Seduction and Democracy in the American Novel* (New York: Columbia University Press, 1997), xi, 91–99.
24. Carla L. Mulford, ed., *William H. Brown* The Power of Sympathy *and Hannah Webster Foster* The Coquette (New York: Penguin, 1996), 102. Emphasis original.
25. Ibid., 103.
26. Mary Louise Kete, *Sentimental Collaborations: Mourning and Middle-Class Identity in Nineteenth-Century America* (Durham, NC: Duke University Press, 2000). See, especially, chapter 4, "The Circulation of the Dead and the Making of the Self in the Novel," 83–102, on *Uncle Tom's Cabin* and *The Gates Ajar*.
27. Harper's poem "Eva's Farewell" appeared in *Frederick Douglass' Paper* on March 31, 1854. She also wrote two other extant poems on the subject of the novel, "Eliza Harris" (1853) and "To Mrs. Harriet Beecher Stowe" (1854).
28. Hedrick, *Harriet Beecher Stowe*, 225.

29. Ibid., 224-25. The poem appeared in the *Independent* above one on the same theme by Mary H. Collier.
30. Harriet Beecher Stowe, *Religious Poems* (Boston: Ticknor and Fields, 1867), 44, 47.
31. George L. Aiken, *Uncle Tom's Cabin; or, Life Among the Lowly. A Domestic Drama in Six Acts* in *Early American Drama*, ed. Jeffrey H. Richards (Harmondsworth, Middlesex: Penguin, 1997), 443.
32. Halttunen, "Gothic Imagination," 117.
33. Dyer notes that representations of death within Christian art have been determined by an aesthetic of beauty that may itself include and be subsumed by the realities of agony and he argues that a "pure ecstasy of death is conveyed in Eva's demise in *Uncle Tom's Cabin*." See Richard Dyer, *White* (London: Routledge, 1997), 208. At one point Ophelia and St. Clare discuss Eva's actions in terms that make her Christ-like actions explicit. See Stowe, *Uncle Tom's Cabin*, 246.
34. Dyer, *White*, 209.
35. Stowe, *Uncle Tom's Cabin*, 247.
36. Lori Merish, *Sentimental Materialism, Gender, Commodity Culture and Nineteenth-Century American Literature* (Durham, NC: Duke University Press, 2000), 162.
37. Stowe, *Uncle Tom's Cabin*, 242.
38. Ibid. 257.
39. Hedrick, *Harriet Beecher Stowe*, 8.
40. Stowe, *Uncle Tom's Cabin*, 258.
41. Hedrick, *Harriet Beecher Stowe*, 191.
42. Stowe, *Uncle Tom's Cabin*, 257.
43. As Karen Sánchez-Eppler has shown, the new technology of the daguerreotype also asserts infant mortality precisely through its modus operandi. Since early daguerreotypes required a fifteen-minute exposure, postmortem images of children were easier to produce than images of live children. See Eppler, "Then When We Clutch the Hardest," 69. For further details on postmortem photography and portraiture and the preoccupation with the physicality of the corpses of the beloved see Gary Laderman, *The Sacred Remains: American Attitudes towards Death, 1799–1883* (New Haven, CT: Yale University Press, 1996), especially chapter 6, 76–78. Laderman notes that one successful painter of postmortem portraits, William Sydney Mount, was a spiritualist.
44. That the death of Charley had an enormous impact upon Stowe is indisputable. She attributed her empathy with slave mothers to the experience of watching him dying, writing that "It was at *his* dying bed, and at *his* grave . . . that I learnt what a poor slave mother may feel when her child is torn away from her." Hedrick, *Harriet Beecher Stowe*, 193. Emphasis original.
45. Stowe, *Uncle Tom's Cabin*, 250.

46. For an example of a photograph of a mourning brooch that combines hair and a daguerreotype of the deceased is reproduced in Jay Ruby, *Secure the Shadow: Death and Photography in America* (Cambridge, MA: Massachusetts Institute of Technology Press, 1995), 109.

47. Lynn Wardley, "Relic, Fetish, Femmage: The Aesthetics of Sentiment in the Work of Stowe," in Samuel's *The Culture of Sentiment*, 204.

48. Stowe, *Uncle Tom's Cabin*, 322.

49. Ibid., 323.

50. Ibid.

51. Kaplan, *Anarchy of Empire*, 24–25. Kaplan uses metaphors of haunting to show the ways in which such a process was threatened: "images of the nation as home were haunted by 'disembodied shades' who blurred the boundaries between the domestic and the foreign." Ibid., 26.

52. Wardley makes the same point on page 213.

53. Ibid.

54. She was very disappointed when her own paper the *Christian Union* gave it "what she regarded as an entirely inadequate review." See Wilson, *Crusader in Crinoline*, 333. She tried to persuade George Eliot to read Dale Owen's work.

55. Owen had met the new editor of the *Atlantic Monthly*, W. D. Howells, on a number of occasions and had discussed spiritualism with him. See W. D. Howells, *Selected Letters: Volume 1: 1852–1872*, 6 vols., eds. George Arms et al. (Boston: Twayne, 1979) 1:381, 1:391–92, 1:401.

56. John Greenleaf Whittier alluded to the article, for example, in a letter to Annie Fields in April 1885. Annie Fields had also had experiences with a fake medium, Rose Darrah. Darrah had claimed to see the spirit of James Fields while at the house of Annie Fields, in the presence of Sarah Orne Jewett and Celia Thaxter. Whittier had a strong desire to believe in the facts of spiritualism but was put off by his knowledge of fakery and trickery of this sort. Stowe herself often expressed distrust of revelations made by paid mediums. In December 1884 Whittier wrote to Annie Fields that "I believe there is such a thing as communication with those who are in another sphere; and that there is in the spiritualistic phenomena, the prophecy of a coming revelation—but there is also much which repels and disgusts me. I am sorry that C. T. [Celia Thaxter] is yielding herself so unreservedly to the baffling and unsatisfactory influence. No real good can come of it, and I am afraid her experience will be a painful one." Letter to Annie Fields, December 1, 1884, in *The Letters of John Greenleaf Whittier*, 3 vols., ed. John B. Pickard (Cambridge, MA: Harvard University Press, 1975), 3:491. References to spiritualism take place in Whittier's correspondence from as early as 1858 in letters to Lydia Maria Child, Annie Fields, Charlotte Fiske Bates, and others, but he always maintained doubts about it. In a

letter of Charlotte Fiske Bates of 1879, he wrote of William Lloyd Garrison that "I have heard Garrison talk much of his faith in Spiritualism. He had no doubts whatever, and he was very happy. Death was to him but the passing from one room to another and higher one. But his *facts* did not convince me" (3:415). Emphasis original. See also 2:357–58; 3:368, 409, 445, 492–94, 498.

57. As Anne Braude has shown, the relationship between the struggle for social justice and the investigation of the spirit world was often close within this period. Braude, *Radical Spirits*, 56–81, in particular.

58. Alex Owen, *The Darkened Room: Women, Power and Spiritualism in Late Victorian England* (London: Virago, 1989), 45.

59. Anonymous, *Spiritualist*, May 29, 1874, 258.

60. All from ibid., 55.

61. Ibid., 46.

62. Robert Owen, "Touching Visitants from a Higher Life: A Chapter of Autobiography," *Atlantic Monthly* (January 1875): 57–69. Owen made detailed comments on the relationship between the two materializations of Katie King at the end of his piece. See ibid., 67–69.

63. Ibid., 67.

64. Ibid., 60.

65. Ibid., 61.

66. Ibid., 66.

67. One citation is to *Robinson Crusoe* (1719) "Having been an old Planter at Maryland, and a Buccaneer into the Bargain."

68. Britten, *Autobiography*, 182.

69. Hedrick, *Harriet Beecher Stowe*, 161–62. Key works on hypnotism and mesmerism remain Darnton, *Mesmerism* and Gauld, *History of Hypnotism*. A good new contribution to the subject is Daniel Pick, *Svengali's Web: The Alien Encounter in Modern Culture* (New Haven, CT: Yale University Press, 2000.)

70. Hedrick, *Harriet Beecher Stowe*, 274–83.

71. Letter to the Duchess of Sunderland August 3, 1857, cited in Fields, ed., *Life and Letters*, 239.

72. Fields, ed., *Life and Letters*, 111–15; Hedrick, *Harriet Beecher Stowe*, 173–85.

73. Hedrick, *Harriet Beecher Stowe*, 367. Hedrick numbers these as "at least four." Ann Braude has shown that the water cure often provided an ideal environment for women to develop and discover "talents incompatible with domestic duties, such as mediumship." See her discussion of hydropathy in Braude, *Radical Spirits*, 154–57.

74. Hedrick, *Harriet Beecher Stowe*, 143–44.

75. Fields, ed., *Life and Letters*, 308.

76. Stowe, *Uncle Tom's Cabin*, 274.

77. Ibid., 275–76.
78. Ibid., 303.
79. Ibid. John J. Kucich makes similar points in his ingenious argument about Harriet Jacobs's use of a spiritualist subtext in her writing. Kucich, Ghostly Communication: Cross-Cultural Spiritualism in Nineteenth-Century American Literature (Hanover, NH: Dartmouth College Press, 2004), 22–31.
80. Stowe, *My Wife and I, or, Harry Henderson's History* (New York: J. B. Ford, 1871), 29–30.
81. Fields, ed., *Life and Letters*, 254. Letter to Calvin Stowe, January 16, 1860.

CHAPTER 5

1. One example of this is a celebrated series of communications from a dead soldier, published as *Private Dowding* with notes by W. T. P. (London: John M. Watkins, 1917). The spirit describes his death as follows: "Think of it! One moment I was alive, in the earthly sense, looking over a trench parapet, unalarmed, normal. Five seconds later I was standing outside my body, helping two of my pals to carry my body down the trench labyrinth towards a dressing station." Ibid., 7.
2. For more on this see Lisa A. Long, *Rehabilitating Bodies: Health, History, and the American Civil War* (Philadelphia: University of Pennsylvania Press, 2004).
3. Emma Hardinge [Britten], *The Great Funeral Oration on Abraham Lincoln* (New York: American News Company, [1865]), 7.
4. Susan-Mary Grant, "Patriot Graves: American National Identity and the Civil War Dead," *American Nineteenth-Century History* 5, no. 3 (Fall 2004): 95–96.
5. Cited in ibid., 85.
6. Elizabeth Stuart Phelps, *Three Spiritualist Novels* (Urbana: University of Illinois Press, 2000), ix–x.
7. A similarly materialist version of heaven is represented in a recent best-selling novel, Alice Sebold's *The Lovely Bones* (2002). Like Phelps' works, it is not spiritualist but bears a strong relationship to ideas within spiritualist thought. An interesting discussion of issues of materiality and embodiment in the novel is in Laura E. Tanner, *Lost Bodies: Inhabiting the Borders of Life and Death* (Ithaca, NY: Cornell University Press, 2006), 215–19. Lucy Frank's fine unpublished essay "Bought with a Price: Elizabeth Stuart Phelps and the Commodification of Heaven" addresses the relationship within the novel of mourning and commodity culture.
8. John J. Kucich makes a convincing case for reading Twain's "Captain Stormfield's Visit to Heaven" as both a satire on Phelps

and an anti-imperialist piece produced after his visit to the Hawaiian Islands. Kucich, Ghostly Communication: Cross-Cultural Spiritualism in Nineteenth-Century American Literature (Hanover, NH: Dartmouth College Press, 2004), 82–90.

9. Walt Whitman, *The Complete Poems,* ed. Francis Murphy (London: Penguin, 1986), 825.

10. See, for instance, Russ Castronovo, *Necro Citizenship: Death, Eroticism, and the Public Sphere in the Nineteenth-Century United States* (Durham, NC: Duke University Press, 2001), 169–71.

11. Jon Butler, *Awash in a Sea of Faith: Christianizing the American People* (Cambridge, MA: Harvard University Press, 1990), 2, 93.

12. Ibid., 295.

13. See, for instance, Garry Wills, *Lincoln at Gettysburg: The Words That Remade America* (New York: Simon and Schuster, 1992), 88–89.

14. Butler, *Awash in a Sea of Faith,* 294.

15. Francis Grierson [Benjamin Henry Jesse Francis Shepard], *Abraham Lincoln: The Practical Mystic* (London: John Lane, 1919); Harriet M. Shelton, *Abraham Lincoln Returns* (New York: Evans, 1957); Nettie Colburn Maynard, *Was Abraham Lincoln a Spiritualist? or, Curious Revelations from the Life of a Trance Medium* (Philadelphia: Rufus C. Hartranft, 1891).

16. Carl Sandburg, *Abraham Lincoln: The War Years* (New York: Harcourt, Brace,1939), 2:261.

17. For further details of her involvement with spiritualism, see Jean H. Baker, *Mary Todd Lincoln: A Biography* (New York: W. W. Norton, 1987), especially 217–22; and Mark E. Neely, Jr., and R. Gerald McMurtry, *The Insanity File: The Case of Mary Todd Lincoln* (Carbondale: Southern Illinois University Press, 1986.).

18. Ann Braude has done a great deal to investigate the relationship between radicalism and spiritualism. See Braude, *Radical Spirits,* 1989.

19. "A Spiritualist medium, Mrs. Nettie Colburn Maynard, who had conducted séances in the White House at which Lincoln was present, claimed that the president had been moved to emancipate the slaves through a spirit message she had transmitted to him. Mary Todd Lincoln, a devoted Spiritualist, declared that she had been present when the message was transmitted. Their son Robert later denied that his father was in any way affected by such communications." Goldsmith, *Other Powers,* 78.

20. Sandburg, *Abraham Lincoln,* 2:344.

21. Ibid., 345.

22. Carl Sandburg, *Abraham Lincoln,* 2:306.

23. See Laderman, "Body Politic," 115–16.

24. See Neely and McMurtry, *The Insanity File,* 20–21.

25. Ibid., 11.

26. Baker, *Mary Todd Lincoln*, 311.
27. William H. Mumler, *The Personal Experiences of William H Mumler in Spirit-Photography* (Boston: Colby and Rich, 1875), 4.
28. For details see ibid., 17 onward; *The Mumler "Spirit" Photograph Case*, argument by Elbridge T. Gerry, of counsel for the people before Justice Dowling, on the preliminary examination of Wm. H. Mumler, charged with obtaining money by pretended "spirit" photographs, May 3, 1869, reported by Andrew Devine (New York: Baker, Voorhis, 1869); Coates, *Photographing the Invisible*, chapter 1.
29. Mumler, *Personal Experiences*, 29–31. See also Coates, *Photographing the Invisible*, 30–31.
30. William Lloyd Garrison, *The Letters of William Lloyd Garrison*, 6 vols., ed. Walter M. Merrill (Cambridge, MA: Harvard University Press, 1979). Letter to Helen E. Garrison and children, December 10, 1861, 5:61–62. See also 5:100.
31. Ibid., 6:323. Letter to Oliver Johnson, May 25, 1874. He adds that "Recently, I have witnessed some extraordinary marvels in the materialization of spirit hands, utterances by spirit voices, &c., &c." Sumner died on March 11, 1874.
32. Ibid., 6:335. Letter to Helen E. Garrison, August 2, 1874. Emphasis original.
33. Cited in William W. Betts, Jr., ed., *Lincoln and the Poets* (Pittsburgh: University of Pittsburgh Press, 1965), 16–17. Emphasis original.
34. Wills, *Lincoln at Gettysburg*, 70. Emphasis original.
35. All the information about the fate of Lincoln's body comes from Gary Laderman, "The Body Politic and the Politics of Two Bodies: Abraham and Mary Todd Lincoln in Death," *Prospects* (1997):109–32.
36. This image (held in a private collection) is reproduced in Dan Meinwald, *Memento Mori: Death in Nineteenth Century Photography* (Riverside: California Museum of Photography, 1990), 27. The process of commodifying Lincoln's memory bears a relation to the commodofication of battlegrounds and what they represent. See, for example, Jim Weeks, "Gettysburg: Display Window for Popular Memory," *Journal of American Culture* 21, no. 4 (Winter 1998): 41–56.
37. Laderman, "Body Politic," 119.
38. Ibid., 117.
39. Wills, *Lincoln at Gettysburg*, 20.
40. Ibid., 21.
41. Walt Whitman, "The Million Dead, too, Summ'd Up," *Complete Poetry and Collected Prose*, 776–77. Emphasis original.
42. Ibid, 777.
43. Anderson, *Imagined Communities*, 9.
44. Ibid. Emphasis original.
45. "The cultural significance of such monuments becomes even clearer if one tries to imagine, say, a Tomb of the Unknown Marxist or a cenotaph

for fallen Liberals. Is a sense of absurdity avoidable? The reason is that neither Marxism nor Liberalism are much concerned with death and immortality. If the nationalist imagining is so concerned, this suggests a strong affinity with religious imaginings. As this affinity is by no means fortuitous, it may be useful to begin a consideration of the cultural roots of nationalism with death, as the last of a whole gamut of fatalities." Ibid., 10.

46. Cited in Gary Laderman, *The Sacred Remains: American Attitudes towards Death, 1799–1883* (New Haven, CT: Yale University Press, 1996), 142. Emphasis original.

47. Louisa May Alcott, *Little Women,* ed. Elaine Showalter (New York: Penguin, 1989), 419.

48. Laderman, "Body Politic," 126.

49. Laderman, *The Sacred Remains,* 130. The same kind of difficulty, Nancy Miller argues, was experienced by those trying to memorialize those killed in the Twin Towers. See Nancy Miller, "'Portraits of Grief': Telling Details and the Testimony of Trauma," *differences: A Journal of Feminist Cultural Studies* 14, no. 3 (2003): 112–35.

50. Castronovo, noting the same quality of speech refers to a "folksy invitation" by Lincoln. Castronovo, *Necro Citizenship,* 169.

51. A selection of these appears in Betts, ed., *Lincoln and the Poets.*

52. Emma Hardinge Britten, *Autobiography of Emma Hardinge Britten,* ed. Margaret Wilkinson (Manchester: John Heywood, 1900), 205.

53. Ibid., 206.

54. Hardinge [Britten], *Great Funeral Oration,* 4. Emphasis original.

55. Ibid.

56. Ibid., 7.

57. Ibid., 22. These highly stylized tropes reproduce the language used by some Northern writers to describe the death of the fictional Little Eva.

58. Ibid., 9. Emphasis original.

59. Ibid., 8–9. Emphasis original.

60. Britten, *Autobiography,* 207. Emphasis original.

61. Roy P. Basler, ed., *Walt Whitman's Memoranda During the War and Death of Abraham Lincoln* (Bloomington: Indiana University Press, 1962), 3. Unless otherwise noted, the pagination here refers to that of Whitman's reading copy of the text which Basler reproduces. Emphasis original.]

62. Ibid., 7.

63. Ibid., 12.

64. Ibid.

65. Anderson, *Imagined Communities,* 11.

66. Walt Whitman, "Song of Myself" (lines 505–518), in Francis Murphy, ed., *Walt Whitman: The Complete Poems* (London: Penguin, 1975), 86–87.

67. On the death of Princess Diana see, for instance, Adrian Kear and Deborah Lynn Steinberg, eds., *Mourning Diana: Nation, Culture and the Performance of Grief* (London: Routledge, 1999). Queen Victoria tried to contact Prince Albert through mediums following his death. Many mediums claim to have communicated with Princess Diana following her death in 1997.

68. Michael C. Kearl, *Endings: A Sociology of Death and Dying* (New York: Oxford University Press, 1989), 307.

69. Karla F. C. Holloway, *Passed On: African American Mourning Stories* (Durham, NC: Duke University Press, 2003), 178.

70. Ibid., 178–79.

71. Robert Bellah and Phillip Hammond, *Varieties of Civil Religion* (New York: Harper and Row, 1980), x, cited in Kearl, *Endings*, 303.

72. Ibid.

73. Ibid. His examples of this include national cemeteries, tombs for the unknown soldier, national days of remembrance and other forms of memorial.

74. In a footnote on this point, Kearl writes that "When the dead are intentionally forgotten, their memories become spirits that haunt the political order. The uninvestigated deaths in El Salvador, for example, led to new antiregime solidarities, including groups never before organized; outraged Salvadorean women created the Committee of Mothers and Relatives of Political Prisoners, Disappeared and Murdered." Ibid., 336.

CONCLUSION

1. For an interesting reading of Weiner's work see Judith Goldman, "Hannah=hannaH: Politics, Ethics, and Clairvoyance in the Work of Hannah Weiner," *differences: A Journal of Feminist Cultural Studies* 12, no. 2 (2001): 121–68.

2. Artemus Ward's take on spiritualism, "Among the Spirits," makes a broad attack on the séance and concludes, like Twain, that professional spiritualists are often frauds. Clifton Johnson, ed., *Artemus Ward's Best Stories* (New York: Harper, 1912), 43–47.

3. George Ellington, *The Women of New York: or the Underworld of the Great City* (1869; repr. New York: Arno, 1972). Two years after this a similar work was published, George M. Beard, "The Delusions of Clairvoyance," *Scribner's Monthly* 18 (May 1879–October 1879): 433–40.

4. See Judith R. Walkowitz, *City of Dreadful Delight: Narratives of Sexual Danger in Late-Victorian London* (London: Virago, 1992), 171–89; and Roy Porter and Helen Nicholson, eds., *Georgina Weldon and Louisa Lowe*, vol. 1 of Roy Porter, Helen Nicholson, and Bridget

Bennett, eds., *Women, Madness and Spiritualism*, 2 vols. (London: Routledge, 2003).

5. Eugene Crowell, *Spiritualism and Insanity* (Boston: Colby and Rich, 1877). Crowell concludes his pamphlet by writing that "Strange indeed would it be if the belief in such a religion tended to insanity, and it should be a source of satisfaction and justifiable pride to every Spiritualist to know that official statistics prove the calumny to be unfounded and unjust," 16.

6. "The room was now pretty well filled with the unmistakable crowd which always attend such meetings. They were mostly artisans, of more intellectual ambition than their fellows, whose love of the marvellous was not held in control by any educated judgment. They had long, serious faces and every man of them wore long hair and a soft hat. Their women were generally sad, broken-spirited drudges, to whom this kind of show was like an opera or a ball. There were two or three shame-faced believers of the better class, who scoffed a little but trembled in secret, and a few avowed skeptics, young clerks on a mild spree, ready for fun if any should present itself." John Hay, *The Bread-Winners: A Social Study* (New York: Harper, 1884), 104.

7. Hay, *The Bread-Winners*, 107.

8. The archives at the University of Southern California contain a significant quantity of material that attests to Garland's interest in the subject. This ranges from spirit photographs and accounts of séances to Garland's own writings.

9. W. D. Howells, *The Undiscovered Country* (Cambridge: H. O. Houghton, 1880), 1. Howells had not finished with the subject of spirits, and in 1897 published *The Landlord at Lion's Head*, which includes a subplot that focuses on spiritualistic belief's effect on a young girl.

10. Henry James, *The Bostonians*, ed. Charles R. Anderson (London: Penguin, 1986), 245.

11. Swedenborg also influenced Sarah Orne Jewett. Both Celia Thaxter and Annie Fields were keen investigators of spiritualism. Josephine Donovan, "Jewett and Swedenborg," *American Literature* 65, no. 4 (December 1993): 731–50. In a letter of January 1898 to Annie Fields, Thomas Higginson notes how profoundly Thaxter was interested in spiritualism. See, Thomas Wentworth Higginson, *Letters and Journals of Thomas Wentworth Higginson, 1846–1906*, ed. Mary Thacher Higginson (Boston: Houghton Mifflin, 1921), 28–29. Sarah Way Sherman notes that, "Celia Thaxter's letters to Jewett's friend, John Greenleaf Whittier, describe a séance in which Annie Fields and Jewett were both present. At one point, the medium roused the spirit of Annie's husband, James T. Fields, and Celia Thaxter later encountered the ghost of her own mother." *Sarah Orne Jewett, an American Persephone* (Hanover, NH: University Press of New England, 1989), 58. See John J. Kucich's pertinent discussion of Jewett, of *The Bostonians*,

and of Pauline E. Hopkins's 1902–1903 novel *Of One Blood* in Kucich, *Ghostly Communication: Cross-Cultural Spiritualism in Nineteenth-Century American Literature* (Hanover, NH: Dartmouth College Press, 2004), chs. 4 and 5.

12. William Leach, *Land of Desire: Merchants, Power, and the Rise of a New American Culture* (New York: Vintage Books, 1993), 225. See also Douglas, *Terrible Honesty*, 32–33.

13. See Joel Myerson and Daniel Shealey, eds., *The Selected Letters of Louisa May Alcott* (Boston: Little Brown, 1987), 287; Myerson and Shealey, eds., *The Journals of Louisa May Alcott* (Boston: Little Brown, 1989), 247 and 252; Madeleine B. Stern, *Louisa May Alcott* (London: Peter Nevill, 1952). Also see indexed referenced to mind cure and mesmerism in each of these books.

14. Stern, *Louisa May Alcott*, 257, 266, 273.

15. See Leach, *Land of Desire*, 225–62.

16. For a carefully composed (and authorized) account of Eddy's engagement with spiritualism see Sibyl Wilbur, *The Life of Mary Baker Eddy* (Boston: Christian Science Publishing, 1941), 52–54. For further details see Willa Cather and Georgine Milmine, *The Life of Mary Baker Eddy and the History of Christian Science* (Lincoln: University of Nebraska Press, 1993), 105–20. See also Cynthia D. Schrager, "Mark Twain and Mary Baker Eddy: Gendering the Transpersonal Subject," *American Literature* 70, no. 1 (March 1998): 29–62.

17. See Bridget Bennett, *The Damnation of Harold Frederic: His Lives and Works* (Syracuse, NY: Syracuse University Press, 1997), 47–58.

18. It was serialized in *McClure's Magazine* in 1907–1908 prior to book publication in 1909.

19. Ella Wheeler Wilcox, *The Worlds and I* (New York: George H. Doran, 1918), 112. She wrote her poem "Illusion" after attending a lecture by Swami Vivekananda, the Indian spiritual teacher. She wrote "It is the only experience of the kind which ever befell me. And oddly enough, it is the only one of my thousands of verses which I was ever able completely to memorize and never forget. Whoever wrote it through me helps me to recall it."

20. Barnes's grandmother Zadel was a celebrated spiritualist and women's rights worker. London's mother was an avid spiritualist. Phillip E. Herring, *Djuna: The Life and Work of Djuna Barnes* (New York: Viking, 1995), 2–5.

21. Lizzie Doten, *Poems from the Inner Life* (Boston: W. White, 1873.) For a discussion of Doten and Poe, see "Resurrexi: Poe in the Crypt of Lizzie Doten," in *The Cryptographic Imagination: Secret Writing from Edgar Poe to the Internet*, ed. Shawn James Rosenheim, 115–38 (Baltimore: Johns Hopkins University Press, 1997).

22. Douglas, *Terrible Honesty*, 228.

23. Sarah Helen Whitman, *Edgar Poe and His Critics* (New York: Rudd and Carleton, 1860).

24. The poem was published posthumously in Sprague, *The Poet and Other Poems*. For more on Sprague's career as a trance lecturer and poet see Braude, *Radical Spirits*, 99–116.

25. Of course this is not just true of U.S. culture. Many writers beyond the boundaries of the United States were also profoundly excited by, and engaged with, such ideas and their expression. Bette London's work on collaborative authorship and mediumship is just one example of the many critical works that show how powerfully British and Irish writers responded to the imaginative potentialities offered by the spirit world in creative terms. Bette London, *Writing Double: Women's Literary Partnerships* (Ithaca, NY: Cornell University Press, 1999.) See especially chapters 5 and 6.

BIBLIOGRAPHY

Abel, Elizabeth, Barbara Christian, and Carolyn Martin Shaw, eds. *Female Subjects in Black and White: Race, Psychoanalysis and Feminism*. Berkeley: University of California Press, 1997.

Adler, Leonore Loeb, and B. Runi Mukherji, eds. *Spirit Versus Scalpel: Traditional Healing and Modern Psychotherapy*. Westport, CT: Bergin and Garvey, 1995. Aiken, George L. *Uncle Tom's Cabin; or, Life Among the Lowly. A Domestic Drama in Six Acts*, in *Early American Drama*, edited by Jeffrey H. Richards. Harmondsworth, England: Penguin, 1997.

Alcott, Louisa May. *Little Women*. Edited by Elaine Showalter. New York: Penguin, 1989.

———. *The Selected Letters of Louisa May Alcott*. Edited by Joel Myerson and Daniel Shealey. Boston: Little, Brown, and Company, 1987.

———. *The Journals of Louisa May Alcott*. Edited by Joel Myerson and Daniel Shealey. Boston: Little, Brown, and Company, 1989.

Altick, Richard D. *The Shows of London*. Cambridge, MA: Harvard University Press, 1978.

Anderson, Benedict. *Imagined Communities: Reflections on the Origin and Spread of Nationalism*. Rev. ed. London: Verso, 1991.

Andrews, Edward Deming. *The People Called Shakers: A Search for the Perfect Society*. New York: Dover, 1963.

Anonymous. *A Reply to Captain Marryat's Illiberal and Incorrect Statements Relative to the Coloured West Indies, as Published in his Work, Entitled, "A Diary in America."* London: E. Justins and Son, 1840.

———. "Black Hawk against Morse and Blaine." In *The Spiritual Telegraph*, edited by S. B. Brittan, 4, 447–48. New York: Partridge and Brittan, 1854.

———. "The Seeress of Prevorst." In *The Spiritual Telegraph*, edited by S. B. Brittan, 4, 122–23. New York: Partridge and Brittan, 1854.

———. [A Guest of the "Community" Near Watervliet, N.Y.] *A Revelation of the Extraordinary Visitation of Departed Spirits of Distinguished Men and Women of All Nations, and Their Manifestation through the Living Bodies of the "Shakers."* Philadelphia: L. G. Thomas, 1869.

———. *Private Dowding*, notes by W. T. P. London: John M. Watkins, 1917.

———. "Spiritual Manifestations among the Indians." In *The Spiritual*

Telegraph, edited by S. B. Brittan, 4, 116. New York: Partridge and Brittan, 1854.

———. "Logan's Speech." In *The Spiritual Telegraph*, edited by S. B. Brittan, 4, 235. New York: Partridge and Brittan, 1854.

———. "Spirits in Keokuk." In *The Spiritual Telegraph*, edited by S. B. Brittan, 4, 409. New York: Partridge and Brittan, 1854.

———. "Charges against a Spiritualist." *Times London*, January 29, 1881, p. 10.

———. *Le Charivari*, June 21, 1853, p. 3.

———. "Untitled." *The Athenaeum*, no. 3212 (May 18, 1889): 633.

———. "Untitled." *Notes and Queries* 7 (1889): 9, 74, 177, 294.

———. *Reynolds Newspaper*. December 19, 1895, p. 8.

Ariès, Phillipe. *The Hour of Our Death*. Translated by Helen Weaver. London: Allen Lane, 1981.

Baker, Jean H. *Mary Todd Lincoln: A Biography*. New York and London: W. W. Norton and Company, 1987.

Bank, Rosemarie K. "Staging the 'Native': Making History in American Theatre Culture, 1828–1838." *Theatre Journal* 45 (1993): 461–86.

Barber, X. Theodore. "Phantasmagorical Wonders: The Magic Lantern Ghost Show in Nineteenth-Century America." *Film History* 3 (1989): 73–86.

Barnes, Elizabeth. *States of Sympathy: Seduction and Democracy in the American Novel*. New York: Columbia University Press, 1997.

Barnes, John. "The History of the Magic Lantern." In *Servants of Light: The Book of the Lantern*, edited by Dennis Crompton, Richard Franklin, and Stephen Herbert, 8–33. Ripon: Magic Lantern Society, 1997.

Barringer, Tim. "The Course of Empires: Landscape and Identity in America and Britain, 1820–1880." In *American Sublime: Landscape Painting in the United States 1820–1880*, edited by Andrew Wilton and Tim Barringer, 39–65. London: Tate, 2002.

Barrow, Logie. *Independent Spirits: Spiritualism and English Plebeians, 1850–1910*. London: Routledge, 1986.

Barthes, Roland. *Camera Lucida*. Translated by Richard Howard. London: Vintage, 2000.

Basler, Roy P., ed. *Walt Whitman's Memoranda During the War and Death of Abraham Lincoln*. Bloomington: Indiana University Press, 1962.

Beard, George M. "The Delusions of Clairvoyance." *Scribner's Monthly* 18 (May–October 1879): 433–40.

Belasco, Susan. "'The Animating Influences of Discord': Margaret Fuller in 1844." *Legacy* 20, no. 1 (2003): 76–93.

Benes, Peter. "Fortune-Tellers, Wise-Men, and Magical Healers in New England, 1644–1850." In *Wonders of the Invisible World: 1600–1900*, edited by Peter Benes, 127–56. Boston: Boston University, 1995.

Bennett, Bridget. *The Damnation of Harold Frederic: His Lives and Works*. Syracuse: Syracuse University Press, 1997.

Bergland, Renée. *The National Uncanny: Indian Ghosts and American Subjects*. Hanover, NH: Dartmouth College, 2000.

Betts, William W., Jr., ed. *Lincoln and the Poets*. Pittsburgh: University of Pittsburgh Press, 1965.

Bloch, Ruth H. *Visionary Republic: Millennial Themes in American Thought, 1756–1800*. Cambridge: Cambridge University Press, 1985.

Boime, Albert. *The Magisterial Gaze: Manifest Destiny and American Landscape Painting c. 1830–1865*. Washington, DC: Smithsonian Institution Press, 1991.

Brandon, Ruth. *The Life and Many Deaths of Harry Houdini*. London: Secker and Warburg, 1993.

———. *The Spritualists: The Passion for the Occult in the Nineteenth and Twentieth Centuries*. London: Weidenfeld and Nicholson, 1983.

Braude, Ann. *Radical Spirits: Spiritualism and Women's Rights in Nineteenth-Century America*. Boston: Beacon, 1989.

Britten, Emma Hardinge. *Autobiography of Emma Hardinge Britten*. Edited by Margaret Wilkinson. Manchester: John Heywood, 1900.

———. *The Great Funeral Oration on Abraham Lincoln*. New York: American News Company, [1865].

Brittan, S. B., ed. *The Spiritual Telegraph*. 4 vols. New York: Partridge and Brittan, 1854.

Bronfen, Elisabeth. *Over Her Dead Body: Death, Femininity and the Aesthetic*. Manchester: Manchester University Press, 1992.

Browder, Laura. *Slippery Characters: Ethnic Impersonators and American Identities*. Chapel Hill: University of North Carolina Press, 2000.

Brown, William H. *The Power of Sympathy*. New York: Penguin, 1996.

Bryant, Sylvia. "Speaking into Being: The Gifts of Rebecca Cox Jackson, 'Black Visionary, Shaker Eldress.'" In *Women's Life-Writing: Finding Voice/ Building Community*, edited by Linda S. Coleman, 63–80. Bowling Green, OH: Bowling Green State Popular Press, 1997.

Buci-Glucksman, Christine. *Baroque Reason: The Aesthetics of Modernity*. Translated by Patrick Camiller, introduction by Bryan S. Turner. London, Thousand Oaks, 1994.

Bullock, Steven C. *Revolutionary Brotherhood: Freemasonry and the Transformation of the American Social Order, 1730–1840*. Chapel Hill: University of North Carolina Press, 1996.

Burgett, Bruce. *Sentimental Bodies: Sex, Gender, and Citizenship in the Early Republic*. Princeton, NJ: Princeton University Press, 1998.

Butler, Jon. *Awash in a Sea of Faith: Christianizing the American People*. Cambridge, MA: Harvard University Press, 1990.

———, and Harry S. Stout, eds. *Religion in American History*. Oxford: Oxford University Press, 1998.

Caddy, Davinia. "Variations on the Dance of the Seven Veils." *Cambridge Opera Journal* 17 (2005): 37–58.

Carnes, Mark C. *Secret Ritual and Manhood in Victorian America.* New Haven, CT: Yale University Press, 1989.

Carroll, Bret E. *Spiritualism in Antebellum America.* Bloomington: Indiana University Press, 1997.

Case, Sue-Ellen, and Janet Reinelt, eds. *The Performance of Power: Theatrical Discourse and Politics.* Iowa City: University of Iowa Press, 1991.

Castillo, Susan. *Performing America: Colonial Encounters in New World Writing, 1500–1786.* London: Routledge, 2006.

Castle, Terry. *The Apparitional Lesbian: Female Homosexuality and Modern Culture.* New York: Columbia University Press, 1993.

———. *The Female Thermometer: Eighteenth-Century Culture and the Invention of the Uncanny.* New York: Oxford University Press, 1995.

Castronovo, Russ. *Necro Citizenship: Death, Eroticism, and the Public Sphere in the Nineteenth-Century United States.* Durham, NC: Duke University Press, 2001.

Cather, Willa, and Georgine Milmine. *The Life of Mary Baker Eddy and the History of Christian Science.* Lincoln: University of Nebraska Press, 1993.

Cawardine, Richard. *Transatlantic Revivalism: Popular Evangelicalism in Britain and America, 1790–1865.* Westport, CT: Greenwood Press, 1978.

Chapman, Alison. "'A Poet Never Sees a Ghost': Photography and Trance in Tennyson's *Enoch Arden* and Julia Margaret Cameron's Photography." *Victorian Poetry* 41, no. 1 (Spring 2003): 47–71.

Chapman, Mary, and Glenn Hendler, eds. *Sentimental Men: Masculinity and the Politics of Affect in American Culture.* Berkeley: University of California Press, 1999.

Coates, James. *Photographing the Invisible: Practical Studies in Supernormal Photography, Script, and Other Allied Phenomena.* London: L. N. Fowler, 1921.

Coale, Samuel Chase. *Mesmerism and Hawthorne: Mediums of an American Romance.* Tuscaloosa: University of Alabama Press, 1998.

Coleman, Linda, ed. *Women's Life-Writing: Finding Voices/ Building Community.* Bowling Green, OH: Bowling Green State Popular Press, 1997.

Collyer, Robert. *Lights and Shadows of American Life.* Boston: Brainard and Company, 1843.

Cottom, Daniel. *Abyss of Reason: Cultural Movements, Revelations, and Betrayals.* New York: Oxford University Press, 1991.

Crowell, Eugene. *Spiritualism and Insanity.* Boston: Colby and Rich, 1877.

Cruikshank, George. *A Discovery Concerning Ghosts: With a Rap at the "Spirit-Rappers."* London: Routledge, W arne, and Routledge, 1864.

Cutler, Edward S. *Recovering the New: Transtlantic Roots of Modernism.* Hanover, NH : University Press of New England, 2003.

Darnton, Robert. *Mesmerism and the End of the Enlightenment in France.* Cambridge, MA: Harvard University Press, 1968.

Davies, Douglas J. *Death, Ritual and Belief: The Rhetoric of Funerary Rites.* London: Cassell, 1997.

Deloria, Philip J. *Playing Indian.* New Haven, CT: Yale University Press, 1998.

Derrida, Jacques. *Specters of Marx: The State of the Debt, the Work of Mourning, and the New International.* Translated by Peggy Kamuf. New York: Routledge, 1994.

Dewedney, Selwyn, ed. *Legends of My People: The Great Ojibway.* Illustated and told by Norval Morrison. Toronto: McGraw-Hill, 1977.

Dickens, Charles. *American Notes for General Circulation.* Edited by Arnold Goldman and John Whitley. London: Penguin, 1985.

Dillon, Elizabeth Maddock. "Sentimental Aesthetics." *American Literature* 76, no.3 (2004): 495–523.

Dimock, Wai Chee. *Through Other Continents: American Literature Across Deep Time.* Princeton, NJ: University of Princeton Press, 2006.

Dobson, Joanne. "Reclaiming Sentimental Literature." *American Literature* 69, no. 2 (June 1997): 263–88.

Donovan, Josephine. "Jewett and Swedenborg." *American Literature* 65, no.4 (December 1993): 731–50.

Doolen, Andy. *Fugitive Empires: Locating Early American Imperialism.* Minneapolis: University of Minnesota Press, 2005.

Doten, Lizzie. *Poems from the Inner Life.* Boston: W. White, 1873.

Douglas, Ann. *Terrible Honesty: Mongrel Manhattan in the 1920s.* London: Papermac, 1995.

Dunkerley, James. *Americana: The Americas in the World, around 1850.* London: Verso, 2000.

Dyer, Richard. *White.* London: Routledge, 1997.

Eliot, George. *The George Eliot Letters.* 12 vols. Edited by Gordon Haight. New Haven, CT: Yale University Press, 1954–1978.

Eliot, T. S. *Collected Poems, 1909–1962.* London: Faber and Faber, 1963.

Ellington, George. *The Women of New York: Or the Underworld of the Great City.* New York: Arno, 1972.

Emerson, Ralph Waldo. *Nature and Selected Essays.* Edited by Larzer Ziff. New York: Penguin, 2003.

Fiedler, Leslie A. *Love and Death in the American Novel.* New York: Criterion, 1960.

Fields, Annie, ed. *The Life and Letters of Harriet Beecher Stowe.* Cambridge: Houghton, Mifflin, and Company, 1898.

Fliegelman, Jay. *Declaring Independence: Jefferson, Natural Language, and the Culture of Performance.* Stanford, CA: Stanford University Press, 1993.

Forrest, Derek. *Hypnotism: A History.* London: Penguin, 2000.

Foster, Hannah Webster. *The Coquette*. Edited by Carla L. Mulford. New York: Penguin, 1996.

Frey, Sylvia R., and Betty Wood. *Come Shouting to Zion: African American Protestantism in the American South and British Caribbean to 1830*. Chapel Hill: University of North Carolina Press, 1998.

Fuller, Margaret. *Summer on the Lakes, in 1843*. Urbana: University of Illinois Press, 1991.

Fuller, Robert C. *Mesmerism and the Cure of American Souls*. Philadelphia: University of Pennsylvania Press, 1982.

Fulop, Timothy E., and Albert J. Raboteau, eds. *African-American Religion: Interpretive Essays in History and Culture*. London: Routledge, 1997.

Garrett, Clarke. *Spirit Possession and Popular Religion: From the Camisards to the Shakers*. Baltimore: Johns Hopkins University Press, 1987.

Gauld, Alan. *A History of Hypnotism*. Cambridge: Cambridge University Press, 1992.

Giles, Paul. *Transatlantic Insurrections: British Culture and the Formation of American Literature, 1730–1860*. Philadelphia: University of Pennsylvania Press, 2001.

Gillman, Susan. *Blood Talk: American Race Melodrama and the Culture of the Occult*. Chicago: University of Chicago Press, 2003.

Gilmore, Paul. *The Genuine Article: Race, Mass Culture, and American Literary Manhood*. Durham, NC: Duke University Press, 2001.

Gilroy, Paul. *The Black Atlantic: Modernity and Double Consciousness*. London: Verso, 1995.

Goldsmith, Barbara. *Other Powers: The Age of Suffrage, Spiritualism, and the Scandalous Victoria Woodhull*. New York: Knopf, 1998.

Gonzalez, John M. "The Warp of Whiteness: Domesticity and Empire in Helen Hunt Jackson's *Ramona*." *American Literary History* 16, no.3 (2004): 437–65.

Gottschalk, Louis. *Lafayette between the American and French Revolution (1783–1789)*. Chicago: University of Chicago Press, 1950.

Gould, Philip. "The Pocahontas Story in Early America." *Prospects: An Annual of American Cultural Studies* 24 (1999): 99–116.

Grant, Susan-Mary. "Patriot Graves: American National Identity and the Civil War Dead." *American Nineteenth-Century History* 5, no. 3 (Fall 2004): 74–100.

Grierson, Francis. *Abraham Lincoln: The Practical Mystic*. London: John Lane, 1919.

Griffiths, Nicholas, and Fernando Cervantes, eds. *Spiritual Encounters: Interactions between Christianity and Native Religions in Colonial America*. Birmingham: University of Birmingham Press, 1999.

Gunn, Joshua. "Mourning Speech: Haunting and the Spectral Voices of Nine Eleven." *Text and Performance Quarterly* 24, no.2 (April 2004): 91–114.

Halttunen, Karen. "Gothic Imagination and Social reform: The Haunted Houses of Lyman Beecher, Henry Ward Beecher, and Harriet Beecher Stowe." In *New Essays on "Uncle Tom's Cabin,"* edited by Eric J. Sundquist, 107–34. Cambridge: Cambridge University Press, 1993.

Hannay, David. *Life of Frederick Marryat.* London: Walter Scott, 1889.

Hardinge [Britten], Emma. *Modern American Spiritualism.* New York: n.p., 1869.

Hawthorne, Nathaniel. *The Blithedale Romance.* Oxford: Oxford University Press, 1998.

———. *The House of the Seven Gables.* Edited by Milton R. Stern. New York: Penguin, 1986.

———. *The Scarlet Letter: A Romance.* New York: Penguin, 2003.

Hay, John. *The Bread-Winners: A Social Study.* New York: Harper and Brothers, 1884.

Hedrick, Joan D. *Harriet Beecher Stowe: A Life.* New York: Oxford University Press, 1994.

Herring, Philip E. *Djuna: The Life and Work of Djuna Barnes.* New York: Viking, 1995.

Higginson, Thomas Wentworth. *Letters and Journals of Thomas Wentworth Higginson, 1846–1906.* Edited by Mary Thacher Higginson. Boston: Houghton Mifflin, 1921.

Philip Hoare, *England's Lost Eden: Adventures in a Victorian Utopia.* London: Fourth Estate, 2005.

Holland, Sharon Patricia. *Raising the Dead: Readings of Death and (Black) Subjectivity.* Durham, NC: Duke University Press, 2000.

Holloway, Karla F. C. *Passed On: African American Mourning Stories.* Durham, NC: Duke University Press, 2003.

Howells, W. D. *Selected Letters: Volume 1: 1852–1872.* 6 vols. Edited by George Arms, Don L. Cook, Christoph K. Lohmann, and David J. Nordloh. Boston: Twayne, 1979.

———. *The Undiscovered Country.* Cambridge: H. O. Houghton and Company, 1880.

Hull, Akasha (Gloria). "Channeling the Ancestral Muse: Lucille Clifton and Dolores Kendrick." In *Female Subjects in Black and White,* edited by Elizabeth Abel, Barbara Christian, and Helene Moglen, 330–48. Berkeley: University of California Press, 1997.

Hulme, Peter, and William H. Sherman. *"The Tempest" and Its Travels.* London: Reaktion, 2000.

Humez, Jean McMahon, ed. *Gifts of Power: The Writings of Rebecca Jackson, Black Visionary, Shaker Eldress.* Boston: University of Massachusetts Press, 1981.

Humphries, Steve. *Victorian Britain through the Magic Lantern.* London: Sidgwick & Jackson, 1989.

Garrett, Clarke. *Spirit Possession and Popular Religion: From the Camisards to the Shakers.* Baltimore: Johns Hopkins University Press, 1987.

Gerry, Elbridge Thomas. *The Mumler "Spirit" Photograph Case.* New York: Baker, Vorhis and Company, 1869.

Gettings, Fred. *Ghosts in Photographs: The Extraordinary Story of Spirit Photography.* Montreal: Optimum, 1978.

Giles, Paul. *Transatlantic Insurrections: British Culture and the Formation of American Literature, 1730–1860.* Philadelphia: University of Pennsylvania Press, 2001.

Gilmore, Paul. *The Genuine Article: Race, Mass Culture, and American Literary Manhood.* Durham, NC: Duke University Press, 2001.

Goldman, Judith, "Hannah=hannaH: Politics, Ethics, and Clairvoyance in the Work of Hannah Weiner." *differences: A Journal of Feminist Cultural Studies* 12, no. 2 (2001): 121–68.

Goldner, Ellen J. "Arguing with Pictures: Race, Class, and the Formation of Popular Abolitionism through *Uncle Tom's Cabin.*" *Journal of American Culture* 24, no. 1–2 (Spring/Summer 2001): 71–84.

Greenblatt, Stephen Jay. *Learning to Curse: Essays in Modern Culture.* London: Routledge, 1990.

Griffiths, Nicholas, and Fernando Cervantes, eds. *Spiritual Encounters: Interactions between Christianity and Native Religions in Colonial America.* Birmingham: University of Birmingham Press, 1999.

Holloway, Karla F. C. *Passed On: African American Mourning Stories.* Durham, NC: Duke University Press, 2003.

Household, G. A., ed. *To Catch a Sunbeam: Victorian Reality through the Magic Lantern.* London: Michael Joseph, 1979.

Howells, W. D. *Selected Letters.* 6 vols. Edited by George Arms et al. Boston: Twayne, 1979.

Humphries, Steve. *Victorian Britain through the Magic Lantern.* London: Sidgwick Jackson, 1979.

Jallard, Pat. "Victorian Death and Its Decline: 1850–1918." In *Death in England: An Illustrated History,* edited by Peter C. Jupp and Clare Gittings, 230–55. Manchester: Manchester University Press, 1999.

James, Henry. *The Bostonians.* Edited by Charles R. Anderson. London: Penguin, 1986.

Johnson, Clifton, ed. *Artemus Ward's Best Stories.* New York: Harper, 1912.

Jorge, Angela. "*Mesa Blanca*: A Puerto Rican Healing Tradition." In *Spirit Versus Scalpel: Traditional Healing and Modern Psychotherapy,* edited by Leonore Loeb Adler and B. Runi Mukherji, 109–20. Westport, CT: Bergin and Garvey, 1995.

Justner, Susan, and Lisa McFarlane, eds. *A Mighty Baptism: Race, Gender and the Creation of American Protestantism.* Ithaca, NY: Cornell University Press, 1996.

Kaplan, Amy. *The Anarchy of Empire in the Making of U.S. Culture.* Cambridge, MA: Harvard University Press, 2002.

Kaufman, Will, and Heidi Slettedahl MacPherson, eds. *Transatlantic Studies*. Oxford: University Press of America, 2000.

Kazanjian, David. *The Colonizing Trick: National Culture and Imperial Citizenship in Early America*. Minneapolis: University of Minnesota Press, 2003.

Kear, Adrian, and Deborah Lynn Steinberg, eds. *Mourning Diana: Nation, Culture and the Performance of Grief*. London: Routledge, 1999.

Kearl, Michael C. *Endings: A Sociology of Death and Dying*. New York: Oxford University Press, 1989.

Kerr, Howard. *Mediums, Spirit-Rappers, and Roaring Radicals: Spiritualism in American Literature, 1850–1900*. Urbana: University of Illinois Press, 1972.

Kete, Mary Louise. *Sentimental Collaboration: Mourning and Middle-Class Identity in Nineteenth-Century America*. Durham, NC: Duke University Press, 2000.

King, W. D. "'Shadow of a Mesmerist': The Female Body on the 'Dark' Stage." *Theatre Journal* 49 (1997): 189–206.

Kolodny, Annette. "Margaret Fuller's First Depiction of Indians and the Limits on Social Protest: An Exercise in Women's Studies Pedagogy." *Legacy* 18, no. 1 (2001): 1–20.

Kucich, John J. *Ghostly Communion: Cross-Cultural Spiritualism in Nineteenth-Century American Literature*. Hanover, NH: Dartmouth College Press, 2004.

Kutchen, Larry. "The 'Vulgar Thread of the Canvas': Revolution and the Picturesque in Ann Eliza Bleeker, Crèvecoeur, and Charles Brockden Brown." *Early American Literature* 36, no. 3 (2001): 395–425.

Laderman, Gary. "The Body Politic and the Politics of Two Bodies: Abraham and Mary Todd Lincoln in Death." *Prospects* (1997): 109–32.

Laderman, Gary. *The Sacred Remains: American Attitudes towards Death, 1799–1883*. New Haven, CT: Yale University Press, 1996.

Leach, William. *Land of Desire: Merchants, Power, and the Rise of a New American Culture*. New York: Vintage, 1993.

Lears, Jackson. *Fables of Abundance: A Cultural History of Advertising in America*. New York: Harper Collins, 1994.

Leavelle, Tracy Neal. "Geographies of Encounter: Religion and Contested Spaces in Colonial North America." *American Quarterly* 56, no. 4 (2004): 913–43.

Leevier, Annette. *Psychic Experiences of an Indian Princess*. Los Angeles: Austin Publishing Company, 1920.

Levander, Caroline Field. *Voices of the Nation: Women and Public Speech in Nineteenth-Century American Literature and Culture*. Cambridge: Cambridge University Press, 1998.

Levine, Lawrence W. *Highbrow/Lowbrow: The Emergence of Cultural Hierarchy in America.* Cambridge, MA: Harvard University Press, 1988.

Lhamon, W. T., Jr. *Raising Cain: Blackface Performance from Jim Crow to Hip Hop.* Cambridge, MA: Harvard University Press, 1998.

Lieberman, Jessica Catherine. "Flight from Haunting: Psychogenic Fugue and Nineteenth-Century American Imagination." In *Spectral America: Phantoms and the National Imagination,* edited by Jeffrey Andrew Weinstock,141–56. Madison: University of Wisconsin Press, 2004.

Lipsitz, George. *Time Passages: Collective Memory and American Popular Culture.* Minneapolis: University of Minnesota Press, 2001.

London, Bette. *Writing Double: Women's Literary Partnerships.* Ithaca, NY: Cornell University Press, 1999.

Long, Lisa A. "'The Corporeality of Heaven': Rehabilitating the Civil War Body in *The Gates Ajar.*" *American Literature* 69, no. 4 (December 1997): 781–811.

———. *Rehabilitating Bodies: Health, History, and the American Civil War.* Philadelphia: University of Pennsylvania Press, 2004.

Lott, Eric. *Love and Theft: Blackface Minstrelsy and the American Working Class.* New York: Oxford University Press, 1993.

Luckhurst, Roger. *The Invention of Telepathy, 1870–1901.* Oxford: Oxford University Press, 2002.

Madden, Etta. "Reading, Writing, and the Race of Mother Figures: Shakers Rebecca Cox Jackson and Alonzo Giles Hollister." In *A Mighty Baptism: Race, Gender and the Creation of American Protestantism,* edited by Susan Justner and Lisa McFarlane, 210–34. Ithaca, NY: Cornell University Press, 1996.

Maddox, Lucy. *Removals: Nineteenth-Century American Literature and the Politics of Indian Affairs.* New York: Oxford University Press, 1991.

Marryat, Florence. *Life and Letters of Captain Marryat.* London: Richard Bentley and Son, 1872.

———. *There Is No Death.* London: Psychic Book Club, 1938.

Marx, Karl. *The Revolutions of 1848: Political Writings: Volume 1.* Edited by David Fernbach. London: Penguin, 1993.

Mason, Jeffrey D. "The Politics of *Metamora.*" In *The Performance of Power: Theatrical Discourse and Politics,* edited by Sue-Ellen Case and Janelle Reinelt, 92–110. Iowa City: University of Iowa Press, 1991.

Mather, Cotton. *The Wonders of the Invisible World to Which Is Added Increase Mather a Farther Account of the Tryals of the New-England Witches.* London: John Russell Smith, 1862.

Maynard, Nettie Colburn. *Was Abraham Lincoln a Spiritualist? or, Curious Revelations from the Life of a Trance Medium.* Philadelphia: Rufus C. Hartranft, 1891.

McCully, Susan. "Oh I Love Mother, I Love Her Power: Shaker Spirit Possession and the Performance of Desire." *Theatre Survey* 35, no. 1 (May 1994): 89–98.

McFadden, Margaret. *Golden Cables of Sympathy: The Transatlantic Sources of Nineteenth-Century Feminism*. Lexington: University Press of Kentucky, 1999.

Meinwald, Dan. *Memento Mori: Death in Nineteenth Century Photography*. Riverside: California Museum of Photography, 1990.

Merish, Lori. *Sentimental Materialism, Gender, Commodity Culture and Nineteenth-Century American Literature*. Durham, NC: Duke University Press, 2000.

Merrill, Walter M., ed. *The Letters of William Lloyd Garrison*. 6 vols. Cambridge, MA: Harvard University Press, 1979.

Miller, Nancy. "'Portraits of Grief': Telling Details and the Testimony of Trauma." *differences: A Journal of Feminist Cultural Studies* 14, no. 3 (2003): 112–35.

Moody, Jocelyn. *Sentimental Confessions: Spiritual Narratives of Nineteenth-Century African American Women*. Athens: University of Georgia Press, 2001.

Moore, R. Laurence. *In Search of White Crows: Spiritualism, Parapsychology, and American Culture*. New York: Oxford University Press, 1977.

———. "Insiders and Outsiders in American Historical Narrative and American History." In *Religion in American History*, edited by Jon Butler and Harry S. Stout, 199–221. Oxford: Oxford University Press, 1998.

Morrison, Toni. *Playing in the Dark: Whiteness and the Literary Imagination*. London: Picador, 1993.

Mott, Frank Luther, ed. *A History of American Magazines*. 5 vols. Cambridge, MA: Harvard University Press, 1957.

Mould, Mrs. *Miss Wood in Derbyshire: A Series of Experimental Seances*. London: J. Burns, 1879.

Mumler, William H. *The Personal Experiences of William H Mumler in Spirit-Photography*. Boston: Colby and Rich, 1875.

Murray, David. "Spreading the Word: Missionaries, Conversion and Circulation in the Northeast." In *Spiritual Encounters: Interactions Between Christianity and Native Religions in Colonial America*, edited by Nicholas Griffiths and Fernando Cervantes, 43–64. Birmingham: University of Birmingham Press, 1999.

Nabokov, Peter, ed. *Native American Testimony: A Chronicle of Indian-White Relations from Prophecy to the Present, 1492–1992*. Harmondsworth, England: Viking Penguin, 1991.

Neely, Mark E., Jr., and R. Gerald McMurtry. *The Insanity File: The Case of Mary Todd Lincoln*. Carbondale: Southern Illinois University Press, 1986.

Nelson, Dana D. *The Word in Black and White: Reading "Race" in American Literature, 1638–1867*. New York: Oxford University Press, 1993.

Nelson, Geoffrey K. *Spiritualism and Society*. London: Routledge and Kegan Paul, 1969.

Nicholson, Helen. "Henry Irving and the Staging of Spiritualism." *New Theatre Quarterly* 16, no. 3 (August 2000): 278–87.

Nordhoff, Charles. *American Utopias* [originally *The Communistic Societies of the United States*]. Stockbridge, MA: Berkshire House Publishers, 1993.

Oppenheim, Janet. *The Other World: Spiritualism and Psychical Research in England, 1850–1914*. Cambridge: Cambridge University Press, 1985.

Owen, Alex. *The Darkened Room: Women, Power and Spiritualism in Late Victorian England*. London: Virago, 1989.

Owen, Robert. "Touching Visitants from a Higher Life: A Chapter of Autobiography." *Atlantic Monthly* (January 1875): 57–69.

Patlin, Thomas. "Exhibitions and Empire: National Parks and the Performance of Manifest Destiny." *Journal of American Culture* 22, no. 1 (Spring 1999): 41-60.

Patterson, Orlando. *Slavery and Social Death: A Comparative Study*. Cambridge, MA: Harvard University Press, 1982.

Patterson, Tom. *A Hundred Years of Spirit Photography*. London: Regency, 1965.

Pease, Donald. "The Global Homeland State: Bush's Biopolitical Settlement." *boundary 2*, 30 no.3 (2003): 1–18.

Phelan, Peggy. "Francesca Woodman's Photography: Death and the Image One More Time." *Signs: Journal of Women in Culture and Society* 27, no.4 (2002): 979–1004.

Phelps, Elizabeth Stuart. *Three Spiritualist Novels*. Urbana: University of Illinois Press, 2000.

Pick, Daniel. *Svengali's Web: The Alien Enchanter in Modern Culture*. New Haven, CT: Yale University Press, 2000.

Poe, Edgar Allan. *The Science Fiction of Edgar Allan Poe*. Edited by Harold Beaver. London: Penguin, 1976.

Porter, Roy, Helen Nicholson, and Bridget Bennett, eds. *Women, Madness and Spiritualism*. 2 vols. London: Routledge, 2003.

Post, Isaac. *Voices from the Spirit World: Being Communications from Many Spirits*. Rochester, NY: Charles H. McDonnell, 1852.

Pratt, Mary Louise. *Imperial Eyes: Travel Writing and Transculturation*. London: Routledge, 1992.

Prins, Harald E. L. "Chief Big Thunder. 1827–1906: The Life History of a Penobscot Trickster." *Maine History* 37, no.2 (1998): 140–58.

Putnam, Allen. *Spirit Invocations: or, Prayers and Praises*. Boston: Colby and Rich, 1876.

Rey, Henri Louis. "Communications Spiritualistses." In *Paroles d'Honneur: Écrits de Créoles de Coleur Néo-Orléanais 1837–1872*, edited by Chris Michaelides, 189–210. Shreveport, LA: Éditions Tintamarre, 2004.

Richards, Eliza. "Lyric Telegraphy: Women Spirits, Spiritualist Poetics and the 'Phantom Voice' of Poe." *The Yale Journal of Criticism* 12, no. 2 (1999): 269–94.

[Richmond, Cora L. V.] *Ouina's Canoe and Christmas Offering, Filled with Flowers for the Darlings of the Earth.* Ottumwa, IA: D. M and N. P. Fox, 1882.

Roach, Joseph. *Cities of the Dead: Circum-Atlantic Performance.* New York: Columbia University Press, 1996.

Robertson, Karen. "Pocahontas at the Masque." *Signs* (Spring 1996): 551–83.

Rogin, Michael Paul. *Subversive Genealogy: The Politics and Art of Herman Melville.* Berkeley: University of California Press, 1979.

Rosenheim, Shawn James. *The Cryptographic Imagination: Secret Writing from Edgar Poe to the Internet.* Baltimore: Johns Hopkins University Press, 1997.

Ruby, Jay. *Secure the Shadow: Death and Photography in America.* Cambridge: Massachusetts Institute of Technology Press, 1995.

Rugg, Julie. "From Reason to Regulation: 1760–1850." In *Death in England: An Illustrated History*, edited by Peter C. Jupp and Clare Gittings, 202–29. Manchester: Manchester University Press, 1999.

Salesa, Damon. "Samoa's Half-Castes and Some Frontiers of Comparison." In *Haunted by Empire: Geographies of Intimacy in North American History*, edited by Ann Laura Stoler, 71–93. Durham, NC: Duke University Press, 2006.

Samuels, Shirley, ed. *The Culture of Sentiment: Race, Gender, and Sentimentality in Nineteenth-Century America.* New York: Oxford University Press, 1992.

Sánchez-Eppler, Karen. "Then When We Clutch Hardest: On the Death of a Child and the Replication of an Image." In *Sentimental Men: Masculinity and the Politics of Affect in American Culture*, edited by Mary Chapman and Glenn Hendler, 64–85. Berkeley: University of California Press, 1999.

Sandburg, Carl. *Abraham Lincoln.* 2 vols. New York: Harcourt, Brace, and Company, 1939.

Schechner, Richard. *Performance Theory.* London: Routledge, 2003.

Scheckel, Susan. *The Insistence of the Indian: Race and Nationalism in Nineteenth-Century American Culture.* Princeton, NJ: Princeton University Press, 1998.

Schrager, Cynthia D. "Mark Twain and Mary Baker Eddy: Gendering the Transpersonal Subject." *American Literature* 70, no.1 (March 1998): 29–62.

Sedgwick, Catharine Maria. *Redwood: A Tale.* New York: E. Bliss and E. White, 1824.

Shaw, Carolyn Martin. "The Poetics of Identity: Questioning Spiritualism in African American Contexts." In *Female Subjects in Black and White*, edited by Elizabeth Abel, Barbara Christian, and Helene Moglen, 349–62. Berkeley: University of California Press, 1997.

Shaw, Ronald E. *Erie Water West: A History of the Erie Canal, 1792–1854.* Lexington: University of Kentucky Press, 1966.

Shelton, Harriet M. *Abraham Lincoln Returns.* New York: Evans, 1957.

Sherman, Sarah Way. *Sarah Orne Jewett, an American Persephone.* Hanover, NH: University Press of New England, 1989.

Showalter, Elaine, ed. *The New Feminist Criticism: Essays on Women, Literature and Theory.* London: Virago, 1986.

Simpson, George Eaton. *Black Religions in the New World.* New York: Columbia University Press, 1978.

Smith, Rita J. "Those Who Go Before: Ancestors of Eva St. Clare." *The New England Quarterly* 70, no. 2 (June 1997): 314–18.

Spires-Robin, Regina, and Peggy McGarrahan. "The Healing Practices of Mexican Spiritualism." In *Spirit Versus Scalpel: Traditional Healing and Modern Psychotherapy,* edited by Leonore Loeb Adler and B. Runi Mukherji, 121–35. Westport, CT: Bergin and Garvey, 1995.

Sprague, Achsha. *The Poet and Other Poems.* Boston: William White and Company, 1864.

Stauffer, John. "Daguerreotyping the National Soul: The Portraits of Southworth and Hawes, 1843–1860." *Prospects: An Annual of American Cultural Studies* 22(1997): 69–107.

Streeby, Shelley. *American Sensations: Class, Empire, and the Production of Popular Culture.* Berkeley: University of California Press, 2002.

Stein, Stephen J. *The Shaker Experience in America: A History of the United Society of Believers.* New Haven, CT: Yale University Press, 1992.

Stern, Julia A. *The Plight of Feeling: Sympathy and Dissent in the Early American Novel.* Chicago: University of Chicago Press, 1997.

Stern, Madelaine B. *Louisa May Alcott.* London: Peter Nevill, 1952.

Stevens, Laura M. "Transatlanticism Now." *American Literary History* 16, no. 1 (Spring 2004): 93–102.

Stoler, Ann Laura, ed. *Haunted by Empire: Geographies of Intimacy in North American History.* Durham, NC: Duke University Press, 2006.

Stowe, Charles Edward. *Life of Harriet Beecher Stowe Compiled from Her Letters and Journals.* London: Sampson, Low, Marston, Searle, and Rivington, 1989.

Stowe, Harriet Beecher. *My Wife and I, or, Harry Henderson's History.* New York: J. B. Ford and Company, 1871.

———. *Religious Poems.* Boston: Ticknor and Fields, 1867.

———. *Uncle Tom's Cabin, or, Life among the Lowly.* Edited by Elizabeth Ammons. New York: W. W. Norton and Company, 1994.

Stowe, Lyman Beecher. *Saints, Sinners and Beechers.* London: Ivor Nicholson and Watson, 1935.

Streeby, Shelley. *American Sensations: Class, Empire, and the Production of Popular Culture.* Berkeley: University of California Press, 2002.

Sundquist, Eric J., ed. *New Essays on "Uncle Tom's Cabin."* Cambridge: Cambridge University Press, 1993.

Swaine, Norman. *Autobiography of Two Worlds.* London: Rider and Company, [1937].

Tanner, Laura E. *Lost Bodies: Inhabiting the Borders of Life and Death.* Ithaca, NY: Cornell University Press, 2006.

Taylor, Helen. *Circling Dixie: Contemporary Southern Culture Through a Transatlantic Lens.* New Brunswick, NJ: Rutgers University Press, 2001.

Thurschwell, Pamela. *Literature, Technology and Magical Thinking, 1880–1920.* Cambridge: Cambridge University Press, 2001.

Tilton, Robert S. *Pocahontas: The Evolution of an American Narrative.* Cambridge: Cambridge University Press, 1994.

Tompkins, Jane P. "Sentimental Power: *Uncle Tom's Cabin* and the Politics of Literary History." In *The New Feminist Criticism: Essays on Women, Literature and Theory*, edited by Elaine Showalter, 81–104. London: Virago, 1986.

Twain, Mark. *The Complete Humorous Sketches and Tales of Mark Twain.* Edited by Charles Neider. New York: Doubleday, 1961.

Underhill, Lois Beechy. *The Woman Who Ran for President: The Many Lives of Victoria Woodhull.* London: Penguin, 1995.

Vaughan, Alden T. "Trinculo's Indian: American Natives in Shakespeare's England." In *"The Tempest" and its Travels*, edited by Peter Hulme and William H. Sherman, 49–59. London: Reaktion, 2000.

Verhoeven, William, ed. *Revolutionary Histories: Transatlantic Cultural Nationalism, 1775–1815.* Basingstoke: Palgrave, 2002.

Wagenknecht, Edward. *Harriet Beecher Stowe: The Known and the Unknown.* New York: Oxford University Press, 1965.

Walkowitz, Judith R. *City of Dreadful Delight: Narratives of Sexual Danger in Late-Victorian London.* London: Virago, 1992.

Wardley, Lynn. "Relic, Fetish, Femmage: The Aesthetics of Sentiment in the Work of Stowe." In *The Culture of Sentiment: Race, Gender, and Sentimentality in Nineteenth-Century America*, edited by Shirley Samuels, 203–20. New York: Oxford University Press, 1992.

Warner, Charles Dudley. "Out of the World." *Scribner's Monthly* 18 (1879): 549–58.

Warner, Marina. "In the Minds Eye: Thought-Pictures and Ethereal Presences in the Photography of Julia Margaret Cameron (1815–79)" *archive*, February 2004, 30–32.

———. *Phantasmagoria: Spirit Visions, Metaphors, and Media into the Twenty-first Century* (Oxford: Oxford University Press, 2006.

Weeks, Jim. "Gettysburg: Display Window for Popular Memory." *Journal of American Culture* 21, no. 4 (Winter 1998): 41–56.

Weinstein, Sheri. "Technologies of Vision: Spiritualism and Science in Nineteenth-Century America." In *Spectral America: Phantoms and the*

National Imagination, edited by Jeffrey Andrew Weinstock, 124–40. Madison: University of Wisconsin Press, 2004.

Weinstock, Jeffrey Andrew, ed. *Spectral America: Phantoms and the National Imagination*. Madison: University of Wisconsin Press, 2004.

Whitman, Sarah Helen. *Edgar Poe and His Critics*. New York: Rudd and Carleton, 1860.

Whitman, Walt. *The Complete Poems*. Edited by Francis Murphy. London: Penguin, 1986.

———. *Complete Poetry and Collected Prose*. New York: Library of America, 1982.

———. *Walt Whitman's Memoranda During the War and Death of Abraham Lincoln*. Edited by Roy P. Basler. Bloomington: Indiana University Press, 1962.

Whittier, John Greenleaf. *The Letters of John Greenleaf Whittier*. 3 vols. Edited by John B. Pickard. Cambridge, MA: Harvard University Press, 1975.

Wilbur, Sibyl. *The Life of Mary Baker Eddy*. Boston, MA: Christian Science Publishing, 1941.

Wilcox, Ella Wheeler. *The Worlds and I*. New York: George H. Doran, 1918.

Willburn, Sarah A. *Possessed Victorians: Extra Spheres in Nineteenth-Century Mystical Writings*. Aldershot, England: Ashgate, 2006.

Wills, Garry. *Lincoln at Gettysburg: The Words That Remade America*. New York: Simon and Schuster, 1992.

Wilson, Forrest. *Crusader in Crinoline*. London: Hutchinson, 1942.

Winter, Alison. *Mesmerized: Powers of Mind in Victorian Britain*. Chicago: Chicago University Press, 1998.

Wood, Marcus. *Blind Memory: Visual Representations of Slavery in England and America, 1780-1865*. Manchester: Manchester University Press, 2000.

Zimmerman, David A. "Frank Norris, Market Panic, and the Mesmeric Sublime." *American Literature* 75, no. 1 (March 2003): 61–90.

INDEX

rhetoric, 8
Richmond, Cora L. V., 188n23
ritual, 15–16
Roach, Joseph, 2, 16
Robertson, Etienne Gaspard, 76–79
Robertson, Karen, 103–4, 207n63,
    208n84
Rochester, 34–35, 91
Rochester rappings, 5–6, 33, 91–93
Rogin, Michael, 28–29, 191n6
Rolfe, John, 103–4
Rowson, Susanna, 124
Ruby, Jay, 191n61

Salem, 63, 92
Sánchez-Eppler, Karen, 213n43
Sand, George, 42, 123
Saunders, William, 161–62
Schnechner, Richard, 15
science, enthusiasm for, 73–74
Scott, Walter, 80
séances, 6–25, 30–32, 36–38,
    43–48, 52–53, 58, 78, 85–90,
    100–101, 111, 115–23, 128,
    137–39, 144, 148, 152–59,
    165, 175, 178–81, 188n23,
    203n10
Sebold, Alice, 216n7
Sedgwick, Catharine Maria, 95,
    104–5
Seneca Falls Declaration, 28–29
sentimental literature, 123–28,
    165–68
Shakerism, 16, 37–39, 76, 84–113,
    174–75, 205n32, 205n35
Shelton, Harriet M., 154
Sherman, Sarah Way, 221n11
Sherwood, Martha Mary, 121
Shockle, Charles E., 155–56
Silko, Leslie Marmon, 10
slavery, 10, 13, 36, 63, 121, 124,
    128; abolitionist movement,
    40–41, 47, 117, 151
Smith, John, 105

Smith, Joseph, 19, 37, 202n88
Smith, Rita J., 121, 210n4, 212n17
Society of Universal Harmony, 71–73
Southworth, E.D.E.N., 212n16
speaking in tongues, 98, 112
Spear, John Murray, 42
The Spiritual Telegraph, 42
spiritualism: definitions of, 5,
    145–46; divergent forms of,
    179; in England, 37–39;
    legacy of, 182–83; opposition
    to, 87, 177–80; origins of,
    39–41, 46–47, 89; spirit
    guides, 10–11, 49; spreading
    of, 28–31, 40, 49; white spirits
    and nonwhite spirits, 99; wide
    appeal of, 179
spiritualists, number of, 7–8
Sprague, Achsha, 93, 183, 205n34
Stedman, Edmund Clarence, 160–62
Stein, Gertrude, 177
Stein, Stephen J., 89, 204n21,
    204n26
Stern, Julia, 56–57, 89, 124
Stone, John Augustus, 108–9
Stowe, Calvin, 118–19, 141–42,
    145, 211n8
Stowe, Harriet Beecher, 13, 29–30,
    42, 116–36, 140–46, 152,
    166–67, 177, 192n15, 210n6,
    212n17, 213n44
Streeby, Shelley, 3, 191n7
Sumner, Charles, 159–60
supernatural phenomena, definition
    of, 8–9
surrogation, processes of, 16
Sutherland, Duchess of, 141
Swedenborg, Emmanuel, 19, 180,
    221n11

Tanner, Laura E., 216n7
Taylor, Bayard, 160
Thaxter, Celia, 214n56, 221n11

Printed in the United States
111640LV00001B/103-237/P